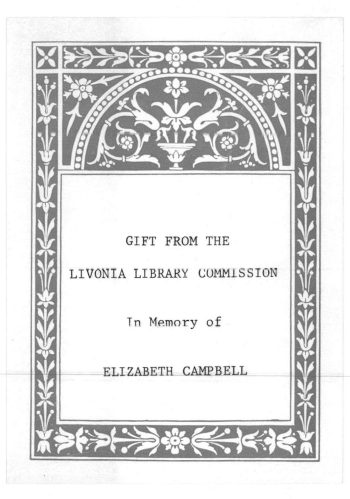

IN SEARCH OF
SCOTTISH ANCESTRY

19

IN SEARCH OF SCOTTISH ANCESTRY

Gerald Hamilton-Edwards

GENEALOGICAL PUBLISHING CO., INC.
BALTIMORE   1980

American Publisher
GENEALOGICAL PUBLISHING CO., INC.
Baltimore, Maryland
First edition, 1972
Second impression (corrected), 1973
Reprinted, 1980

Published in England by
PHILLIMORE & CO. LTD.
Shopwyke Hall, Chichester, Sussex, England
First edition, 1972
Second impression (corrected), 1973
Reprinted, 1980

Library of Congress Catalogue Card Number 72–86
International Standard Book Number 0–8063–0506–1

Text set throughout in 10 on 12 Times Roman

Printed in Great Britain by
COASBYPRINT LTD.,
Portsmouth, Hants.

CONTENTS

ILLUSTRATIONS

PEDIGREES

Endpieces by Joan Harris

ACKNOWLEDGEMENTS

THERE ARE SO MANY who must remain unnamed, such as the helpful messengers at the Scottish Record Office whose patient willingness has smoothed many paths, the kind assistants in libraries who have ferreted out some small but vital piece of information and correspondents who with detailed care have answered questioning letters.

Particular mention must be made of the staff at the Scottish Record Office; Mr J. Imrie, the Keeper; Mr A. Anderson, Curator of the Historical Records; Mr John Bates of the Records Liaison Section, who has been most helpful with information about the local and sheriff court records of which he and his staff are making a survey; Dr. Athol L. Murray; and Miss Alma Calderwood, expert decipherer of early documents, whose kind assistance has been much appreciated.

I am grateful also for help received from Professor Gordon Donaldson of Edinburgh University and for his permission to quote from his *Scots Overseas* in my introduction, and also for assistance from Mr C. P. Finlayson, Keeper of the Manuscripts in that university; Mr R. G. Ball, Assistant Keeper Scottish United Services Museum, Edinburgh Castle, for much information on Scottish Army records; Miss Joan Ferguson, Librarian of the Royal College of Physicians of Edinburgh; Sir James Fraser, Honorary Secretary, and Miss Wardle, Librarian, of the Royal College of Surgeons of Edinburgh, for information about their medical records; Dr T. I. Rae, of the Department of Manuscripts, National Library of Scotland; and the Librarians in the Reference Library, Edinburgh Library and Scottish Library at the Edinburgh City Central Library.

Gratitude is also due to Sir Thomas Innes of Learney, former Lyon King of Arms, to Malcolm Innes of Edingight, Carrick Pursuivant and Lyon Clerk, to Lt-Colonel H. A. B. Lawson, Rothesay Herald, and to Major D. M. Maitland-Titterton, Falkland Pursuivant Extraordinary, for much helpful assistance in matters of Scottish titles, clans and armory.

Mr R. MacLeod, Deputy Registrar General, General Register Office, has shown that help and kindness outweigh and override bureaucracy.

I am grateful too to several members of the Scottish Genealogy Society; in particular, to Mr and Mrs J. Fowler Mitchell, inveterate copiers and publishers of monumental inscriptions in Scottish graveyards; to Mr Donald Whyte, who among other acts of kindness supplied me with the censorious remarks of the parish clerk at Glassary quoted in Chapter III, the source of a foundling's name at Livingston mentioned in Chapter IV and for drawing my attention to the interesting registers of Old Luce and Abercorn quoted in Chapter III; to Mr David C. Cargill, senior, Mr David C. Cargill, junior, and to Miss Patricia M. Baxendine, Director, Secretary and Treasurer, Scots Ancestry Research Society, for information about their work; and to the Right Rev. Monsignor David McRoberts, Editor of the *Innes Review*, for information on Roman Catholic records.

Coming south of the border, I owe thanks in many ways to Mr Donald Steel, whose work, *Sources for Scottish Genealogy and Family History*, will be so valuable to Scottish searchers. He has co-operated with me in a number of ways. Much of the factual matter in the early part of my introduction came from him. Mr A. J. Camp, Director of Research at the Society of Genealogists in London, has been his usual helpful self, Mr Lawson Edwards, the Librarian there, has supplied information, and an example on naming patterns used in Chapter V, and Miss J. M. Masters has given me information about local records in Orkney.

A bouquet paragraph must go to Miss Joan Harris, constant and reliable perceiver of textual errors and humorous terminal illustrator of chapters. I am sure her endpieces will add greatly to the reader's enjoyment of this book.

Gratitude is also felt towards Captain J. A. S. Trydell, Mrs Penelope Shelton and Gervald Frykman of Magdalen College School for willing assistance with checking proofs; to Mr Peter John, who has been so helpful in typing parts of the book from tape recordings, and to his able and careful typist, Mr Victor Springall, who has been responsible for the typing of most of the final version. Then to the publishers: Mr Philip Harris, Managing Director of Phillimore, Mr Jeremy Gibson and Mr Noel Osborne, who have been particularly responsible for seeing the book through the press, my appreciation of much encouragement, help and hospitality.

Oxford
20 October 1971

GERALD HAMILTON-EDWARDS

INTRODUCTION

AN OUTLINE OF SCOTTISH HISTORY

I T IS ALWAYS advantageous for the genealogist to have some knowledge of a country's history, especially her social and economic
history. This is particularly desirable in Scottish research.

Scotland's history has been influenced by many factors, among the
more important of which are: the division of the country by its language
because of its Gaelic speaking population in the Highlands; the infiltration
in the Middle Ages of the feudal system from England; the Reformation
in Scotland and the influence of the Calvinists in the Lowlands in extending
Presbyterianism throughout the country, then mainly Episcopalian or
Roman Catholic. Her history has been a struggle also by the central
Government to extend its authority over the independently-minded Highlanders and Highlands. At the same time the introduction of the Norman
feudal system in the Highlands created an amalgam of feudal tenure and
the tribal system.

All through this period the English Government were trying to impose
their will on the Scottish people and to institute the English legal system.
When James VI of Scotland succeeded Queen Elizabeth as James I of
England and the two countries came under the same sovereign, the
English made further attempts to dictate to the Scottish people their
methods and ideas – legal, political, social and economic.

The anglicization of the Lowlands began during the reign of Queen
Margaret, and her son, King David I, further encouraged it by receiving
Norman barons from England and granting them tracts of land. These
included such names as Bissett and Chisholm, which are today thought of
as Scottish rather than English names.

In this process Scottish chiefs who had held their land up till now by
traditional right were granted charters and they were glad to receive this
confirmation of their land holdings by document. Thus gradually the

1

whole of the Highlands came under feudal tenure. By the time of the death of Alexander III in 1286 almost the whole of the Lowlands were English speaking but because of their remoteness from the central Government the infiltration of anglicization in the Highlands was less pronounced and slower. Nevertheless in due course the feudal system was implanted in that area also. It possessed much in common with the clan system in its loyalty to its chief rather than to a central government, for the chief was in the same position as the feudal lord in England.

The clan system was based on the ownership of land which was vested in the chief of the clan, though there was much overlapping of clan territory which led to disputes and fights between the clans. It does not seem that the territory was ever held or owned by the clan itself but by its chief and thus the system was feudal rather than allodial.

The clans probably owed their origins as much to the topographical features of the Scottish countryside as to any other reason. Professor Gordon Donaldson has written:

No one has yet explained the origin and the precise nature of Highland clans. They certainly did not consist, as is so often supposed today, of people all bearing the same surname. And it is impossible that they could have, for the very good reason that until the seventeenth century few Highlanders had surnames at all. A clan consisted of men bearing a great variety of names. But the concept of accepting the leadership of a chief persisted in the Highlands until well into the eighteenth century. It was probably fostered not only by the physical obstacles which prevented the normal system of law and order from spreading through the Highlands, but also by the physical obstacles within the Highlands themselves, especially the mountains which cut off one glen from another and tended to make the people of each glen an exclusive, self-sufficient community.[1]*

When surnames came into use in the Highlands many of the clansmen adopted the surname of their chief. Some were related to him, though most of them only very distantly. The surname of the chief came to be to a certain extent eponymous. The clans early absorbed other families, some of whom took the chief's name, though not related to him, but later tended to keep their own surname and were known as septs of the clan. Thus the MacIvers are a sept of the Clan Campbell and the MacKails of the Clan Cameron.

The chief stood in relation to the clan rather as a father to his great family and the clansmen looked up to him with filial affection or at any rate with filial respect. In this way he was not unlike the Russian Tsar who, although an autocrat often greatly feared and held in dread reverence, was referred to by his humblest peasant as 'Little Father'. George F. Black in the introduction to his *Surnames of Scotland* (New York 1946)

---

*Notes and References appear on pp. 215–7.

shows how the Clan Mackenzie greatly increased in the 16th and 17th centuries through its absorption of numerous families settled on its lands.

He also mentions how in these centuries chiefs coerced or bribed other families to come into the clan; how some Frasers were brought in by a bribe of a boll of meal, being poor people of the surname of Bissett who changed their name to Fraser, but were known as 'Frasers of the boll of meal' to distinguish them from the true-blood Frasers; how also when the protection of Gilbert Cumin was sought by oppressed people in his neighbourhood, he adopted them by baptizing them at the stone hen trough of his castle, an act which resulted in their being thereafter known as 'Cumins of the Hen Trough', to distinguish them from the Cumins of the true blood. The Campbells are one of the best examples of the absorption of other family groups and by this means they extended their influence over the whole of the Western Highlands.

The clan system was basically territorial and the chief of the clan was the owner of the lands on which the clansman lived. In some cases, however, where the chief of the clan was removed and replaced by another landowner the clansman refused to recognize the new feudal chief. These were known as broken clans. The chief of a clan held his position by his ownership of the land on which the clan lived. This might be by out-right ownership as a feudal tenant, by the ownership of a lease or feu, or even he might hold it by sword-right, his position in the last-mentioned case being strengthened by the comparative impotence of the central Government in the Highlands area.

Scottish historians have made much of the divisions of the country into the Highlands and the Lowlands and have referred to it as 'the two kingdoms', but this may be an exaggerated view and the merging of cultures was a gradual but perpetual process. The range of the Grampian Mountains has been regarded as the division between the Highlands and the Lowlands, though others have thought the division should be taken further south along the Ochil hills as Galloway was predominantly High-land in its attitudes. Certainly, on the east coast, the port and town of Aberdeen, the kingdom of Fife, the Lothians and the counties south of the Pentlands can be regarded as the true Lowlands, extending on the west to Dumfriesshire and Kirkcudbright. The division of the kingdom was more the division of countrymen and townsmen and when, driven by economic reasons, Highlanders found their way into the towns in search of employment they were cutting themselves off from everything which their social life and clan kinship meant to them.

This loss of the sense of belonging was no doubt the reason why clan associations were formed in the great cities and even among those who migrated to other parts of the world. Even today, the clan feeling, though greatly diluted, is still strong.

The clan sense was echoed in the strong loyalties among the households and families of the Lowland aristocracy and these loyalties were found also in the northernmost counties of England. Innes of Learney states that at the time of the Union of England and Scotland (1707) when the population of Scotland was about a million, some ten thousand of these bore titles of chiefship or minor titles as lairds. This 'noblesse' formed a circle of aristocracy greater than any in Europe in proportion to its population, and accounts not only for the family pride of Scotsmen in general but the ease with which the lowest and highest in the land intermingled socially.

This situation was greatly aided by the existence of sub-infeudation, which was abolished by the Plantagenets in England. Thus even the younger branches of the families in Scotland would inherit a small part of the family land, which they would add to their surname and even sign their name by the name of their lands until 1672, when an Act of Parliament forbade their doing so and confined signature by title to peers and bishops. Other people were forced to use their Christian and surnames, though they were not forbidden to add 'of' and the name of their estate as an epithet to their name, and this was later regarded legally as part of their surname.

The Building of National Unity

Scotland's early history is one of a continual struggle with its neighbouring and more powerful country south of its border. Border raids and border wars left the southern part of the Lowlands in a continual state of uncertainty, but resistance to the English was largely and temporarily broken down on Edward I's annexation of the Lowlands in 1296. There then followed the wars with Robert Bruce, who by 1313 had taken so many castles in Scotland that Stirling alone was left to England. This decided Edward to resume the war and led to the Battle of Bannockburn the following year and the defeat of the English by the Scots.

This renowned Scottish victory brought independence to Scotland and by the Treaty of Northampton in 1328 England acknowledged this independence.

The death of Bruce the following year led to the dispute between Edward Balliol and David Bruce for the Scottish throne. Balliol was assisted by the English lords, and when he was defeated Edward III came to his help. In 1333, Berwick was captured by the English and Balliol made king, but the following year he was expelled from Scotland. In 1335 when Scotland was invaded by King Edward and Balliol, Philip of France helped to repel them.

During the 15th century the Hundred Years War and its results absorbed England's attention but after Henry VIII came to the throne disputes arose again between the two countries and in 1513 the Scots, urged on by the French, their old allies, declared war upon England. This led that year to the Battle of Flodden Field in which the Scots were defeated and the flower of their nobility were killed, but adversity strengthened national unity and pride.

Centralizing Tendencies
The struggle of the King and the central Government to impose its will on the whole country increased in the late 15th and early 16th centuries and a determined attempt to curb the power of the clan chiefs was made by James IV. He cancelled the feudal charters to the western chiefs and offered them instead tenancies at will. At the same time, on the principle of 'divide and rule', the central Government fanned the differences and disputes between the clans which were always on the verge of conflagration.

Scotland was in a sorry state during the second half of the 16th century. James V's embittered and gloomy remark when he lay dying at Falkland after the Battle of Solway Moss in 1542 and was brought the news that his wife had been delivered of a daughter was long remembered. 'The Devil go with it. It will end as it began. It came with a lass and will go with a lass'.[2] James was succeeded by an infant daughter, and the country was torn by the internecine strife of the powerful nobles. Mary of Guise, the widow of James V and Regent of the kingdom, capable though she might be, was not strong enough to suppress the rival faction among the nobles. Mary, Queen of Scots, one of the most fascinating characters in Scottish history, was married when only fifteen to the Dauphin of France who succeeded as Francis II but died a young man in 1560. That year also, Mary of Guise died, and Mary, her daughter, Queen of Scots and Queen Dowager of France, returned to her kingdom one gloomy August morning, landing at Leith to be grimly welcomed to a country torn by strife and hostile to her Roman Catholic religion.

Roman Catholicism versus Presbyterianism
Hostility to French influence in Scotland had grown under the Regency of Mary of Guise, and had led to her deposition as Regent shortly before

her death. Parallel with this had grown up a jealousy of the vast lands and wealth of the Scottish abbeys and cathedrals and this, coupled with the growth of the reformed doctrine, led in 1557 to the establishment of the first National Covenant and the revolt of the Scottish Protestants. This was further inflamed in 1559 by the return from Geneva of John Knox. His bitter opposition to the Queen Regent and the rule of 'the monstrous regiment of women' further stirred the revolt. The effect was an onslaught on the monasteries, and one disastrous result of this to historians and genealogists was the almost total destruction of the ecclesiastical records of Scotland together with their paintings and illuminated manuscripts. As these records were concerned with the daily life of the people their loss was irreparable. There was successful resistance in a few places, such as Glasgow, to the destruction by the zealous Protestants of their art treasures and church records, but such cases were unfortunately exceptional.

The religious fervour burnt high and fiercely. Following the deposition of the Queen Regent an alliance was formed with Queen Elizabeth of England. In 1560, the Scottish Parliament abolished Roman Catholicism and established Calvinism, forbidding the celebration of Mass under dire penalties. The civil war which ensued after Mary, Queen of Scots' return from France in 1561 continued throughout her brief reign until 1568, when her abdication was followed by her flight to England.

The Presbyterian system was established throughout Scotland although resistance to it was great in the Highlands. This system had a penetrating influence on the population and gave them a sense of independence, for unlike the Church of England where the clergy came mostly from the upper classes, the Presbyterian system gave every churchgoer a say in the government of the Church, and the ministry of the Scottish Church was mainly filled from the lower or middle classes.

A less fortunate effect of the establishment of Calvinism was the loss of many Scottish customs, but on the credit side must be counted the translation of the Bible into Gaelic and the establishment of that tongue as a written language. In the influence of the Church of Scotland over the ordinary inhabitant and its encouragement of the reading of the Bible lay the foundations of that respect for education and learning which has since characterized the Scottish nation. In the Highlands also the sense of participation in the affairs of the church had a binding influence on the clans.

James VI, when he was old enough to take the power into his own hands, having accepted the Protestant faith obtained a large measure of control over the Church. He also took steps to suppress the Highlands, and one of these was the establishment of three royal burghs in them. These were Campbeltown, Fort William, and Stornoway in the Isle of Lewis.

In 1598 he forced the chiefs to produce charters and, as in many cases they were unable to do so, having held their lands and positions by tradition rather than by any written deed, he gave them the security of a new crown deed after a substantial payment. He forbade the carrying of guns, bows and swords and demanded that the children of the chiefs should be sent as hostages to Edinburgh. He considered the abolition of the heritable jurisdictions but found this impracticable.

The National Covenant

In spite of the repressive measures of James VI the chieftains continued to exercise their ancestral hold over their clans, administering the traditional forms of justice. The loyalties within the clans were strong, though their conditions of life were primitive and they enjoyed a far lower standard of life than people in the south realized.

In other parts of Scotland a better standard of life was developing. One such part was the north-eastern area and, in particular, the City of Aberdeen, the centre of a prosperous district because of the east-coast sea trade. The Aberdonians prided themselves on their orderly style of life and were proud also of their university.

After James VI's succession to the English throne in 1603, the border country also enjoyed a more peaceful and prosperous existence. Here agriculture was the principal means of support. Many of the ordinary people lived on the borderline of poverty, for there was little trade except on the eastern coastline and hardly any established industry.

At this stage in Scotland's progress the feeling of national unity was slight. The Highlanders placed their clans before any pride of country and the upper classes were more internationally- than nationally-minded. The nobility frequently sent their sons to French and Dutch universities and adventurous Scotsmen of all classes accepted employment abroad, in particular in the armies of the Netherlands, Sweden and France.

In religion also the nation was disunited. Though Protestantism had reached Caithness and the Orkney and Shetland Isles by means of sea traffic, the Western Highlands knew little of it apart from that area in the Earl of Argyll's domain. In the 17th century, priests from Ireland had come as missionaries to the islands and Western Highlands and their work in this field established many devout and loyal Roman Catholics whose faith survives in certain areas to the present day.

The strength of the Presbyterian Kirk lay in the south and central Scotland. The support of the laymen for their ministers was strong. Roman Catholic practice was viewed with horror and the Church of England was thought of as only a step removed from Rome, its bishops being viewed with suspicion as agents of a near-Catholic king. Only around Aberdeen was there a strong episcopal tradition. Charles I, who succeeded his father in 1625, was far more divorced from his Scottish subjects and had little understanding of them. He had spent practically all his life in England and did not visit Scotland until 1633. The little that he understood of the Scottish Church gave him no affection for it and he had no appreciation of the hold which the General Assembly had on the affections of the ordinary people.

When Charles came to Edinburgh in 1633 he held a coronation service in St Giles's with full Anglican rites, believing that the Scots would find them so impressive that they would be completely won over to the Anglican ritual. At the same time he founded the bishopric of Edinburgh and shortly afterwards appointed Spottiswoode, Archbishop of St Andrews, to be his Chancellor in Scotland. He then set about abolishing the presbyteries and appointed a commission to draw up a revised prayer book for Scotland.

When the new liturgy was read for the first time on 23 July 1637 in St Giles's Cathedral in Edinburgh, there were shouts from the congregation and people flung stools and bibles about; after they had been driven out of the cathedral by armed guards the rioters threw stones at the windows.

Charles could not understand this hatred of his high-handed interference with the Scots' religious liberty. He merely sent instructions to the Privy Council there that all who protested against the prayer book were to be punished and the book itself was to be taken into regular use. The great surge of resistance to the autocratic methods of the King culminated in the National Covenant, signed on 28 February 1638 in the Greyfriars Kirk at Edinburgh by many of the nobility of Scotland. Copies of it were quickly made and soon signed on the two following days by a great mass of ministers and other delegates then assembled in the Scottish capital. This National Covenant represented in the words of Lord Warrington 'the great marriage day of this nation with God'.

The National Covenant incorporated the confession of faith which had been signed in 1581 by the young James VI. It detailed the many Acts of Parliament establishing the true religion and the maintenance of the Church's liberties. It incorporated a protest against the recent changes forced upon the Church and ended with a vow of loyalty to the Protestant religion.

Copies of this covenant were swiftly taken by mounted messengers to all parts of Scotland and even abroad, so that soldiers serving in foreign armies might sign it. Support for it came from men of every class.

The Covenant nearly achieved what previously had seemed impossible, the uniting of the Scottish nation. A wave of enthusiasm for it swept the country. Scotland was fortunate in having two great leaders whose enthusiasm for the Covenant inspired the rest of the country. One of these was James Graham, 5th Earl of Montrose. Although a Calvinist, he was not a typical one, being tolerant, gay, and generous, loving life and enjoying friendship. His sense of humour and personal charm helped him to spread enthusiasm for the Covenant. His influence was particularly strong in Perthshire, for his home lay at Kincardine in the Ochil Hills, but he also succeeded in carrying the cause of the Covenant into Aberdeenshire, the heart of the episcopalian land.

The Covenant's champion in the west was Archibald Campbell, 8th Earl of Argyll, a man of very different character from Montrose, a strange and, as it turned out later, a dangerous partner in this enterprise. With his seat at Inveraray, his sphere of influence covered Argyll.

When King Charles learnt of the resistance of the Scots he told an English council that he would have to use force, but meanwhile he agreed to the recall of the General Assembly, hoping that some of the Scottish critics would quarrel among themselves.

This Assembly met in November 1638 and after violent debates deposed all the bishops, rejected the service book, and appointed a commission to enquire into various abuses. The King's Commissioner had been the Duke of Hamilton, who had walked out during the proceedings, and the King therefore declared its decisions were illegal. The actions of the Assembly kindled further enthusiasm for the Covenant and the Covenanters began to form a force, aided by the Scottish officers and soldiers returning home from long service in continental armies. They found in Alexander Leslie an outstanding general with valuable campaign experience gained in Germany.

In 1639 and 1640 the King made unsuccessful attempts to use force against the Scots and his failure forced him to summon the English Parliament. But already among the Covenanters disputes were arising between the extremists and the more moderate elements led by the Earl of Montrose. Meanwhile, Argyll was taking every advantage he could to

B

build up his own power and even advocated deposing the King. Montrose, on the other hand, although he signed a pact with some of the supporters at Cumbernauld in Dunbartonshire reaffirming his belief in the Covenant, also pledged his loyalty to the King.

At this stage in 1641 Charles, hoping to play off one faction against the other, decided to accept the decisions of the General Assembly of 1638.

When the Civil War broke out in August 1642, Montrose, disgusted by the idea of taking up arms against the King though still loyal to the Covenant, had no ideas of betraying his Sovereign. On the other hand, Argyll remained hostile to the King and identified himself with the English Parliament.

In the early years of the Civil War events did not go too well for Parliament and in 1643 they decided to negotiate with the Scots for active help from them. The latter agreed to assist on being paid £30,000 a month for expenses and, what was more important to them, 'a reformation of religion in the kingdoms of England and Ireland in doctrine, worship, discipline and government, according to the word of God and the example of the best reformed Churches, and that popery and prelacy should be extirpated'. This treaty was known as the Solemn League and Covenant. After its signature the English Parliament reorganized its army under Cromwell, and from 1644 onwards it became apparent that the King's cause was lost. That year Parliament defeated him at Marston Moor, and the following year at Naseby.

The Royalists in England were encouraged on hearing that Montrose had taken up arms in Scotland on behalf of the King. He defeated the Covenanters at Tippermuir, capturing Perth in the autumn of 1644. Crossing Scotland by Blair Atholl and over the barren mountains westward he brought the war into Argyll's own stronghold of Inverary so unexpectedly that Argyll himself only just escaped capture. He later defeated the supporters of Argyll at Inverlochy.

In 1645, Montrose captured Dundee and established his hold on both Edinburgh and Glasgow. September that year brought his first defeat at Philiphaugh. He still remained optimistic about redeeming the King's cause in Scotland until he heard the distressing news that Charles had surrendered to the Scottish army at Newark in England. One of the conditions of this surrender was that Montrose should disband his followers and leave the country.

This was a sorrowful blow to Montrose, who was one of the most loyal and single-minded supporters of the King, but Charles was becoming more and more opportunist and was now playing off one rival against another and seeking the support of Argyll. Meanwhile, the disillusioned Montrose made his way to Norway.

By now the Scottish army in England was in a predicament. It was short of money, as the English Parliament had not paid the promised sums to them and following their recent victories no longer needed the Scots' help. Though the Scots held the King he was unwilling even in his extremity to agree to support the Covenant. Had he done so, he might have won great support among the Scottish people but in the circumstances the Scottish leaders handed him over to the Parliamentary Commissioners, receiving a promise from them of £400,000 towards their expenses. Then followed, as so often, second thoughts, and the Scots, dismayed at Charles' rebuke that they had sold him, began to think that if he was reinstated matters might get better. The Earl of Lauderdale and some others visited him secretly and said they would support him if he would agree to England being made Presbyterian for a trial period of three years. Charles agreed, though with some modifying conditions. The treaty was known as the Engagement, but some of the Covenanters were very angry with the persons concerned, feeling that they were watering down the strength of the Covenant.

The execution of Charles I in 1649 was a great shock to Montrose and even to Argyll who, though he had opposed Charles, would never have countenanced his execution. Both Montrose and Argyll offered their support to Prince Charles, the heir. Montrose returned to the Orkneys and made his way down through Scotland; but he was betrayed by a laird into the hands of extreme Covenanters, taken to Edinburgh and after a mock trial was condemned to death and hanged, drawn, and quartered. Prince Charles then had no alternative but to rely on Argyll. He came to Scotland, agreed to the Covenant and was crowned at Scone, Argyll himself placing the crown on his head. However, the Scots army was shortly afterwards defeated at Dunbar and Prince Charles, or King Charles II as he afterwards became, suffered further defeat at Worcester and was forced to escape to France, where he was nine years in exile.

The military suppression of Scotland which Cromwell considered necessary took him eighteen months, but by August 1652 resistance was ended and by a treaty of union the Scots were allowed to send thirty representatives to the Parliament at Westminster. This was a surprise innovation, forestalling the later union of England and Scotland.

Seven commissioners, four English and three Scottish, were appointed by Cromwell to supervise the administration of justice in Scotland. New sheriffs were commissioned for the Scottish counties and an attempt was made to end the violence in the Highlands.

Cromwell's relations with the General Assembly were unfriendly. He wished to allow freedom of worship to all religions except the Episcopalians and Roman Catholics, an idea which shocked the General Assembly. Cromwell became impatient of its deliberations and forbade its meeting. It was natural thenceforth that he was hated by the Presbyterians.

Cromwell's rule over Scotland was a military one. There were nine regiments at one time in the kingdom. The Scots hated this rigidly enforced dictatorship and after Charles II was restored to the throne in 1660 there was a wave of rejoicing throughout the Scottish kingdom.

The Sufferings of the Covenanters

Charles II was not a vindictive man and he did not wish to avenge himself on those who had brought about his father's end, but neither did he wish to offend those who had brought about his restoration and he eventually agreed that fifteen of the surviving men who had caused his father's execution should themselves suffer the same fate. In Scotland, the Marquess of Argyll (created such by Charles I, and who had crowned his son at Scone) rather hoped to receive some reward for his services; but his many enemies thought otherwise and pressed for his punishment. They could not designate him a regicide but they were able to show that he had committed treason and for that offence he was executed. The Scottish Parliament was summoned to meet in 1661, the King's agents making sure that it was well packed with his supporters. This Parliament cancelled all legislation which had been made since 1633, thus bringing about the restoration of the bishops and also the church patronage which had been abolished in 1649.

The staunch supporters of Presbyterianism were adamant in their resistance to these changes. The ministers who had been admitted to parishes since 1649 had to obtain formal presentation from their patrons. Some 300 of them refused to do so and abandoned their churches. In the south-west, which was the main centre of opposition, many ministers continued to hold meetings in barns, kitchens, and any other places they could find, and even out in the open fields on the hillside.

As a result, the Privy Council introduced fines for people failing to attend church and the parish ministers were encouraged to forward lists of absentees. Later, the ministers who had left their churches were forbidden to live within twenty miles of their former parishes or within three miles of any royal burgh. Troops were quartered in this part of Scotland to try to enforce these regulations.

These illegal services were known as conventicles. They became so numerous that the Government had to take severe steps to try to crush them, but though the punishments were made more and more severe the stout Scotsmen became more determined to resist. A number formed an ill-organized rebellion, doomed to failure, which was defeated in 1666 at Rullion Green, on the outskirts of Edinburgh. Fifteen of the leaders were hanged in Edinburgh, others in Glasgow and Ayr. A number were imprisoned and subjected to torture.

The murder of Archbishop Sharp in 1679 led to further repression. The Duke of Monmouth was sent to carry this out and at Bothwell Bridge the Covenanters were mown down by English forces; 1,200 of them were made prisoner and driven into an improvised concentration camp in the churchyard of Greyfriars in Edinburgh. Some gave way under this pressure, but others remained firm in their faith. A number of them were executed, and about 250 of them condemned to slavery in the West Indies. The ship in which they were to be transported was sunk in a storm off the Orkneys and they were all drowned.

Though these repressive measures continued and were even intensified under James II, engendering a bitter hatred of English rule, many of these brave Scotsmen remained firm in their faith. The fate of numbers of them can be read in the registers of the Privy Council of Scotland of this period. In 1684 the Lords of His Majesty's Privy Council deliberated on the fate of some of these prisoners in the tolbooths at Edinburgh and in the Canongate 'for there alleadged being in the late rebellione, ressett of rebells and for church disorders, and examination of the saide persones taken by the comittie of Councill for Publick Affairs'. These prisoners had 'refused to engadge not to ryse in armes against the King or his authoritie or to oune the King as their lawfull soveraigne except with ther oune treasonable limitations and according to the Covenant, or to take the oath of alleadgeance, and having considered his Majesties letter authorizeing them to restrict their punishment to banishment, have ordained the foresaide [here follows the list of names] to be banished to the Plantationes in Carolina and discharges them ever to return to this kingdome'[3]. These proceedings are full of distasteful details about the banishment of these men. John Edward in Dalgaine, for instance, was banished to America as one of the prisoners in the Tolbooth of Glasgow 'who are to be carried in shackles and put aboard Walter Gibson's ship called the Pelican in the Clyde'[4] and at Edinburgh on 22 June 1685 there were recorded declarations of prisoners sent from Glasgow. These included Robert Edwart who came from Cumnock in Ayrshire. He swore that 'he will never ryse in armes against his Majesties authority and promises to keep the kirk [that is, to attend church regularly]'[5] but in spite of this submission he was banished to the plantations of Carolina and ordered to have his left ear cut off, which was a quite common additional punishment. His destination was later altered to the plantations of Jamaica.

This period in Scottish history was known as the 'Killing Time', but a welcome respite came to them in 1688 with the Revolution in England when James II was driven out, and William of Orange and his wife, the Princess Mary became King and Queen as joint sovereigns in 1689. In 1690 episcopal government in Scotland was abolished, the Presbyterian government of the church by the General Assembly, synods, presbyteries and kirk sessions was confirmed and patronage of livings was again abolished. Nevertheless, there were sad events. John Graham of Claverhouse, the hero of Scottish song and tradition, whose unwavering loyalty to James II is one of the happier memories of this time, was killed in the narrow gorge of Killiecrankie in 1689 and his forces dispersed. There is the melancholy story, too, of the massacre at Glencoe in 1692. The last four decades of the 17th century in Scotland's history were filled with sad and tragic happenings.

The Union
For some time the union of the two kingdoms of England and Scotland had been discussed and debated, and this finally came about in 1707. Although there was much resistance to it by many Scotsmen it ultimately proved greatly beneficial to the Scottish nation. Scotland was given representation by forty-five members in the British House of Commons, and sixteen of their peers were elected to the House of Lords. Scotland retained its own legal system, as it does to this day. A benefit to the Scots was that their ships were now classed as British, so that they avoided the prohibitions of the Navigation Acts. The standardization of coinage and the fiscal system, and of weights and measures, eventually proved beneficial to the northern kingdom. The main benefits of the Union to the Scots were that it brought them peace, law and order and an opportunity to develop under a stable economy.

The 18th Century
The decades following the Union began to see improvements in Scottish life and conditions. Progress was made in commerce and trade and this gradually brought with it better standards of life, improved education and a developing culture, particularly in the Lowlands. But in the first half of

the century the Scottish people were to experience and suffer two rebellions, the Fifteen and the Forty-five. Had dour James possessed the gay charm of his son, Charles Edward, the result of the Fifteen might have been different. At that time the Hanoverians had only just come to the British throne and were not particularly popular, but by the time Bonnie Prince Charlie landed on the west coast of Scotland the Georges had been established over thirty years and the chances of ejecting them were negligible. The Forty-five was doomed from the outset and it was only the winning personality of the Young Pretender that brought him any support at all.

The repression that followed Culloden was harsh and the Scots were even forbidden to wear the most significant part of their dress—the kilt. Such attempts to break their native spirit failed. As so often, adversity united rather than broke the nation.

Both rebellions were followed by long-drawn-out trials. Some Scots were executed, others banished. There were a few who had joined in both rebellions – Lord Balmerino was one of them. As a young man he had joined the forces of the Old Pretender, and thirty years later had been won over by the Young Pretender. He had been pardoned for his part in the Fifteen but it was too much to expect that he would receive a second pardon, and this generous-hearted and gallant Scotsman was executed at Tower Hill in 1747, mourned by his countrymen and admired by his enemies.

The hard measures following the Forty-five did little to endear the English to the Scottish people, and the English redcoat was an object of hatred. Nevertheless, there were good things to come out of the occupation. Among these were the roads built in the 1720s by General Wade across the Highlands, which made this part of Scotland more accessible.

The escape of Charles Edward himself, for many months in hiding in the Highlands and Western Isles and protected by the incredible loyalty of his followers – who were not tempted by bribes which would have made them wealthy for the rest of their lives – is one of the romantic sagas of Scottish history. These two rebellions had disrupted Scottish life and brought tragedy and misery to the ordinary people. Perhaps the feelings of such people are expressed in a letter dated 18 August 1746, written by the author's own ancestor, John Edward of Coupar Angus, from St Andrews, where he had been staying, to his brother Thomas in London. 'As for news I have none but what is common. I thank God pace is restored once more in our Native Country.'

The latter half of the 18th century brought this peace to the country and enabled it to develop. The Highlands began to be opened up to travellers.

Even Dr Johnson, the most English of Englishmen, enjoyed his journey with Boswell to the Highlands and to the Western Isles, rejoicing in that hospitality and kindness of heart which often seems strongest among the poorer section of the community.

The two rebellions, coming in the half-century following the Union, brought feelings of insecurity in England and retarded the fusion of the two kingdoms, and the benefits which had been visualized as a result. However, the economic conditions in Scotland gradually improved, particularly in the second half of the 18th century. This was mainly because for the first time for almost 500 years Scotland was able to enjoy a period of peace and a sense of security. As a result, agriculture, industry, and the transport systems developed and the country entered an epoch when its literature, art, and architecture began to flourish and in which many Scotsmen found fortunes in the developing colonies.

Agriculture
Scottish farming methods had before the Union been unenlightened and primitive and this was largely responsible for the poverty of the countryside. In the early 18th century wages were extremely low. Labourers in 1730 earned only 40s. a year, and thirty years later the annual wage had only risen to 60s. Even though food was cheap the standards of life were bound to be miserable. Many of the lairds lived in great discomfort because their rent was paid in kind and they had, in consequence, no money to invest and no capital with which they could bring about improvements on their lands. A great deal of the Scottish soil was poor and better transport was necessary to allow proper manuring to be carried out. Drainage, too, was another essential since much of the kingdom's best soil was waterlogged. But this planning and fertilization could only be carried out by wealthy landowners or by tenants with money who enjoyed the security of a long lease. In the 18th century improved methods for farming were much discussed and written about, and some of those lairds who were able to afford it began to improve their lands with beneficial results both to themselves, their employees and the rest of the country.

One of these was Sir Archibald Grant, who succeeded to a poverty-stricken estate at Monymusk, about twenty miles from Aberdeen. Although Grant was an advocate and not able therefore to give a great deal of time to his estate until he retired, he had a good factor to whom he sent instructions; he spent £1,200 on enclosing fields, building dykes, planting trees and draining the land, with the result that his nurseries during the five years following 1726 produced over a million trees of various kinds, which were either sold or transplanted. Grant, in 1726, engaged an English farmer called Thomas Winter, who cultivated turnips by means of the drill, and instituted hoeing. These turnips provided food for the cattle during the winter and thus improved the breed. Monymusk was one of the first estates in Scotland to make use of turnips. In 1733, Grant bought a copy of Jethro Tull's book *Horse-Hoeing Husbandry*, but by that date he had already learnt from his own experience much of what was in the book. Grant encouraged those of his tenants who were willing to accept new methods and stimulated them with his own enthusiasm. As a result, when he died he left Monymusk one of the best farms as well as one of the most beautiful estates in the country.

Grant's efforts were followed by other great landowners. As a result rents and profits increased and the whole standard of life improved. Lairds and their wives and families began to make visits to the capital and enjoy the developing luxury of Edinburgh life. The homes of the farmers' wives began to be improved. George Robinson, writing about 1765, noted that these farmers were exchanging their old box beds for fourposters, covering their floors with carpets, buying sofas and even elegant pianofortes. The minister of Kilsyth, making his report for the Old Statistical Account in 1790, stated that 'formerly the most respectable Scottish farmers used to wear nothing but Scotch cloth of their own making, plaiding, hose, and bonnets. Now the servantmen on holidays wear nothing else than English cloth, cotton, and thread stockings and hats . . . every maid servant wears a silk bonnet and cloak, and generally muslin or printed gowns and thread stockings. So that the men and women are more gayly dressed than their masters and mistresses were formerly'.[6]

The Old Statistical Account
Scotland is fortunate in having Sinclair's Statistical Account (known as the Old Statistical Account) of all the parishes in the kingdom in 1790, for at that date the parishes were probably not very different to what they had been for the previous hundred years or more and many of the families settled in them had been there for generations.

The accounts of the parishes, frequently written by the minister, vary according to the personality and ability of the writer, but the basic information follows a pattern.

The parish of Lintrathen in Angus on the borders of the Highlands, which today's gazetteers picture in quite attractive terms, was then given a depressing description. The author of it writes under the pseudonym, 'A Friend to Statistical Inquiries'. After describing the locale he goes on to portray the 'state of the people &c.' 'In this sequestered district', he writes 'there is no town, no village of note, no seat, no mines nor minerals, no natural curiosities, few manufactures, and little trade; no innkeeper, no baker, no writer, no surgeon, no butcher, no apothecary and one Seceder only'. He describes how 'a mean village composed of despicable huts, crowded together on the rocky bank of the Melgam, almost opposite to the church, indicates the poverty of the inhabitants, who seem to be in a rude state of society'. Of the people he writes, 'From the register of baptisms and burials, the number of inhabitants at present may be computed at nearly ninety. Of these about fifty are denominated farmers who occupy certain proportions of land, out of which they tear a scanty subsistence. Few improvements have been made there in agriculture. The old system prevails. Some plots of turnip, flax, and sown grass appear, but oats and barley are the principal productions of the ill cultivated soil. Of these a sufficient quantity is raised to supply the necessities of the natives; but there is no proper encouragement to industry'.[7]

He goes on to describe critically the free labour which the tenants were bound to give to their landlord. 'This is a disgraceful remain of a system humiliating to men and hostile to all improvements; a system which, about fifty years ago, prevailed in all its rigour throughout the northern part of Scotland, but which every enlightened landlord, desirous of the prosperity of his country, and of his own interest, has now abandoned.'

Nevertheless, he admits that the inhabitants in all their poverty seemed contented. 'There is no trade nor manufacture in this corner, but such as is necessary to the accommodation of the natives, and their wants are few. Destitute of the elegances, and most of the conveniences of life, their desires are limited. They enjoy little, and with that little are contented. Attached to their naked soil, they are temperate and sober.' The state of the church then comes in for scathing comment. 'The church is an old, dark, dis-proportioned fabrick, built at two different periods. The manse is a wretched hovel, covered with thatch . . . the stipend is L400 Scots and 40 bolls victual . . . The parochial schoolmaster has a salary of six or seven bolls oats, collected from the tenants and some trifling fees. On this miserable allowance he has contrived to support a family upward of sixty years. The hut in which he resides is hardly fit to accommodate the meanest beggar.'

Of the place-names he writes, 'The names of the parish and many places in it seem to be partly Gaelic and partly Anglo-Saxon; but the language spoken by the inhabitants is English, or a dialect of it peculiar to North Britain.'

The account of Lethendie in Perthshire, written by Mr Laurence Butter, the minister there, is more cheerful. He speaks of the quiet contented simple lives of the inhabitants and of their good manners and of the absence of any desire on their part to be concerned with politics or events in the outer world. He has, however, a sly dig at the established church. In mentioning that there were three churches, the established church, the church of the Antiburgher Seceders and that of the English Episcopalians he states, 'Of these the Established Church is by far the worst in point of structure and accommodation'.

The wages of a manservant are stated to have been from £10 to £12 sterling a year, a woman-servant from £4 to £5 with victuals. Day labourers were receiving 15d. to 18d. a day in summer and about 1s. a day in winter, without victuals. 'Oat-meal is the principal food of the people, and generally sells at 1s. the peck. Butter sells at 9d. per lib; cheese from 4s. to 5s. per stone, Amsterdam; beef and mutton at from 3d. to 4d. per lib.'[8]

The account of Coupar Angus in common with the account of a number of parishes, emphasizes the difficulties of calculating the population because of the failure of persons to register their children's baptisms. 'The average number of births and deaths cannot be accurately ascertained from the unwillingness of many to register their children, and from there being no regular register of deaths.'[9] Genealogists should bear this in mind when searching unsuccessfully for a baptism.

Highland Developments

For many centuries there had been a great demand for Scottish cattle in England and these used to be driven in for many miles from the Highlands to centres like Crieff and Falkirk. A. R. B. Haldane, in his fascinating book *The Drove Roads of Scotland*,[10] tells his story of these drovers in their long distance nomadic treks across the Highlands to these sales. These Highland cattle were skinny, small, ill-fed beasts but the English bought them avidly because after a period of fattening from the rich English pastures they provided succulent meals for English diners and the special flavour of Scottish beef was much appreciated.

In the late 18th century a number of improvements were made with agricultural machines and implements, though these were not always welcomed, particularly by the more suspicious and superstitious of the people. Andrew Meikle of Dunbar invented, in the 1770s, a horse-drawn threshing machine (later adapted to water-power) which however produced an artificially-created wind which some countryfolk soon denounced as a wind created by the Devil.

The demand for home-produced food during the Napoleonic Wars gave the more progressive Scottish farmers a ready market with high prices. Those who benefited were the farmers of the Lowlands and the eastern border who modernized their methods. The situation was different in the Highlands, where new methods and ideas were resisted, the crofters continuing to farm their isolated and scattered patches of land in the traditional and un-economic ways. The digging stick or caschrom was still in use until well into the 19th century.

These Highlanders, although sturdy and hardened by their adverse conditions, because of their poor living were ill-nurtured and small in physique. Statistics of prisoners captured in the Forty-five reveal that the average Highlander was only 5 ft. 4 ins. in height. The Board of Commissioners who took over the forfeited estates of the rebels introduced improvements, but the Highlanders resisted these more enlightened methods and their plight was worsened by years of bad harvest and consequent famine in the latter half of the 18th century. Only toward the end of that century was turnip cultivation, the key to real progress in farming, introduced into the Highlands.

Difficulties were increased by the chiefs and chieftains, now that they were deprived of their power and privileges, becoming absentee landlords, only interested in the rents from their lands. The Highlands provided poor pasture and many of the Highland cattle failed to live through the harsh winters. It was only in the latter half of the century that it began to be realized that the Blackfaced sheep were the only breed able to survive the hard climate, the Cheviots being confined to the glens.

During the Napoleonic Wars some of the crofters supplemented their incomes, and thus kept themselves going, by making kelp, which is an alkaline ash, produced by burning seaweed, used in the manufacture of soap and glass. In peacetime, alkaline substances from abroad such as barilla were preferred, but in wartime these could not be procured and the price of kelp rose so that by 1800 it was £22 a ton. Unfortunately for these people, when the war ended the price of kelp dropped rapidly and many families, deprived of this addition to their income, were driven to emigrate rather than face starvation.

The emigrating Scots went mainly to the New World and their flight there was accelerated greatly by the potato blight in 1846 which had particularly serious effect in the Highlands, where whole districts were deprived of their main source of food. Although relief measures were taken by the Government, the Church, a number of organizations and the more enlightened and humane chiefs, these were insufficient to stem the disaster and emigration increased to such an extent that in one year 106,000 people left the kingdom. Others crowded into the cities in the hope of some relief, as did many emigrants from Ireland. This only increased the difficulties and terrible conditions of over-population.

In the more prosperous and mild south and east of Scotland agriculture was making real progress. The breeding of cattle was greatly improved so that the shorthorns, the Ayrshire and Galloway cattle became renowned and commanded high prices. Many of the best specimens of the more famous herds, such as the Aberdeen Angus, were exported to the Argentine, and the Clydesdale horse became known throughout the agricultural world.

In the 19th century the lowland farms made real progress. A system of ley farming was introduced, with its rotation of crops, and in these rich lowland lands modern methods produced grain, seed potatoes and fat stock which became famous. These prosperous agriculturists of the Lowlands were a contrast to the poor emigrants forced to leave their homes and the land they loved, their hearts filled with embittered feelings.

Transport

General Wade's road-building following the Fifteen Rebellion was the beginning of the opening up of the Highlands. His roads were built from the towns of Crieff and Dunkeld, which met at Dalnacardoch and continued to Dalwhinnie, where they separated again, the easterly road finding its way to Inverness and the westerly one to Fort Augustus. Then Inverness, Fort Augustus and Fort William were linked with a road running beside Loch Lochy and Loch Ness. This was the first time these rough Highland mountains and hills had been crossed by properly surfaced roads. Then, following the Forty-five Rebellion, more military roads were built by the British Army. The Highlanders themselves thought poorly of this opening up of their countryside. Typical of their views was that of a countryman, recorded by Ramsay of Ochtertyre in 1761, who 'saw no use of them but to set burghers and redcoats into the Highlands, none of whom in his father's time would have durst venture beyond the Pass of Aberfoyle'.[11]

Nevertheless, these roads were the salvation of the Highlands and later in the century throughout Scotland turnpike roads began to pattern the countryside, surfaced by the methods of that famous road-making engineer, McAdam, whose name was given to his particular system of road building.

These were the great days of the mail coach. In 1749 the first coach to ply between Glasgow and Edinburgh began its twice-weekly schedule, covering the forty-four miles in just under two days, but by 1760 after the introduction of the turnpike system this journey could be covered in one-and-a-half days. In that year a regular coach service between Edinburgh and London was established, although it only ran once a month. Glasgow people wanting to travel to London had first to make the journey to Edinburgh, and it was not until 1788 that they had their own direct service to the English capital. Its duration was then 65 hours and its cost £4 16s. By 1798 Aberdeen also had an independent coach to London.

Postal services were of course equally slow and in Edinburgh for many years after 1707, when the postal arrangements were recognized, only one letter carrier was required for delivering the mail in the Scottish capital; even in 1780 only six post boys were required for such work. The arrival of the post in Glasgow was such an event that a gun used to be fired when the letters had been sorted and were ready for distribution.

The late 18th-century development of canals in Scotland, as in England, greatly influenced trade and communications. The cutting of a Forth-Clyde canal was long discussed by Scottish engineers and eventually implemented. The canal was opened in 1790. As important was the Monkland Canal which brought the coal supplies from the Coatbridge area into Glasgow. Scotland's famous Caledonian Canal was designed by Telford in 1803 and took over seventeen years to build. This allowed shipping from the North Sea to make the journey to the west coast and Ireland without having to go round the dangerous North Passage of Scotland but, financially, it never paid.

In the 18th century Port Glasgow was what its name implied, and Glasgow itself was a quiet town with a riverside meadow named Broomielaw, because the broom grew attractively along its banks. The dredging and opening up of the Clyde by Telford and Rennie transformed all this so that the shipping came right up to Broomielaw and even in Telford's lifetime the ship tonnage using the port rose from nothing to over one million a year. This was the beginning of the great commercial and shipbuilding era at this end of the then pleasant little riverside town.

Glasgow was the cradle of the steamship. Henry Bell's Clydeside-built *Comet* was launched there in 1812. Bell was Provost of Glasgow and ran there the Baths hotel, later the Queen's hotel. Shortly before the end of the Napoleonic Wars the Clyde Shipping Company was founded, a company which continues to the present day.

In 1838 the Atlantic was first crossed by a steamer – the *Sirius*, which had been built in Leith but engined in Glasgow. Her crossing took eighteen days and she used up 450 tons of coal.

Many of the famous wooden tea clippers were built in Scotland. The famous *Thermopylae* was built in Aberdeen, and the even more famous *Cutty Sark* in Dumbarton in 1869, but by the end of the 19th century the tramp steamer had taken the place of these enchanting windjammers.

The coming of the railways further opened up Scotland and in spite of the outburst of Lord Cockburn that 'Britain is at present an island of lunatics, all railway-mad'[12] the railways were a great success. By 1850 you could travel by train from London as far as Aberdeen on the east and Glasgow on the west coast.

It was no mean achievement that during the long French wars in which Scotland herself played no insignificant part, she was able, as Telford himself wrote to a friend, 'to construct canals, roads, harbours, bridges – magnificent works of peace – the like of which are probably not to be found in the world. Are not these things worthy of a nation's pride?'[13]

Commerce and Industry

Just as the agriculture of Scotland began to adopt new methods and consequently make progress, so the old industries of Scotland adapted themselves to more modern conditions. In 1727 a Board of Trustees for Manufactures had been set up by Parliament to stimulate Scottish industry. One of the earliest established of these was the manufacture of linen, taught to the people by foreign weavers and flax dressers. This industry was successfully established in many towns and Scottish woven linen began to be in demand abroad. In the 18th century these linen workers were cottagers, working in their own homes with hand-made wheels and frames. The agents who distributed the flax and later collected the spun yarn provided the capital. In 1746 the British Linen Company was founded to assist these workers in organizing their business. The Company's branch banks which were set up all over Scotland continued long after the Company's service to the linen industry had ceased.

Although new and improved methods of manufacture were introduced, hand-made linen continued well beyond the turn of the 18th century. These cottagers were busy making holland sheeting and shirtings, linen for umbrellas and window blinds, the famous shawl cloths, calicoes and muslins, besides the stiff linens used mainly for hat linings. Individual towns had their famous products, such as the fine lawns and damasks of Glasgow and the coarse linens and bleached canvas, much used by the Navy, of Fife, the table linen from Dunfermline, and the renowned Paisley twisted thread.

Nevertheless, the prosperity of the linen trade began to diminish by the end of the 18th century because the mechanically-produced cottons were taking their place both in the foreign and home markets. A melancholy report of 1040 showed that spinning had practically disappeared and that this was a great distress for the old people who were cut off from work to which their age and disposition particularly suited them.

In fact, after 1820 only a few places like Dunfermline continued to produce linen. A more cheaply produced cotton began to be worn by the women, and gentlemen wore cotton waistcoats instead of woollen ones. Since cotton manufacture was an English development the English cotton trade benefited at the expense of the Scottish linen trade.

The first successful Scottish mills were opened on the Isle of Bute and cotton manufacture started to develop in Renfrewshire and Lanarkshire. Water power from the swift-flowing streams began to be used and raw cotton to be imported through the avenue of the Clyde. From the end of the 18th century the newly-invented spinning wheel was used for spinning, but weaving for a long time continued to be a hand trade. The weavers obtained high wages as a consequence of the demand for their work. In four days a week they could earn £2, but in 1807 the power loom made its appearance at Catrine and this spelt the end of the hand weaver, though it was not until about 1840 that the hand loom finally disappeared.

The prosperous hand weavers were thrown out of work and many were forced to emigrate to the New World. Among those who sailed there with his family in May 1848 was William Carnegie, whose son, Andrew, was later to bring such benefit to Scots all over the world.

While the cotton industry prospered in the 19th century the manufacture of tweed was developing and Scottish tweed soon became as renowned as the earlier Scottish linen.

Another Scotsman who at this time contributed much to his own and the rest of the world's prosperity was James Watt. His steam engine brought power to the looms of the mills and released a force which was to be of incalculable value in the industrial world.

Another industry of great development in the late 18th century was the iron industry. Originally timber had been burnt for smelting the iron, resulting in the denuding of the Scottish forests, but the discovery that coke could be used for this purpose brought the iron foundries to the areas of the coalfields. Improved methods and the increasing demand for iron encouraged the rapid expansion. This greatly affected towns like Falkirk, which until the late 18th century had been renowned only for its autumn cattle trysts, but in the next century was transformed by the establishment there of the famous Carron Iron Works.

The Scottish Mines

Coal-mining in the 17th and 18th centuries had been limited to parts of Fife, Ayrshire and Lanarkshire and mainly to surface mining. With the increase in demand for coal in the 18th century a number of new pits were opened and older seams extended. In the early 19th century the industry expanded, particularly in Ayrshire, Lanarkshire, the Lothians, and Fife, so that by the middle of that century the Scottish mines produced some seven and a half million tons a year, a considerable amount of which was exported. By 1900 this total had reached thirty-three million tons.

This went hand in hand with the development of the engineering industry; it began to produce machines for use in farming and tools for factories and mills, and much of this production was for the export trade and largely concentrated around Glasgow and the Clyde. The increase in coal and development of engineering helped to bring into being another of Scotland's great industries – shipbuilding. Though later this was mainly concentrated in the Clyde area, earlier on it was more dispersed and the ports of Aberdeen, Leith, Port Glasgow, and Greenock for some time were building a greater tonnage of ships per year than Glasgow. However, from about 1830 onwards the Glasgow shipyards took the lead. The first four ships of the Cunard Steamship Company were built on the Clyde, their engines being designed and built by Robert Napier, the great Scottish marine engineer. Glasgow, being the centre of both the engineering and iron industries, proved a natural centre when iron ships came in, and when later steel ships were required, the steel works of the locality took the place of the iron works.

Cultural Growth

In the early 18th century Glasgow, as previously mentioned, was a pleasant, quiet, countrified town. Its population was scarcely 13,000 inhabitants. Defoe, in 1727, described it as 'one of the cleanliest, most beautiful and best built cities in Great Britain',[14] and nine years later a Scotsman, McUre, wrote of it as 'surrounded with cornfields, kitchen and flower gardens, abounding with fruit of all sorts, which, by reason of the open and large streets, send forth a pleasant and odoriferous smell'. Among the still familiar buildings of that time were the cathedral and the university, with meadows beside the college buildings, where they bordered the placid Clyde.

C

Edinburgh was a very different place. It was then confined within the area of the old city walls, with the north loch as a 'nearly impassable fetid marsh, a stinking swamp, open on all sides, the receptacle of many sewers and seemingly of all the worried cats, drowned dogs and black-guardism of the city'.[15] Cramped in their building area the Edinburgh people made their homes in tall buildings on each side of the famous High Street leading down from the Castle to Holyrood Palace. Many writers have remarked on the filthiness of the cobbled wynds, though this overcrowded form of living had its compensations in that everyone knew each other and there was a genial friendliness about the place. The first two or three storeys of these tall houses would be occupied by the aristocracy and professional men and their families, while the upper storeys housed in great congestion the working-classes. On the narrow ill-lit stone staircases the whole gamut of society would meet and pass and sometimes collide with each other. This cobbled High Street, the Royal Mile as it is called, was the spinal cord of the old city, the scene of most of its historical and often tragic events, for which reason it has been called the Via Dolorosa of Scottish history. It links the Royal Palace at the lower end with the rock-founded Castle towering above everything at its upper limit. In the Luckenbooths close to St Giles's Cathedral were the city shops, the street itself being used for the shopkeepers' stalls and counters.

Edinburgh expanded slowly. George Street was built in 1765 but the more spacious homes there were regarded as too far from the centre of things, the North Loch barring easy access to them. In the 1770s work was begun on its drainage, though this took fifty years to complete. At the same time the North Bridge was built across the gulley to link the old town with the new.

With this increasing ease of access the wealthy people moved from their cramped quarters to the new town and George Street, Queen Street and Charlotte Square became the fashionable places of residence. Much of the new town bears the imprint of Robert Adam and others, and the great architectural beauty of such splendidly proportioned streets and squares as Moray Place, Ainslie Place, Queen Street and Heriot Row are still almost unspoiled monuments of their talents and achievements.

With the more peaceful years following the forty-five rebellion an awakening of interest in literature and the arts grew. The father of Alan Ramsay, the artist, was a bookseller whose shop had drawn around it a literary circle of Edinburgh people. In 1754 he founded the Select Society for Encouraging Art, Science and Industry, a group which was supported by Adam Smith, the economist, and David Hume, the philosopher; it also attracted a number of distinguished men like Lord Kames, the Adam brothers, William Robertson, George Dempster, James Boswell and John Home. Alexander Nasmyth was discovered and encouraged by Ramsay, and Nasmyth's two sons and six daughters all became artists in the capital. The most famous of Edinburgh's portrait painters was Sir Henry Raeburn, who was knighted by George IV on his visit to Edinburgh in 1822.

In Glasgow the Foulis brothers founded the Foulis Press, which produced some of the finest printed works of the century. These two brothers also founded the Glasgow Academy of Arts which, although it failed to find sufficient support, was a forerunner of a developing culture in Glasgow.

Robert Adam was much sought after by the aristocracy of England and houses designed by him south of the Border are well-known and appreciated features of our national heritage. A Scottish architect famous for the design of many English churches was James Gibbs. St Mary-le-Strand and St Martin-in-the-Fields are among his most noted works in London and he also built the Radcliffe Library in Oxford, the Senate House in Cambridge, and the buildings of King's College, Cambridge, which stand at right angles to the 15th-century chapel.

This period saw also the rise of the philosophers led by William Robertson and David Hume. The latter's cousin John Home, although a minister of the Church, wrote the play *Douglas* which was produced in Edinburgh in 1754 and much disturbed and disgusted some members of the General Assembly there. The play did well and was highly praised, though John Home had to give up his church.

The poems of Robert Burns had preceded him to Edinburgh, where he arrived in November 1786. The people appreciated his strong sense of understanding of the Scottish character, his piquant humour and his terse, down-to-earth style. In consequence he was much lionized and welcomed into every Edinburgh literary drawing-room, but he grew rather tired of these formal gatherings and much preferred meeting people in the easier atmosphere of the home of William Creech, his literary agent.

Burns never cared particularly for the Scottish capital, but Sir Walter Scott much enjoyed his life there and the friendships he made with other literary and cultured people. Lord Cockburn, whose delightful racy memoirs are such a source of information on this period, wrote with affection of Scott's 'plain dress, the guttural, blurred voice, the lame walk, the thoughtful heavy face with its mantling smile, the honest, hearty manner, the joyous laugh, the sing-song, feeling recitation, the graphic story'.[16]

The early 18th century capital was a place of slums and vulgarity but all this changed by the end of the century when Edinburgh's culture became known and recognized south of the Border to such an extent that, during the French wars, when young sons of the aristocracy were prevented from making their grand tour they were sent instead to Edinburgh to study and learn something of the culture and life of the Scottish capital. Among them was the young Hicks-Beach whose tutor, Sydney Smith, imbibed the cultural life of the capital with relish and became a welcome guest in its literary circles.

Sydney Smith was instrumental in founding the Friday Club, and he and two other members of it, Francis Jeffrey and Francis Horner, also founded in 1802 the *Edinburgh Review* which startled the reading public with its liberal ideas and ideals at a time when there was great reaction to any change, people fearing it would lead to a revolution such as had occurred in France. The *Edinburgh Review* is remembered for its attack on the Lake poets and Keats, but many of its outspoken comments in other directions were the forerunners of a more liberal outlook. No small number of English statesmen like Lord Palmerston derived benefit from their stay in Edinburgh during their youth, when the continent was closed to them.

The cultural ascendance of Edinburgh began to diminish after about 1830. Some maintained that this was because it had burnt itself out, but it is more likely that when the continent was once more free for travel the grand tour again became the fashion.

Religion and Education

In the 18th century the Scots people took their religion more seriously than did the English. Their ministers worked hard and their weekly sermons were the subject of much discussion and debate among their parishioners afterwards. The General Assembly of the Church of Scotland in Edinburgh each year was a meeting at which the ministers met other ministers, and people other than their own parishioners, and talked about national affairs, besides replenishing their shelves from the bookshops in the Luckenbooths.

A less pleasant feature of religious life in Scotland was the intolerance of the Kirk Sessions. The people found guilty of breaking the sabbath, of swearing or of immorality were subjected to humiliating examination by the Session and later had to stand and be rebuked before the whole congregation by the minister and sometimes made to wear sackcloth garments. Social historians and genealogists will come across many references to such events in the Kirk Session records, many of which are now held in the Scottish Record Office.

Another matter of importance was that of patronage, restored in 1712, by which the landowners were able to appoint ministers to churches on their own property. It was a cause of much bitter feeling, resulting during the 18th century in the break-away of a number of groups from the Presbyterian Church. The bodies principally concerned were the Burghers and the Anti-Burghers, but there were also the 'Auld Lichts' and the 'New Lichts'.

The persecution of Roman Catholics continued in this century and in many places they had to worship in secret and were deprived of normal citizen rights, being still suspect because of their association with the Stuarts. Some measures of emancipation proposed in 1779 produced such an outburst in Edinburgh and Glasgow, as well as in London, that it was another fifty years before toleration was extended to the Roman Catholics in Scotland. After the Penal Laws of 1829 were abolished the number of Scottish Roman Catholics increased, largely on account of the crowds of Irish workers who came over to the industrial south of Scotland, driven there by the potato famine of 1846 in their own country.

The Episcopalians in Scotland met with almost as much hostility from the Church of Scotland as did the Roman Catholics. Their stronghold was the north and north-east where they were comparatively undisturbed. The Toleration Act of 1712 allowed episcopal form of worship, provided it was conducted by persons who had abjured the Pretender. Many of them, however, would not do this and their continued sympathy with the Jacobites was constantly bringing them trouble.

Until the middle of the 18th century the General Assembly looked with great disfavour on all organized amusements and, in particular, on the theatre, as John Home had found when he tried to produce his play *Douglas*. By the end of the century their attitude had changed and in fact, in 1784, when Mrs Siddons visited the capital, the General Assembly actually arranged their sittings to allow for their younger members to attend her theatrical performances. Dr William Robertson, the historian, was one of those who helped to produce in the Church a more liberal attitude towards the theatre. His scholarship was respected not only in Scotland but throughout Europe. He was Principal of Edinburgh University in 1762 and the following year Moderator of the Church of Scotland. He numbered among his friends Adam Smith, the economist, and Tobias

Smollett, the novelist, and the breadth of his outlook is shown by the fact that he also included among them the sceptic, David Hume.

In May 1843 further division within the Church took place over the matter of patronage, and 474 ministers, representing a third of the total, broke away and formed the Free Church of Scotland. As they gave up their churches and stipends the congregations who supported them had to find buildings and also finance their livings.

Some improvement in the matter of patronage was made by the passing of the Benefices Act in 1843, but lay patronage was not completely abolished until 1874. Another regrouping of the Church took place in 1847, when the United Presbyterian Church was formed. This came about as a result of a series of reunions between splinter groups which had left the established church in the 18th century. There were thus after this date three main groups of Presbyterians in Scotland, the Church of Scotland (the state church), the new Free Church, and the United Presbyterian Church.

Until the end of the 18th century Scotland was largely an illiterate nation, but many years earlier John Knox had seen that the Church ought to assume responsibility for education because he thought, like Calvin, that people who could not read nor write could hardly understand the Christian faith. He had planned, therefore, to found grammar schools and colleges in all the towns, and village schools even in the smallest parishes, considerable progress was made in the 17th century and further action taken by the Scottish Parliament at the end of the century further improved the education. A statute of 1696 required heritors in each parish to provide a school building and a salary of £10 a year for the schoolmaster. This was never fully implemented and in the 18th century there were still many parishes possessing no school at all.

Boys of proved ability could move from the parish school to a grammar school. This would sometimes have only one teacher, but in the larger schools one would take charge of the class for the first three or four years, then the rector (headmaster) would continue with the top boys. Some of these grammar schools had conscientious and efficient teachers and sent their quota to the Scottish universities. Among these was Thomas Carlyle, who in 1809, at the age of fourteen, walked the hundred miles between his home in Ecclefechan and Edinburgh University to have a chance of reading for a degree. The discipline in the schools was hard and Lord Cockburn, who went to Edinburgh High School in 1787 when he was about eight, records that during his first four years he was beaten almost every day; but he admits that being afraid of his master caused him to learn his work.

Until the middle of the 19th century education in Scotland was mainly developed through the Church, but from then onwards the state gradually took over the responsibility. Scotland has always had a high regard for education and in the days when there were only two universities in England she maintained five: St Andrews, Glasgow, Edinburgh, and in Aberdeen, King's College and Marischal College.

The Scotsman in Parliament

At the time of the Union Scotland was allocated forty-five members in the House of Commons and sixteen in the House of Lords. The latter were elected by their fellow peers, but the Scottish members who sat in the House of Commons were elected by a medieval process which meant that they represented a very small section of the population. Thirty members were elected by the shires and the remaining fifteen by the burghs. In the shires only the tenants-in-chief to the King had a vote, which meant that a number of lairds who held considerable property had no vote. As a result the number of voters in the shires was small and in the whole of Ayrshire, for instance, although it was a large county there were only 214 voters in 1788, and even by 1821 only about 3,000 people had a vote in all the shires, at a time when the population was nearly two million. Furthermore, these representatives from the shires contributed little to democratic government at Westminster since they were frequently won over to Government support by offers of posts for themselves or their relations and friends in the East India Company or in some public office.

The situation in the burghs was even worse. Only royal burghs were represented and this excluded large towns like Paisley and Greenock. As they had only fifteen members between them it meant that a member had to represent several burghs. Nor was any account taken of the size of the burgh and Glasgow, for instance, with a population in 1821 of 150,000 had no greater proportion in the representation than a place like Rutherglen with only 10,000 population.

In any case the only persons who had a vote in these burghs were the town councillors, and these town councils were self-perpetuating bodies; since vacancies were usually caused in them by the death of one of the members, these were filled by the town councillors' votes. In this way some councils had fallen into the control of one family. Bribery to obtain the councillors' votes was quite common in the burgh parliamentary elections.

The Scottish members at Westminster were not a very effective body. The difficulties of travelling to London, the expense of maintaining two homes, and the unfamiliar and unfriendly atmosphere among a body of people who regarded Scotsmen as strange oddities, mitigated against the Scots members' regular attendance and effectiveness. The Scots people themselves were indifferent to the events of Parliament. Westminster was remote from them and little was heard of Parliamentary proceedings.

The French Revolution brought some changes in this attitude. Scotsmen began to take an interest in European events and to discuss and argue about the ideals of the revolutionaries. Edmund Burke's *Reflections on the Revolution in France* was read with avidity and when Thomas Paine's reply, *The Rights of Man*, was published in two parts (1791 and 1792) at twopence each it proved a best-seller. It was the subject of discussion in almost every household and Robert Burns championed it in such poems as 'Man was Made to Mourn' and 'Is there, for Honest Poverty'.

The Government tried to suppress Paine's publications, announcing that it was seditious to possess or disseminate any of them; a number of men were tried on very slender evidence and in some cases sentenced to transportation to Botany Bay. The trial judge was Lord Braxfield, whose name became as hated in Scotland as that of Judge Jeffreys in England; but a number of political organizations had been formed, such as the Association of the Friends of People, and although these were driven underground by repressive measures their ideals continued and the Reform Bill of 1832 brought considerable changes to Scotland as well as to England. There were eight new burghs created, Edinburgh and Glasgow were each given two members, a number of royal burghs were recognized, and the franchise was widened to include a household which paid £10 or more in rates. Similarly, in the shires owners of property worth £10 a year and occupiers of land on a long lease worth £50 were given the vote. The following year the election of local councils was made more democratic. As a result, a far greater interest began to be taken by Scotsmen in political affairs.

Migration

People are inclined to think that the great number of Scots who migrated in the 18th and 19th centuries did so in search of adventure. This may have been true in some cases but in the majority of cases they were driven abroad by economic necessity. The Scots have always lived a hard life, but the coming of industry intensified their difficulties, particularly in the cities where the slums increased and became the breeding grounds for sickness and crime. The 1861 census showed that 35 per cent of Scottish families were living in one room of about eighty to a hundred square ft. in area, and seven or eight ft. in height. These terrible conditions encouraged Scotsmen to emigrate and all through the 18th and most of the 19th centuries shiploads were leaving, mainly bound for Canada and the United States. They left in crowded and often unseaworthy vessels and were overwhelmed by shipwreck and cholera to such an extent that the Commons in 1848 learnt that of the 106,000 Irish and Scots who had emigrated the previous year 12,200 of them had died at sea or immediately after their arrival; a further 7,100 died within a few weeks of their landing. This was indeed a harsh example of the survival of the fittest.

Those who lived settled mainly in family groups, a very natural arrangement. A number from Arran settled round Quebec, and in the Cape Breton district were settlers from the Isle of Skye, while Nova Scotia was populated by Ross-shire families. In 1815 a settler in New Caledonia wrote home to his nephew, 'Your mother will meet with more of her relations here than in Breadalbane'.[17]

The Scots settlers in the new lands had at first a hard time, especially those who went to settlements some way inland. Some suffered unbelievable hardships on their journey into Upper Canada but the very struggles hardened their characters and, forged in the fires of adversity, they brought an energy and drive to their new life and a sense of devotion and support to each other that resulted in the building of a sturdy, determined and hardworking community.

Many Scotsmen entered the employment of the Hudson's Bay Company and in 1800, three-quarters of the Company's servants were said to be Orcadians. Another company which attracted Scotsmen in great numbers was the North West Company, a rival fur trading firm working in the same area as the Hudson's Bay Company. Naturally, there was fierce rivalry between the two and frequent fighting among their men until they were finally amalgamated.

One of the most famous emigrants in the 19th century, Andrew Carnegie, has been mentioned before. His parents had realized that the weaving trade in which they had been engaged in Dunfermline was now finished and so made their way to the New World. Carnegie built a huge fortune in the iron and steel business and came also to control a vast network of newspapers, railroads and other businesses. His generosity to libraries and research centres throughout the world and particularly in his native Scotland caused his name to be blessed by many a working man intent on self-education.

Missionary work in the more primitive countries was well supported by the Scottish people and among their most famous missionaries was David Livingstone, who, as a doctor with a passionate desire for exploration, worked under the London Missionary Society in Central Africa, travelling across the Kalahari Desert and up the unknown reaches of the Zambesi

River. His idealism fired the imagination of many other Scotsmen. Eugene Stock in the *History of Church Missionary Societies* states that 'Scotland has given a far larger proportion of its ablest and most cultured men to Foreign Missions than any other country in the world'.[18]

Although Scotsmen travelled as missionaries and explorers in central Africa, migration to South Africa was less pronounced, being mainly confined to men in the late 19th and early 20th centuries able to purchase farms and employ native labour.

Apart from convicts shipped from Scotland, as from England, to Australia and Tasmania, there were considerable numbers of Scots free settlers in this continent, which being largely agricultural was attractive to the Scottish race and many Scotsmen made great contribution to the development of this dominion.

New Zealand also in the second quarter of the 19th century attracted numbers of Scotsmen. Although the first New Zealand Association in 1827 was not a great success, the New Zealand Company of 1839 bought up some 20,000,000 acres of land from Maori chiefs and settled Scotsmen on them, mainly on the North Island, apart from Nelson at the northern part of South Island. This accounts for the great number of Scottish names among the New Zealand towns.

The Scottish emigrants, by their enterprise and industry, brought great benefits to the countries in which they settled, but a lingering nostalgia for their homeland remained and many of them saved for a return visit to Scotland, some, having grown wealthy, to shower generosity on the place of their birth or the homeland of their ancestors. There were some like the Macneil of Barra who came back and purchased Kismul Castle, the ancient stronghold of the chief of the clan, and put it in good repair and order.

Many Scotsmen in the early 19th century migrated to England, particularly to the north of England, and to the developing port of Liverpool. Among those who came to this growing town were the MacIver brothers, who jointly with George Burns, who remained in Glasgow, and Samuel Cunard, a Scotsman who had already migrated to Canada, founded the Cunard Steamship Company. Shipping became a great Scottish industry and later in the century a number of Scotsmen were prominent in the shipping world, men like Sir Donald Currie and Andrew Weir, Lord Inverforth.

The Clyde shipyards became known throughout the world and the building of ships went hand in hand with marine engineering. By 1890 the iron ships had given way to steel ones and the Clyde was a river of shipyards.

Scotland has become noted for its heavy industries, the smelting of iron and later of steel, and for the building of ships. These developed into her great activities, but there were other outlets. Agriculture in Scotland made great advances in the 19th and 20th centuries and by the middle of the latter the value of Scottish cattle, sheep and grain were around seventy million pounds. The fishing industry also has grown in importance and over a third of all the fish landed in Britain today comes from Scottish ships. The textile industry employs over 10,000 workers in the area round Galashiels. Scottish distilleries produce all the whisky of Great Britain, and the tweeds and hosiery of the border towns have gained a world-wide reputation.

Culturally, too, Scotland has made great strides in this century. Not only does the Edinburgh Festival attract people from all over the world, but lesser centres like Pitlochry which hold their own festivals have made a name for themselves.

In all these ways Scotland has developed, particularly in the Highlands, from a country of hard toil and sometimes grim poverty, which often drove people to overseas territories, into a progressive prosperous and forward-looking nation.

I

FAMILY INFORMATION

I T IS NATURAL that your first step in finding out information about your family and in tracing its pedigree should be to discover all you can from living members of it, particularly of course the older generations. You may feel reluctant to do this and think you are being a nuisance to them, especially if you are rebuffed at first by those who do not seem particularly interested.

Very often, however, one of the family, possibly a maiden aunt, has taken some interest in the subject. There is usually one person in each generation who does so. They may be reluctant to talk about it at first and you may not have known that they had any special knowledge.

It is a good idea to send out a questionnaire to all the members of the family and a suggested pro forma for this is given in an appendix to this book. You can get this duplicated or reproduced by some other method. This will show that you are in earnest in your search for information and by doing this you will not only get your information in a more systematic form but also be saved asking the same questions of a great number of people.

Some members of the family will probably ignore your questionnaire and not bother to reply, but it will no doubt stimulate some interest in the family history and cause members to talk about it among themselves. The replies may reveal a great deal.

From them you will be able to build up some kind of picture of the family background. It is often noticed that members of the family who begin by saying that they know nothing about it in the end are able to tell you a considerable amount. Scottish people are proud of their ancestry and often there are traditions in the family which, though possibly exaggerated by the course of time, nevertheless have a basis of truth. It is always therefore worth while following up any such traditions. Beware, however, of the more pretentious assertions. It is surprising how many families have a story that they are entitled to some money in chancery which they could claim if only they had enough money to fight the case, or that they are the rightful owners of some estate or title. Such claims and beliefs are nearly always pipe-dreams. They are linked with the almost universal human delusions of wealth and grandeur.

Very often a few deeds or documents relating to the family survive and you should try to collect these or, at any rate, make copies of them. The kind of materials you should particularly seek are originals or copies of wills, marriage settlements, deeds of family arrangement, and birth, baptism, marriage, death and burial certificates, as well as deeds relating to graves and their upkeep. If you are lucky you may even find someone who has an old family Bible in which the entries of baptisms, marriages and burials have been made, as was the custom in the past. Naturally, a discovery like this is particularly fortunate and may allow you to construct straight away a pedigree running back several generations.

The Scottish nation have always been a closely-knit race, proud of their family ties. In the Highlands the clan system helped to bind them together. It is hoped that the brief outline of Scottish social and political history in the introduction to this book will help you to appreciate the background of your kin.

There are, of course, factors which affect the ease or difficulty of tracing a family. Naturally, one which has held high position in the social structure of the country will be easier to trace than one in more humble circumstances. The ancestry of a laird from a family which has held its land for generations should be traceable through that land as far back as there are records of them holding it. Scotland is particularly fortunate in having a good record of such ownership in its register of sasines. England has nothing equivalent to this.

Inevitably, in higher society tracing a line is easier. The hereditary peers, for instance, are easy to trace, for the very essence of such a peerage is its hereditary element, but many families of commoners are linked with the peerage, though possibly only remotely. Scotland is fortunate in having an excellent peerage, *The Scots Peerage*, edited by Sir James Balfour Paul,[1] the nine volumes of which are a mine of information. The ninth volume consists of an excellent index and it is worth looking in this early on in your searches.

The existence and survival of the necessary records is an *a priori* factor which affects your search. If you find you come from a family which lived in the Outer Hebrides where often little record was kept and sometimes the parish registers only begin at the end of the 18th or even the beginning of the 19th centuries, then your task will be paved with increased difficulties.

The surname which you are tracing is another influence. It is natural that a very uncommon surname is far easier to trace than a very common one. Scotland abounds with such names as Mackenzie and Campbell, but people are often surprised to learn that the most common name of all in Scotland, as in England, is Smith, and the reason for its frequency is that a smith, as in England, was about the most common of trades.

Even when the surname is a common one there are certain helpful factors. Probably the most important of these was the very conservative attitude to Christian names which the Scots nation possessed, even more so than in England and Wales. For instance, the eldest son was almost invariably named after the paternal grandfather and the eldest daughter frequently after the mother's mother. The second son was usually named after the mother's father and the third son after the father. This name pattern is something to be taken closely into account and is discussed more fully in Chapter V. Almost inevitably the child was named after someone of an earlier generation. Exceptionally he or she might be named after a particularly important godparent. The introduction of a strange Christian name into a family is therefore something to be eyed with much suspicion and carefully investigated.

Sometimes an unusual Christian name in a family can be a valuable clue. D. J. Steel has made some researches into Christian names, although, as he admits, a great deal more needs to be done in this field. His article on 'The Descent of Christian Names' will be found in the June 1962 issue of *The Genealogists' Magazine*.

The same writer has devoted a section in the *Register and Directory 1966* of the Society of Genealogists to 'Hereditary Unusual Christian Names', which he hopes may be the beginning of an index of such names. Of Scotsmen, the rare Christian name of Aeneas in the family of Lord Reay is mentioned and to this may be added another Scottish example, the name of Ninian in the family of the Marquess of Bute. These are well-known families, but there must be many examples of distinctive Christian names being perpetuated in lesser known ones.

Continuance in the same trade or profession for some generations is also helpful. Even the most obscure family which never reached any prominence may be traced as far back as the registers stretch if they have continued to live in the same parish and have been members of the Church of Scotland.

You need to make certain that no printed account of your family has been previously made, for it is annoying to find after doing a long search that it has all been done before. It is probably unlikely that there is any such printed account of which you are unaware, but the number of family histories in print is considerable, and is growing every year; there is always the possibility that you may link up with one of them. T. R. Thomson's *Catalogue of British Family Histories*[2] is a valuable book, and one particularly dealing with Scotland is Joan Ferguson's *Scottish Family Histories Held in Scottish Libraries* (1960). An earlier book of special value is Margaret Stuart's *Scottish Family History* (1930), which refers to innumerable sources, MSS. and otherwise, on various families which are listed alphabetically. A new edition of this, bringing it up to date, would be very welcome.

The *British Museum Catalogue of Printed Books* is another source which should be consulted. Family histories are listed in this under each surname at the beginning of that name. As the catalogue up to 1955 has been printed and can be found in many large reference libraries, its consultation is reasonably easy. There have been supplementary volumes published bringing the catalogue up to date. You can also discover any recent publications of family histories in the *British National Bibliography* under the Dewey classification number of 929. The National Library of Scotland has many accounts, both printed and MSS. of Scottish families; other Scottish libraries may have good genealogical collections and their catalogues should also be consulted. More details of such collections are mentioned in Chapter XVIII.

In addition to separately printed family histories a number of printed pedigrees and accounts of families have appeared in various publications. *Landed Gentry* has been published since 1840 and there are numerous Scottish families within its covers, for there has never been a separate 'Landed Gentry' for Scotland as there has been for Ireland.

There have been from time to time a number of genealogical magazines, such as *The Genealogist*, *Miscellanea Genealogica et Heraldica*, and *The Ancestor*. George Marshall's *Genealogists' Guide* (last edition 1903) with J. B. Whitmore's supplement to it, *A Genealogical Guide* (1947), indicates 'any descent of three generations in male line' which has been discovered in a wide range of publications.

The possibility of your family having had a rightful claim to armorial bearings (and there are almost sure to be rumours that they had) needs investigating. You can be sure of a courteous and kind reception at the office of the Lyon King of Arms, now in the New Register House in Princes Street, Edinburgh, and the possibility of any right to arms can be investigated there. Should such a right be substantiated the genealogical assistance derived from the Lyon Court records may be considerable, but even apart from a right to arms the library of the Lyon Court is naturally very rich in genealogical material. The Lyon Office records are more fully described in Chapter XVII.

From the start of your searching you should aim at keeping records of your discoveries in some systematic manner. *In Search of Ancestry*[3] has a chapter on 'Keeping your Records', and all that is said there refers equally to Scottish ancestral records. Certainly you should get a filing cabinet and file your information on cards or slips of 8 in. x 6 in. and 3 in. x 5 in. in the way suggested, either in alphabetical order or in some other classified order, according to the circumstances.

Since that chapter was written, various means of copying documents have been devised and produced commercially, in particular, the Rank Xerox system. Most record offices today have means of copying documents so that students and researchers can obtain copies of them inexpensively. This saves a great deal of time: you can examine the documents at leisure at home, and be certain that you have not missed out any points, which may happen when you merely make abstracts.

Early on you should get out a rough pedigree showing how far you have progressed. A chart pedigree is one of the clearest ways of doing this and will help you in your future work. The above-mentioned chapter describes how you can do this by using a dye-line process, reproducing from a transparency. The Xerox method may be an even less expensive method of doing this, but there are not a great number of Xerox machines which take paper larger than foolscap size. However, a larger pedigree can be drawn in two or more sections and these can be joined together quite neatly.

II

CIVIL REGISTRATION

C IVIL REGISTRATION BEGAN in Scotland later than in England and it was not until 1855 that Scottish law required it. However, its late start is its only disadvantage, for the registration itself in the details which it gives is far superior to that in England and Wales and to most registrations elsewhere.

The 1855 registration was the finest of all years. The amount of information it gives in all certificates is quite astonishing. Unfortunately, it was decided that the difficulties of obtaining in every case this very full information made it impracticable; the details required were reduced in 1856 and these were again slightly modified and improved upon in 1861. From then onwards the registration details have remained virtually the same, only the marriage certificate being slightly altered in 1922.

The details given in 1855 in the various certificates are as follows:

Birth Certificate

The name and baptismal name, if different; sex, year, date of month and hour of birth; place of birth (if in lodgings, so stated); father's name, rank, profession or occupation, his age and birthplace; when and where he was married and his other issue, both living and deceased; the mother's name and maiden name, her age and birthplace; the signature of the father, mother or other informant, and residence if out of the house in which the birth occurs; when and where registered and the signature of the Registrar.

Marriage Certificate

The date and place of the marriage and in what form the marriage took place; and for both bride and bridegroom, the present and usual residence; age, rank or profession and, if related, the relationship of the parties; status (widow or widower and if so whether second or third marriage and the number of children by each former marriage, living and deceased); birthplace, and when and where registered; the names with the rank, profession or occupation of both the parents in each case; if a regular marriage, the signature of the officiating minister and of the witnesses, or if irregular, the date of the extract, sentence or conviction or decree of declarator and in what court pronounced; the date and place of registration and signature of the Registrar.

Death Certificate

The name, rank, profession or occupation; sex and age; place of birth and length of time in the district of the deceased; names, ranks, professions or occupations of both parents; if deceased was married, the wife's name, the issue in order of birth, both living and deceased, their names and ages; the year, date of month and hour of death; place of death, cause and how long the disease continued, medical attendant certifying and when he last saw the deceased; burial place and name of undertaker certifying it; signature of informant (usually mentioning relationship if related); date and place of registration and signature of the Registrar.

Searchers will notice at once the information additional to that given in the English certificates. For instance, in the birth certificate the parent's age and place of birth and their other issue are mentioned and the place and date of their marriage. In the marriage certificate is given the birthplaces of bride and bridegroom, details of any former marriage, with the issue if any. In the death certificate the place of birth of the deceased, the names of the deceased's parents, the details of any marriage and the issue of it are all particularly useful pieces of information.

Even the modified certificates give far more information than the corresponding English ones. The birth certificates from 1856 to 1860 only omit the age and birthplace of the parents and details of their marriage and details of any other issue. In the certificate of 1861 onwards the date and place of the parent's marriage is restored. In the marriage certificates from 1856 to 1860 the heading 'Residence' is substituted for 'Residence, Present, Usual', and details of any former marriage and issue and the birthplace of the parties are omitted. From 1861 onwards the information is substantially the same, the heading 'Residence' being altered to the more useful 'Usual Residence'. In the 1922 certificates the information is similar, except that the names of the parties, in addition to their signatures, are given in full, the only information being omitted is the relationsip, if any, of the bride to the bridegroom. The death certificate from 1856 to 1860 omits the deceased's place of birth and details of any marriage and its issue. From 1861 onwards the information is in effect the same, except that the burial place and the undertaker's certification are not included.

There are of course occasions when some of the columns will be marked 'unknown' or left blank. This is particularly so in the death certificate. When, for instance, the deceased died in lodgings, the lodging-house keeper perhaps did not know the names of the deceased's parents or of any relatives. In general, however, the details have been completed fully, the Scottish people being conscientious in matters such as their ancestry.

It is particularly valuable that such full information is given in the death certificate, which in England is peculiarly uninformative, not even telling whether the deceased was married or single. Two examples of Scottish death certificates for 1855, and one for 1857 are given below.

1855 Deaths in the Parish of Stornoway in the County of Ross. Registered by Colin Crutch, Registrar.

MORISON, Kenneth, Flesher. Male *Aged* 50 years *Born* Lionel (Ness) 39 years in Stornoway *Parents' Names* Roderick Morison, Flesher, Margaret Morison, Maiden Name, Ross. *Married to* Mary Morison, maiden name Gunn. *Issue in Order:*

1.	Alexander	25
2.	Ann	23
3.	John	21
4.	Margaret	19
5.	Malcolm	17
6.	Annabella	15
7.	Louisa	13
8.	Mary	11
9.	Donald	9
10.	Roderick	7
11.	William	5

Died April twelfth 7h 0m PM *at* Bayhead.
Cause Gangrene of the Lungs as certified by Roderick Millar, Surgeon, who saw deceased April 12.
Burial Place Sandwich. Not certified.
Signature of Informant Donald Morison His × Mark. Brother.
Registered 1855 April 16 at Stornoway.

1855 Deaths, Rothesay Isle of Bute.

MORISON, Elizabeth, Female *Aged* 70 years
Born Jamaica *How long in this District* 30 years
Parents' Names William Gauntlett, Proprietor in Jamaica (Deceased), Elizabeth Gauntlett, Maiden Name Hinxman (Deceased) *Married to* William Morison. *Issue (in order of Birth, their names and ages):*

1.	James Mitford	28
2.	Henrietta Elizabeth	27
3.	Marianne Francis	25

Died 1855 May thirteenth 5h. 30m. PM.
Where died Glenfauld Cottage, Rothesay.
Cause of Death and how long Disease continued, Medical Attendant by whom certified and when he last saw deceased Schinis uteri for years. As certified by Thomas Gibson, MD, FRCPS, Rothesay.

Burial Place, Undertaker by whom certified Rothesay Burial Ground. As certified by J. McKechnie, Undertaker.
Signature of Informant James Mitford Morison Son of the deceased.
When and Where Registered and Signature of Registrar 1855 May 17th. At Rothesay. John Palmer. Registrar.

1857 Deaths, District of Hutchestown.

MORISON, Roderick Supervisor Inland Revenue (Married) *Died* 1857 April fourteenth 2h. 30m. am. 3 Apsley Place (South) Glasgow.
Sex M *Age* 80 years *Parents' Names* Alexander Morison, Officer of Excise (Deceased) Janet Morison, Maiden Name McKenzie (Deceased).
Cause of Death Paralysis 3½ years as certified by David Tindal, Surgeon, who saw deceased April 13th.
Burial Place Southern Necropolis Glasgow, as certified by Wylie and Lochhead, Undertakers. *Signature of Informant* (Present) C. Morison, Son. *Registered* 1857 April 14th at Glasgow. Jno M. Thomson, Registrar.

The amount of information in these certificates will be quickly appreciated. In that of Kenneth Morison, from his age we can tell that he was born in 1804 or 1805 at Lionel in the Isle of Lewis and that he had lived for thirty-nine years in Stornoway in that island, that his father, Roderick, was, like himself, a flesher; that his mother was born Margaret Ross and that his wife was Mary Gunn. The names of the children in order are particularly valuable, not only for the direct information but in indicating the Christian names which existed in the family. We have also the exact date of his death at Bayhead in the parish of Stornoway and where he is buried. The signature of the informant, being his brother, gives a collateral relative.

The certificate of Elizabeth Morison, who died at the age of seventy in Rothesay, reveals the important detail that she was born overseas in Jamaica and that her father was a proprietor in that island. Although the date of the marriage is not given the age of the eldest child gives some indication of this. The death certificates of the older people will often provide a considerable link with the past. In the case of Roderick Morison, for instance, his having died in April 1857 aged eighty shows that he must have been born about 1776 or 1777 and his parents may have been born some thirty years before that, which takes us back to the years just following the Forty-five rebellion.

Where the surname is rare or even comparatively rare the information from a number of certificates of people living in the same area, even including quite a wide distance around, and dying in 1855 with their combined information may provide considerable family links and build up a pedigree collaterally which can be most valuable, taking the pedigree also backwards.

The records of the civil registration, and also the old parish registers of the Church of Scotland described in the next chapter, are housed in the New Register House, Edinburgh EH1 3YT, under the care of the Registrar General for Scotland.

A particular search in these records, and also in the census records described in Chapter XI, can be made by the Register House staff on receipt by post of sufficient details and the fee. A general search can only be made by the applicant or by someone acting on his or her behalf. Full details of the fees and conditions for particular or general searches can be obtained from the Registrar General.

III

PARISH AND NONCONFORMIST REGISTERS

T HE EARLIEST REFERENCE to the keeping of parish registers in Scotland is in a synod enactment of St Andrews in the 14th century which ordered incumbents of parishes to bring with them each year in writing the names and numbers of all who had died in their parish. This enactment was introduced so that the bishops might check that any testamentary dispositions, particularly of course those leaving gifts to the Church, were handed in and granted probate.

Unfortunately, none of these lists survive, so that it is not known to what extent notice was taken of this statute, but it is likely that Scotland was influenced by Thomas Cromwell's ordinance in England regarding the keeping of parish registers. The General Provincial Council of Scotland in 1552 did in fact enact that each parish should keep a register in which the curate should enter the names of the infants baptized together with those of their reputed parents and godparents, and also a register of the proclamations of banns of marriage and that these registers should (in Dr Patrick's translation) 'be treasured among the most precious Jewels of the Church'.[1]

This ordinance was passed at a period when the old Church was in decline and thus had little effect. The new reformed Church at first merely renewed the earlier enactment regarding the registration of deaths, this being done only as a means of helping the Commissaries in the administration of testators' estates. In 1616, however, the General Assembly passed an edict, later confirmed by the Scottish Privy Council, that every minister should keep a register of baptisms, marriages and burials.

Unfortunately, these instructions were never carried out effectively and a canon of the Scottish Church of 1636 proved no more successful. Even so there are a number of registers in existence which started before 1616, presumably as a result either of the statute of 1552 or else through the

46

ministers, having noticed the introduction of registration in England, adopting it themselves.

There was little supervision over the maintenance of these registers, and the presbyteries were only able to recommend and not to enforce their instructions. The keeping of the registers was mainly in the hands of the session clerk who did more or less as he pleased, but in some parishes the minister or reader showed a sense of responsibility in their upkeep.

In a few cases the ministers took too much interest in their registers and there are, unfortunately, signs in some country parishes in the 17th and early 18th centuries that they occasionally revised entries in them.

The number of parishes in which the registers commence before 1600 is only twenty-one and very few of these have been kept continuously since their beginning. Some thirty-five registers do not begin before 1801. The care with which they were kept and the details of information given vary from parish to parish, and from period to period as one session clerk succeeded another.

Very few of these registers have been printed or copied. The Scottish Record Society has published registers of the Edinburgh and Canongate marriages, Greyfriars Burial Ground and a few others. In 1872 was published *A Detailed List of the Old Parochial Registers of Scotland*. It was a very limited edition and is consequently only to be found in a few of the largest reference libraries. At Appendix A of this book will be found an alphabetical list of all the parishes in this publication.

A valuable work has been the indexing of all the entries of baptisms in the old parish registers of Selkirkshire up to 1854. This was organized by Dr A. B. Taylor, when Registrar General, who invited a few of his friends to collaborate in this task.

Selkirkshire was chosen for the experiment because it was the county with fewest parishes. In 1854 it contained only six. These, with the date of their earliest entries, were as follows: Ettrick (1693), Galashiels (1714), Kirkhope (1851), Roberton (1679), Selkirk (1697) and Yarrow (1691). The surnames of the children were arranged alphabetically, illegitimate children under the mother's name and also under the father's name when known.

If this enterprising work could be continued we might one day have an index of baptisms up to 1854 for all the counties of Scotland.

It is not surprising that the registers which are best kept and which begin at the earliest dates are mainly those in the large towns. The Canongate register of Edinburgh, which begins in 1564, records the marriage proclamation and subsequent marriage of Mary, Queen of Scots with Lord

Darnley. In more remote parts like the Western Isles the registers were irregularly kept and began at a much later date. In Stornoway in the Outer Hebrides no register was kept until 1780 and the reason for its being started then, as stated rather naïvely in the beginning of its earliest register, is revealing:

The Session taking into consideration that the Town and Parish of Stornoway is daily increasing in number and in trade and several of the youth going abroad to the Army, Navy and other Occupations, it may at some future period be a detriment to families that there is no authentic Register for recording the Marriages & Births of the Inhabitants; Have agreed that such a Register shall be kept in this Parish in time coming narrating the date of marriages and births within the parish as they occur, and at the same time invite all the inhabitants of this parish to give in to the clerk appointed to keep this register a state of their respective families narrating their marriage and birth of their children as soon as possible that they may be inserted before any of the new occurrences, at the same time every person is at Liberty to record the state of their families or not as they see convenient: and the Session constitutes Patrick Downie, Cooper in Stornoway, to be Clerk of this Register appointing him to sign every page at the bottom and to bring the book to the Session as often as he is required to do so that it may be examined and attested. Closed with prayer.

This opportunity in Stornoway for families to record details of the baptism and marriages of their members before the start of the new register was unfortunately only taken by the minister, his session clerk, and a few others. Had everyone done so there would have been a convenient account of all the families of the parish.

The same opportunity occurred in the parish of Kilmonivaig in the heart of the Highlands near Glengarry and the Caledonian Canal. This register also only started in 1780 and contains mostly Camerons, Macdonalds, and some Macnaughtens. An account of the minister's family is given early in the register, stated as 'Account of Children of the Minister, Mr Thomas Ross, who married Miss Louisa Cameron, daughter to John Cameron in Fassfern 20 Apr 1780'. This shows their seven sons and three daughters, born between the 6 October 1781 and 18 January 1801.

Some other families registered in this way, for example, Mr John Mitchell in Donie and his wife Mary McDiamid registered their children born between 1807 and 1816. Duncan McIntyre in Muwachan and his spouse, Catherine Kennedy, recorded their children born between 1793 and 1817. Alexander Cameron in Braehaldar and his spouse, Mary Stewart, registered their children born between 1812 and 1821, as did John Macdonald in Achaneich and his spouse, Jane Macdonald, their children between 1812 and 1819.

An unusual entry occurs in the Old Cumnock register of baptisms in 1782. There is an entry stating:

James l.s. of John Nicol in Bonland Mains and Agnes Crawford his wife was born on the 3d of July 1782.
N.B. Inserted at the request of the above James Nicol, as extracted from the Family Register, kept by his father, September 6th 1848.

There follows a list of the children of the above James Nicol and his wife Sarah Murdoch born between 1808 and 1826.

After the establishment of civil registration in 1855 the old parochial registers of Scotland were called in and are today housed in the New Register House, Edinburgh, where they are well looked after and have been suitably repaired and rebound where necessary. It is convenient to have them all available for consultation in one place, though the possibility of their destruction by fire or other causes is a serious threat, especially as so few have been copied. During the 1939–45 war they were moved for safety to Borthwick Castle.

In 1855 there were under 1,000 parishes in the kingdom and the total registers brought in were some 4,000 volumes. Some of them had been badly kept and a contributory cause of this was an act passed in 1783 imposing a tax of three pence on every entry. This resulted in parishes and in some cases whole counties discontinuing registration almost completely for a number of years. The registers were also affected adversely by the secession of 1733. Those who seceded regarded registration as connection with the established Church and declined to have the baptism of the children registered; some even went to the absurd length of paying the dues to the session clerk but not allowing him to make the registration.

Thus it is found that, though the English registers often contain the registration of dissenters, this is exceptional in Scotland.

No doubt the entries were frequently written up from some rough note-book kept by the session clerk and in a number of cases this is all that survives. Nor can the accuracy of the details be relied upon. It must be remembered that in a close community, such as existed in the country parishes, the session clerk would probably be among the guests at the ceremony and after enjoying the convivial hospitality of such occasions he may not have remembered too clearly the details when he came to write them in his note-book after returning home. Much depends on the conscientiousness of the session clerk. Sometimes in country parishes there are gaps in the registers for ten or even twenty years.

In Old Cumnock, Ayrshire, the minister, Mr Muir, after making some entries of proclamations which had apparently been omitted by the clerk notes: 'These marriages were all expede in the year 1763. What other neglects the clerk hath been guilty of in his management of this register from the year 1758, at which it begins, I cannot pretend to recollect' and he also has a more detailed and lengthy note headed, 'Cumnock 15th Febry 1757. I having at the desire of the Kirk Session revised this register of Baptisms, Find it has not been faithfully kept'. He went on to elaborate six points, among them were that, 'In different places there are Large Chasms whole pages left blank whereon it is presumable many names should have been recorded', and that in a number of instances, 'one of the parents' names, or their place of Abode and sometimes the very name of the Child baptis'd, are awanting', and that the numbering of the pages had been neglected, and that the clerk had failed to insert whether the child was lawful or natural, and finally that the writing was not plain nor were the margins properly laid out.

Criticism was not always by the minister of his session clerk. Sometimes it was the other way round. In the beginning of the year 1768 in the Glassary Parish Register of Births the session clerk inserted the following note:

N.B. Let not Posterity be surprised that the Register is not complete. It is and has been the Custom of the Revd Mr Peter Campbell ever since the Incumbency of the present Clerk to baptize Children without a certificate of their names being registered. In consequence of which it may safely be averred that one third if not one Half were never given in.

The neglects of Mr Campbell are certainly regretted by that portion of posterity who are genealogists, and as a son and grandson of ministers, and as a minister much consulted on his knowledge of Church law, it might have been expected he would have had more care.

In general, the information in entries varies considerably. It may be far fuller than that found in the English registers, or it may be more scanty. On the whole, where the entry exists, the information tends to be better than that found in England. One great advantage in the baptismal entries is the recording of the maiden name of the mother. In Scotland a married woman was not considered to have lost her maiden name on her marriage. Thus a Miss Jean Gordon marrying a Mr Robert Mackenzie would be designated in legal documents as 'Mistress Jean Gordon or Mackenzie'.

Baptisms
As mentioned the baptismal entry gives you the maiden surname of the mother. A typical entry taken from the previously mentioned Old Cumnock parish register reads as follows:

Robert Johnston Son Lawfull to Mr Daniel Johnston Surgeon in Cumnock and Mary Mackie his Spouse was Baptized the 4th of Jany. 1754 years.

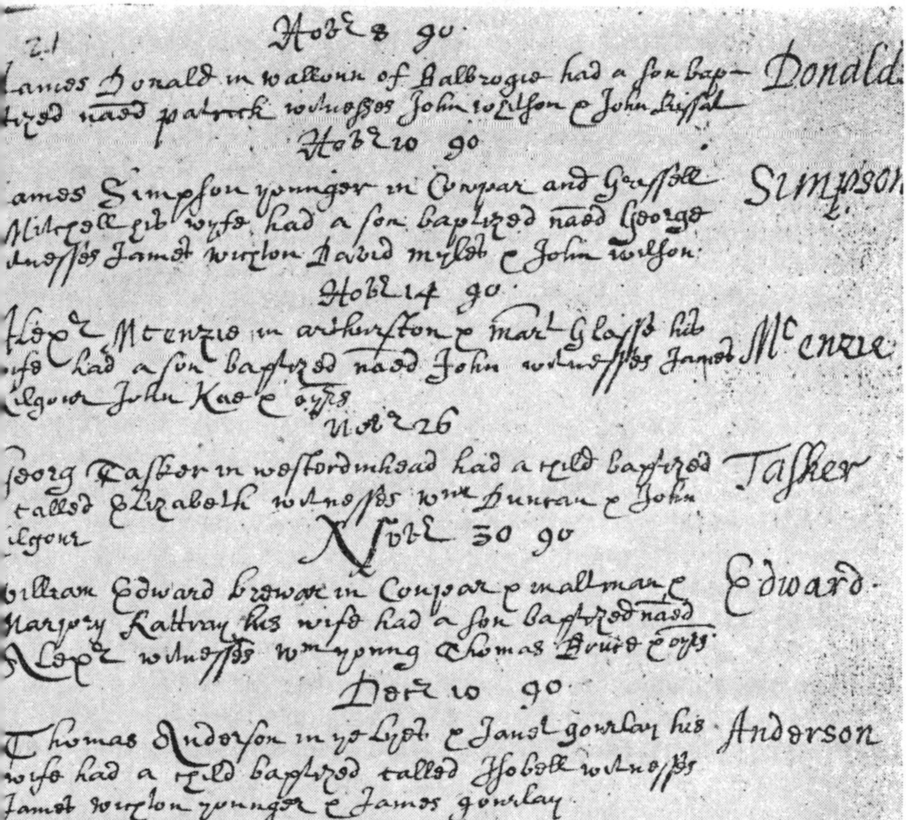

FIG. 1

Part of a page of baptisms of November and December 1690, from the earliest Coupar Angus parish register *Reproduced by Courtesy of the Church of Scotland and the Registrar General for Scotland* [R.G. ref. no. OPR/372/1]

Such entries greatly assist in identification. Genealogists in England know well the vexed problem of dealing with a very common surname like Smith, where there are several Smith families in the same parish, Identification in such cases sometimes becomes virtually impossible. It cannot always be assumed that, for instance, Jane daughter of John and Mary Smith is a sister of Richard, son of John and Mary Smith. There may be other John Smiths in the parish whose wives were called Mary. But in Scotland one can be reasonably certain that the daughter of 'John Smith and Mary Robertson his spouse' is a sister of other children of 'John Smith and Mary Robertson his spouse'.

Another advantage in Scotland is that often the names of the sponsors or godparents, usually called witnesses, are recorded. They were, of course, often relations. Sometimes the relationship is mentioned. There appears to be no fixed or universal Church rule as to the number of sponsors in Scotland. The medieval practice in England was two men and one woman for a boy and one man and two women for a girl. The custom has been in general carried on to the present day and was followed also in Scotland. The Aberdeen register, which starts at a particularly early period, from the beginning of its baptisms in 1563 and up to 1584 shows every boy with two godfathers and one godmother and every girl with one godfather and two godmothers, thus following the English custom. In this register the name 'godfather' rather than 'witness' is used for the period 1623 to 1704, as it is also in Glasgow parish from 1609 to 1651. After 1600 the names of female witnesses are seldom found and therefore after that date the names of godmothers are not known from this source.

As stated earlier, the relationship of witnesses is sometimes mentioned. Occasionally the information is extensive. Here is an unusually good example from Ayr parish register:

1739 John Hamilton son lawl. to John Hamilton merch. at present in Jamaica and Mrs Margarit Montgomery his spouse was born on Wednesday the 24th of Octr. 1739 bapt: thursday the 25 of the sd month by Mr Hugh Hamilton Mintr. of the Gospell at Garvine Uncle to the Child. Presented by Alexander Montgomery of Coylsfield uncle to the child in absence of the Parent. Witnesses Thomas Garvan prit. Provost of Ayr uncle in law to the Child, Mr Patrick Woodrow minst. of the Gospell at Tarbolton.

This kind of entry is exceptional and one cannot normally hope for such good fortune as this, a registration of a child of good social position. The registering of upper class children is usually fuller than that of those further down the social scale, but this is not always so. From the same parish comes this entry of a son of a coal-heaver, which is very remarkable in its information:

1734 Mathew Hall son lawl. to Mathew Hall Coalheaver in Newton & Helen Hunter his spouse was born friday the 8th of Feby. 1734 bapt. at Supra [i.e. Ayr] witnesses James Hall grandfather to ye child & John Hall uncle to the child.

On the other hand, sometimes an entry form from parents in a higher social position may be disappointing. Below is an entry from Maybole parish in Ayrshire:

Margaret Hall procreate betwixt Mr and Mrs Hall spouses in Auchindrain was born the 12th of July 1774 and baptized said day at her father's house by the Ordinary Minister.

Here, because of the parents' higher social position we actually get less information, losing all information of the parents' christian names and of the mother's maiden name. Also, perhaps because the baptism took place in the house, there are no witnesses recorded.

In contrast, in the larger town parishes, the list of witnesses can be lengthy. Thus in the registers of the Canongate parish, Edinburgh, we get:

January 1701. John Hamilton of Bardonoch, Bailie of the Abbey of Hallyroodhouse and Catherine Arbuthnot alias Arbuckles his lady had a sone born upon monday ye 30 Oct 1700 and baptized upon fryday ye 10 January 1701 Named Gerard after ye Surname of Elizabeth Dutchess of Hamiltoun: witnesses – Sir Archibald Cockburn of Lantourne, Sir John Johnstoun of Westerhall, John Cunninghame of Ba'ndalloch, Mr Gavin Johnstoun brother to Westerhall and several others.

The father was very remotely related to the ducal family but the Duke was hereditary Keeper of the Palace of Holyrood and John Hamilton of Bardannoch was his deputy. It may incidentally be of interest to note that the duchess referred to was the wife of the famous James Douglas, 4th Duke, who was killed in a duel in 1712 with Charles, Lord Mohun, immortalized in Thackeray's *Henry Esmond* as 'the Lord Murderer'. The Duke had married as his second wife Elizabeth, daughter and heiress of Digby, Lord Gerard. It is also worth noting that here, in accord with Scottish practice, the Laird of Westerhall is referred to by his estate instead of by his surname.

The baptism of the father himself provides an example of a baptism in the Edinburgh 'High Kirk' parish register of the mid-17th century:

Baptism 25 Januarii 1642 Johnne Hamiltoun of Murehouse (and) Anna Elphinstoun a S[on] N[amed] Johnne, Witn. Johnne Mr of Balmironoch, Mr Johnne Cockburne, Mr Johnn Elvis Advocat.

It will be noticed that the abbreviation for the title 'Master' for the Master of Balmironoch (or Balmerino) is the same as the ordinary 'Mr' which suggests that at this period they were both still pronounced 'Master'. It will also be noticed that the Christian name of all the witnesses is the same as that of the child baptized. This occurs elsewhere in this parish and in some other parishes.

Four examples from 17th-century baptisms in Brechin parish in Angus are given below.

4 June 1651 George Edward Chepman husband to elspit Louchars had a maid child bapt named Marat Wit: William Leuchars David Gray & Andrew Guthrie.

24 Jany 1657 George Edward hus to Isoble Leuchars had a man child baptized named William Witness William Leuchars William Gray Wm Livingston.

1687 22 August George Edwart husband to Janet Webster had a man child bapt James James Foorde, James Watt, James Davidssone Witts.

2 Dec 1792 James Carnegie of Cookston husband to Anna Livingstone had a man child bapt James (witnesses) James Lord Carnegie, James Carnegie of Balnamoon elder & yor.

It will be noticed that it is only in the case of the boys that the witnesses have the same Christian name as the baptized child. This could not be done in the case of the girls because women at this period were practically never witnesses to baptisms. It would seem for the boys that the witnesses were chosen because they had the same Christian name as the boy being baptized. The names given to the children were probably following the usual Scottish customs, which will be discussed in the next chapter.

The form 'had a man child' and 'had a maid child' is unusual but by no means unique.

It may also be noticed that in the first entry George Edward's wife has the Christian name 'Elspit' (Elspeth) and in the second entry 'Isobel'. Both these names were forms of Elizabeth.

Abercorn register is unusual in having entries of copies from a presbyterian register in England:

April 30th London Vestry in Swallow Street
                                                    8th Decr. 1803
John Son of General John Hope and Louisa Dorothea his wife was born the 15th Novr. last in Charles Street, Berkley Square in the parish of St George Hanover Square and baptised this day.
Copied from the Register of Births and Baptisms belonging to the Scotch Church in Swallow Street licensed according to Act of Parliament this 20th Decr. 1803 (Signed) John Trotter DD.
Abercorn 30th April 1807. The above this day copied from the original contract by W. Brown Sess. Clk.

This entry referred to the local laird's family and there is another entry of a baptism in this family which is an example of how much more information would often be given in registering members of prominent families.

George Johnstone Hope Esqr. Captain in the Royal Navy, and Lady Jemima Johnstone Hope, his Spouse, had their first child, a Daughter, born at their House in Charlotte Square, Edinburgh, on the 10th of April 1807 and Baptized by the Revd Dr Andrew Hunter Minister of the Tron Church on the 1st of May, in presence of James Earl of Hopetoun and Colonel John Hope named Helen. NB. Lady Jemima stood Sponsor for her Daughter, Captain Hope being abroad, in the Service of his Country.

The Scots were hard on the parents of base children. The kirk session records are full of notices of penance performed by such parents. Entries of base children are frank and often reflect on the social history of the times. Such a one is that given below from the Lintrathen baptisms:

Baptisms Sept. 30 1783.
Jean Ramsay, Daughter to John Ramsay in Dryburgh, had a Child begot in uncleanness baptized named David. The said John Ramsay being Sponsor.
The young man whom she accuses to be the father, having fled the bounds last Summer & resides sometimes in parish of Kirk Michael & at other times in parish of Alyth, shifting about from one place of the Country to another.
N.B. James Paterson, whom she accused as the father, has at last compeared before the Session, and confessed. Vide Session Minutes.

Marriages

In Scotland the registers often record only the proclamations of the banns of the marriage. This is not therefore a record of the marriage itself, nor is there any certainty that the marriage took place, though it may be assumed that it normally did. It is an advantage, however, that the proclamation is usually recorded in the parishes of both the bride and bridegroom. In some cases the parish in which the marriage took place will record this fact. For example, in Inch parish, Kirkudbrightshire, there is the following entry:

August 19th 1797. Alexr. Kelly in this parish and Catherine Hall in the Parish of Ayr gave in their Names in Order for Proclamation of marriage

and in Ayr Parish, Ayrshire, the following:

Ayr. 26th August 1797. Quo Die Alexander Kelly in the parish of Inch and Katherine Hall in Ayr parish gave in their Names to be proclaimed in Order for marriage and After proclamation were married Accordingly.

It will thus be noticed that in Inch parish the proclamation only is recorded, but in Ayr parish it is stated that they were married, thus showing that the marriage took place in that parish.

Occasionally there is an entry of a marriage without proclamation. This was only made in special circumstances, perhaps to a certain extent comparable to the licence or special licence in England, though far less common. An example of this is in the register of Kilbride on the Isle of Bute.

Marriage Proclamations. 1729 July 30th.
Gerard Hamilton and Margaret Stewart were married without proclamation by appointment of Elders for certain honourable causes.

Marriage proclamations sometimes give the name of the bride's father but seldom that of the bridegroom's father. Even this is an advantage over the English register where, until 1837, neither is normally given; but it is a disadvantage that, as these are records mainly of proclamations, there are no names of witnesses of the marriage such as you get from 1754 onwards in England.

Apart from cases where the elders gave special permission, the celebration of a marriage without proclamation in Scotland was a serious offence, making the marriage a clandestine one and rendering the minister liable to transportation. Even so, clandestine marriages were not uncommon. Sir John Sinclair in his *Statistical Account of Scotland* says that the authorities connived at rather than discouraged such marriages. Those which took place at Gretna Green were mainly English runaway couples and usually with one or perhaps both parties under age.

In a different category is Mordington, a parish near the border in Berwickshire. In its registers are a number of marriages recorded of people whose banns had been called in some parish on the English side of the Border and the details of these English banns have been recorded in the Scottish parish. It would seem that these couples wished or found it convenient to celebrate their marriage in this Scottish parish.

In England and Wales the marriages are the fullest and most nearly complete of the registrations, but in Scotland the baptisms are the most complete.

Burials

The recording of deaths was, as we have seen, the earliest obligation on the ministers of the parishes but, unfortunately, it has been the obligation least observed, and in many parishes no records of deaths or burials exist before the civil registration began in 1855. It has been suggested that one reason for this was that some small parishes had as many as seven or eight burial places.

Where there are surviving burial registers these often cover years spasmodically, and frequently consist merely of the account for the mortcloth kept by the parishes for use at funerals. This will indicate the approximate date of the burial, but it will only include those able to pay for the hire of the cloth. This means that the poorer people go unrecorded and also some of the well-to-do, as usually the presentation of the mortcloth to the parish was made by the laird or by some other prominent person, and in such cases no fee was normally charged for himself or his family when they required its use.

In the larger towns a register was sometimes kept for the burial ground and this may have an index indicating the approximate place of the grave. Often no stone will be found, as until quite recent times people were frequently buried with no headstone over their graves. Sometimes the older stones have been used again on the back, as they have been at Coupar Angus. In country parishes monumental inscriptions may be found on the stones in the churchyard and there will possibly be tablets on the walls of the church for people locally prominent.

Nevertheless, there are parishes in which the records of burials have been well kept. One of these is the parish of Old Luce, Wigtownshire, where in the 18th and early 19th centuries there are good tabulated lists of burials, including a separate list of burials of children under twelve. The previously mentioned parish of Abercorn, West Lothian, has also well-kept records of burials, in which the date of death is frequently also given, with the age and often the relationship to others, such as 'son of . . . ', 'spouse of . . . ', and quite often the cause of death, for instance – died 'of a pineing sickness'. This register of deaths usually has such details even in its earliest period of such records from 1645 to 1661, although this portion is unfortunately very fragmentary and damaged. The register of burials is unfortunately wanting from 1661 to April 1700, after which it is clearly written and gives the details indicated. This parish has also in its registers 'A True List of Contributors to the Mortcloaths Residing within the paroch of Abercorn at the Thirtieth day of December [1724]'. This valuable list gives considerable genealogical information about the contributors. For instance, entry No. 10 shows 'John Moffat there spouse to Jannet Shaw has a right by his said Spouse she being Daughter to John Shaw procreat betwixt him & Jannet Wood his spouse & grandchild to John Wood in Gallowscrook a Contributor in person pr. Second list', and No. 15 (headed 'In Hoptounhouse') 'Gavin Robertson herdsman Yr son to George Robertson fewer in Duntervie & Grandchild to George Robertson fewer there Contributers in person'.

There are 125 such entries in the first list. The second list only contains a further nine names as having been admitted by the session 10 January 1727. These were presumably a few names which required further investigation.

A great deal of valuable work has been done by members of the Scottish Genealogy Society in taking down the essential genealogical information from monumental inscriptions. Clackmannanshire, Dunbartonshire,

E

Kinross-shire and West Lothian have been covered by Mr and Mrs J. F. Mitchell, assisted in some counties by Miss M. A. Churchmichael, Miss H. M. Woodford and Mr Duncan McNaughton. Messrs. D. C. Cargill, senior and junior, have covered much of Berwickshire and Mr George Gilchrist of Annan with the assistance of Messrs. M. Cowan, A. Shannon, M. Shannon, R. A. Shannon and Mr C. H. Moore, have covered a number of the graveyards in Dumfriesshire. These have mostly been published, reproduced from typewriting, and are indexed and usually have a plan of the burial ground. Mr Sydney Cramer has covered a number of graveyards in Angus, Edinburgh and elsewhere and copies of his transcriptions are available on microfilm at the Scottish Record Office. Mr and Mrs James A. Thompson have transcribed Kettle churchyard, Fife. This work is particularly estimable in that these monumental inscriptions are deteriorating and becoming difficult or impossible to read and in some cases the stones are being removed in the course of town or country development.

Episcopal Church of Scotland Registers

Information about the surviving registers of this church must be sought from the individual parishes. The extent of their survival varies considerably. There is no central point of information about these records. Some reference to this matter and the possibility of having some list made of known pre-1855 registers was made in the Scottish Genealogy Society Council Report for October 1969. A useful list of known surviving registers will be found in an Appendix in Donald Steel's *Sources for Scottish Genealogy and Family History* (1971).

Roman Catholic Church Registers

A certain number of these registers survive among the older Catholic churches in Scotland, varying much in their content, some having only baptismal registers, others having also marriage and burial registers. Few, unfortunately, go back further than the 19th century. It is necessary at present to apply to the parish priest for information, but there is a survey in progress and the registers are being photocopied (1970). It is hoped that this work may be completed in about two years' time, when the photocopies will be available for researchers centrally. The list, when completed, will be published in *The Innes Review*.

Quaker Records

The Society of Friends never appeared in any strength in Scotland. Cromwell's Edict of Toleration in 1657 allowed a few brief years of

Quakerism in country areas like Aberdeenshire, and at Urie in Kincardineshire, where the Quaker, Robert Barclay, was the laird in mid-17th century. He was the author of the *Apology* which was accepted for many years as a classic exposition of the Quaker creed.

In the 18th century Quakerism declined in Scotland to a greater extent than it did in England and its almost entire survival was in Edinburgh, where the family of Miller of Craigentinny encouraged its existence. At the end of that century some increase was experienced with the establishment of the Half-Yearly Meeting of North Britain in 1786. The 19th century saw little growth in the numbers of this sect, which was then mainly concentrated in Edinburgh and Glasgow.

Although the importance of keeping records was stressed by the Society of Friends in England, the survival of records of this society in Scotland is poor. The records of the monthly meetings are principally those at which births, marriages and burials were recorded. These and the lists of members, with some accounts of 'Sufferings', constitute the principal genealogical Quaker records in Scotland, together with the *Annual Monitor*, which was a compilation of obituary records of members.

Scottish Quaker records are held by the three centres, Aberdeen, Edinburgh and Glasgow, and for better preservation some of the earlier documents have been sent to the library at Friends House, Euston Road, London. The others are retained in the meeting houses in Aberdeen, Edinburgh and Glasgow. There is a proposal to centralize them in Edinburgh. Dr George B. Burnet's *Story of Quakerism in Scotland* contains a list of the principal records as an appendix, though these are not always quite accurate in some details.

In London are preserved minute books of the Aberdeen Monthly Meetings from 1690 to 1786, which contain references to marriages and deaths, though these are infrequent. There is also a register of marriages at the Aberdeen Monthly Meetings from 1700 to 1786, but unfortunately these are largely illegible through damp. The register of births from the Aberdeen Quarterly Meetings from 1784 to 1795 contain printed forms of birth certificates, but there are very few entries. The register of burials given in the Quarterly Meetings of Aberdeen from 1783 to 1795 also contain few entries. A register of marriage certificates for this centre from 1786 to 1792 has full page entries in copperplate, but few in number.

The *Aberdeen* records include a digest of births etc. to 1872 (this appears to be duplicated in the Glasgow records mentioned below); a register of births recorded at the Monthly Meetings from 1795 which has been kept up to date; and a marriage register from the Aberdeen Monthly Meetings from about 1797 on. There are various other volumes and documents relating to the Monthly Meeting and the General Meetings of ministers[2] and elders.

At *Glasgow* records are held in the Meeting House at 16 Newton Terrace. Probably the most valuable of these is the 'Digest of births, marriages and burials in Scotland' which appears to have been kept up to 1872 with a few later entries. Here also are the minutes of the Aberdeen Monthly and Quarterly Meetings 1672 to 1692, which include death notices; minute books of Aberdeen Montly Meetings 1690 to 1786; a minute book of the Aberdeen Quarterly Meetings 1697 to 1773 and of Kinmuck Monthly Meetings 1701 to 1782; register book of Aberdeen Montly Meetings, including the births from 1664 to 1715 and marriages 1669 to 1696; minute book of Urie Monthly Meetings, which includes births 1670 to 1787, marriages 1669 to 1762 and deaths 1671 to 1782; the register books of Aberdeen Monthly Meetings, marriages 1700 to 1786, births 1796 to 1866, marriages 1797 to 1862 and burials 1795 to 1865; and the register of the Quarterly Meetings containing the births 1784 to 1795, burials 1783 to 1795 and marriages 1786 to 1792.

At *Edinburgh* minutes and register books for the Monthly Meetings there from 1710 to 1786 exist, though badly kept. There are minute books of the Edinburgh Monthly Meetings 1669 to 1706; and 1730 to 1794; Edinburgh Quarterly Meetings 1669 to 1737; Edinburgh Monthly Meetings register books of births, marriages and deaths 1786 to 1794; Edinburgh Two-months meetings register book of births, marriages and deaths 1794 to 1864; Hamilton and Glasgow Monthly Meetings 1695 to 1722; Kelso Monthly Meetings minute book 1748 to 1787 and of Preparative Meetings 1787 to 1792; West of Scotland record book 1656 to 1703, which includes notices of births, marriages and deaths, and the General Meeting for Scotland register book 1795 to 1867.

A more detailed account of these records, with a number of examples of information found in them is contained in an article by William H. Marwick entitled 'Scottish Friends Records', *Scottish Genealogist*, Volume 7, No 3. Most of the information in the preceding paragraphs is based on this article, which is recommended to all searchers of Quaker records in Scotland.

IV

SURNAMES AND CHRISTIAN NAMES

Scottish Surnames

SURNAMES IN SCOTLAND were adopted for the same reasons and at about the same time as they were in England and Wales, and they were mainly formed from the same sources – from the father's Christian name, from the estate, from a trade or from a nickname. People who migrated to other parts were often called after the district or country from which they came. This accounts for such names as Scott, England, Sutherland.

In the Highlands and Islands, being Gaelic-speaking, descendants of the same ancestor can have very different surnames, depending upon whether they derive from the Gaelic or from an English translation of the name. An example of this is found in the Morison family of Lewis, who are said to derive their surname from an ancestor called in Gaelic 'Gille-Mhuire', that is "Servant of Mary", possibly someone who was a servitor or other worker in a chapel dedicated to the Virgin Mary. The descendants who kept the Gaelic names were MacGhillemhuire, which in the course of time became shortened to Gillmore or Gilmour, or even to Milmore, then sometimes contracted to Miles or Myles. The name, however, translated into English became Morison or Morrison or, less frequently, Maryson.

Because Gaelic names were thought by some of those who bore them to be long, cumbersome and difficult for strangers to pronounce, their possessors sought to change them to their English equivalent. Blain's *History of Bute* (1880), edited by William Ross, mentions (p. 31) that some inhabitants of the island made such changes. People of the name of MacKemies, which is a corrupted form of MacHamish (son of Hamish, i.e. of James) changed their name to Jamieson, and a number of others made, or tried to make, similar changes. In some cases, the father and

61

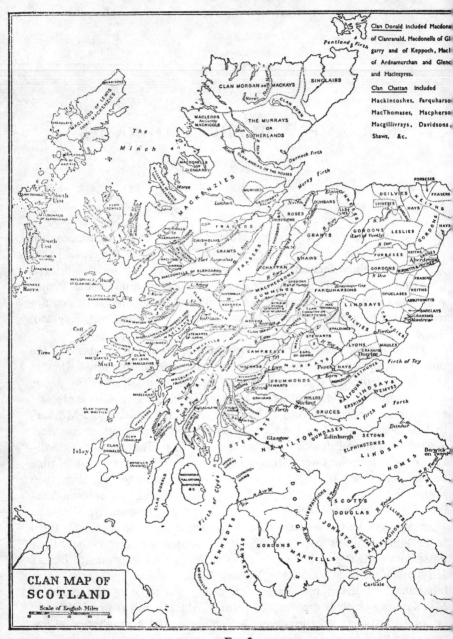

FIG. 2
Map showing the Homelands of Clans and Lowland Families *Reproduced from* The Clans, Septs and Regiments of the Scottish Highlands, 8th Edn. (jacket map) Johnston and Bacon (1970) *by courtesy of Geoffrey Chapman, Publishers, a Division of Crowell Collier and Macmillan Publishers Ltd.*

certain of his children still kept their traditional surname while others took the new one. The confusion was, of course, considerable.

The minister of Rothesay of the time, who possessed an affection for the Gaelic tongue, vehemently objected to these changes and refused to do anything to aid or encourage persons wanting to make them or, indeed, to sanction their adoption.

Certainly the Scots attached less permanence to surnames than the English. Mention has been made earlier of the clansmen taking the surname of their chief. Another change, far less uncommon than in England, was the adoption of the mother's name. This was often through the inheritance of estates in the female line. The retention of the maiden name by a married woman is indicative of the importance attached to it and in consequence of a greater willingness to adopt the female surname. This is a factor which genealogists searching Scottish records must bear in mind.

As a result of the clan system people of the same name were indentified with the clan country, and therefore the name was prevalent in that area and often rare in other areas. Even today Scottish names tend to be confined mainly to certain areas. Sir Iain Moncreiffe and Don Pottinger have produced an excellent *Map of Scotland of Old*,[1] which shows the different districts in which the clans and their names exist.

In the Isle of Lewis in the Outer Hebrides even now the families bear mainly three names, Morison, Macleod and Nicholson. The Mackays are largely confined to Strathnaver in the north and the Sinclairs to that part of Caithness in the north-east corner. The great clan of the Mackenzies stretch across Ross from east to west. The Camerons occupy the west portion of the Lochaber district and the great Campbell clan cover Argyllshire as one would expect them to do, but also have a smaller settlement in Ayrshire. The McDonald clan, once known as McDonald of the Isles, occupy the Isles of Islay and quite a proportion of the Isle of Skye and the northern portion of Uist.

The Lowland families also occupy distinct areas. In Galloway we have the Kennedys and the Maxwells and the great family of Hamilton occupy much of Strathclyde. In the eastern Lowlands the Homes lived in Berwickshire, and the Kerrs, Scotts and Hepburns on the Border, but all these families have pockets of occupation in other areas. The great family of Mackintosh, with their chief, the Mackintosh of Mackintosh, a vast landowner, occupy much of Moray and Inverness-shire. The Gordons extend through Marr and Buchan. The Ogilvys were mainly in Angus though earlier they came from further south.

The Gaelic 'Mac' means 'son of' as did the Norman 'Fitz'. Thus in the Highlands you get few names ending in '-son', which is so common in England. Those that do often have a Scandinavian derivation, possibly from migrants from Orkney and Shetland, where names ending in '-sen' have sometimes been anglicized to '-son'.

For the above reason the letter 's' is not a common ending to Scottish names, though it frequently gets added to those of Scots who move to England. Names like Gibb and Cumming are constantly designated Gibbs and Cummings, and the author's own surname of Edwards was so altered when an ancestor went to India in the East India Company's service. The name, originally Edward, is a comparatively rare one, found principally in Angus from where this family came.

Shetland Surnames

The north of Scotland as a whole in early times was affected by Norse invasion, and the Shetland and Orkney Isles particularly so; and in these islands patronymics, that is, the practice of each generation being named after the father's Christian name, persisted far longer than it did elsewhere in Great Britain. This means that a name like Peterson means literally 'son of Peter' and the father will perhaps be called Peter Johnson, meaning 'son of John', while his father in turn might be called John Robertson. Patronymics are therefore descriptive and not hereditary as are surnames.

Patronymics did of course exist in Great Britain in Norman and early Angevin times and it was the inconvenience of their use which caused Edward II to require that people should adopt surnames; many surnames did, of course, derive from Christian names with 'son' added to them.

Mr A. Sandison, in his article on 'Shetland Surnames' in *The Genealogists' Magazine* for June and September 1959,[2] shows that patronymics continued to be used there even as late as the early 19th century. He gives an example of a Gilbert Sandison who, when he died in 1870 aged seventy-six, was described in his Scottish death certificate as 'son of Alexander Harrison'. This shows that people were even being named by patronymics as late as the 1790's, for Sandison is only an abbreviated form of 'Alexanderson'.

None of the Shetland parish registers begin before the 18th century, but a number of them start around 1735. In these you can see the patronymics and the surnames side by side. Some of the parish clerks recorded the child's name separately in addition to the father's second name. Others, unfortunately, did not do so. Mr Sandison says that by the year 1820 children were keeping their father's surname though many adults retained the patronymic. This change, he explains, depended greatly on the parish clerk and he gives entries from the Northmavine register of baptisms to show this. Thus there is baptized in 1781, 12 August, to 'Peter Christi & Donaldsdaugh^r. in Stenness, a son Christopher' and two years later, '1783, 10 Aug. Peter Sandison, & Donaldsdaughr. in Hogaland, a son Arthur'.

It will be noticed that in the first entry the father is called by his surname, but in the second is described by his patronymic, and it will also be noticed that the mother is described both times by her patronymic, 'Donald's daughter'. This female form of patronymic for daughters, sometimes 'daughter', sometimes abbreviated to 'daugh.' or 'dr,' and sometimes 'dochter', did not survive as long as the 'son', perhaps because it was rather a mouthful, and later daughters, somewhat illogically, also have the patronymic '-son' added to their father's name. Thus at later periods Joan Donaldson may be used for a daughter of Donald.

The Christopher born in 1781 as son of Peter Christi is shown in his death certificate as Christopher Sandison, son of Peter Sandison and Margaret Donaldson. You here have a good example of the patronymic and surname existing side by side, Peter being described in one entry by his probably newly-adopted surname of Christi and in the other by his patronymic of Sandison because he was the son of Alexander; the mother, though in both baptismal entries described by her patronymic as Donaldsdaugh^r. without her Christian name, in the death certificate of the son Christopher is given her Christian name Margaret and the later form of female patronymic, Donaldson, rather than Donaldsdaugh^r.

Mr Sandison quotes a good example of the use of patronymics from an account of a wedding in the *Shetland Times* of 1907. The later generations follow the modern practice of surnames, but when we get back to the earlier generations of the bride we find 'Charles Hoseason of Dalsetter, born in 1722, a son of Hosea Anderson of Aywick', the father being in turn described as Andrew Johnson, whose father was John Francisson: He was the son of Francis Johnson of Aywick (1667); son of John Lawrencson, Foude of Yell 1622, who died in 1635, who was in turn a son of Laurence Sjovaldson, a son of Sjovald of Aywick.

Sir Francis J. Grant in his *County Families of the Zetland Islands* (1893) also mentions this Hoseason family as a splendid example of patronymics for eight generations and gives a number of other examples of the use of patronymics in the Shetlands. These include the descent of Magnus (or Mans) Norsk, the descent running: Magnus Norsk – Thomas Magnussen – Magnus Thomasson – Thomas Manson (or Magnusson) (no sons) – Grizel Thomasdaughter, married Gilbert Arthurson of Sandvoe (son of

Arthur Anderson of Sandvoe) and had issue Arthur Gilbertson – Thomas Arthurson – Anne Eliza Arthurson (died 1837). It will be noticed how the last patronymic 'Arthurson' becomes established as a surname for the daughter Anne Eliza.

In the pedigree of the Grays of Cliff in the parish of Unst we have William Gray of Cliff, died in February 1634, having married Sinnevo Schewartsdochter, who survived him and had issue – Walter Gray of Cliff, married Dorothy Thomas, daughter of Thomas Manson (or Magnusson) and granddaughter of Magnus Norsk, minister of Unst, and had issue.

Mr Lawson Edwards, (the present librarian of the Society of Genealogists,) has provided me with another example of the existence of patronymics into the 19th century. His ancestor, Edward Donaldson, a fisherman of Unst in the Shetland Isles, who was born about 1752 and was living at the time of the census of 1841 and married to Bretta Jack on 21 December 1779, had an eldest son Daniel with the surname Edwardson, being a patronymic, who was born in 1781 and died in 1861, when his death certificate showed his father with the surname of Donaldson. Daniel had a son, Robert, who retained the now-established surname Edwardson, but he joined the Royal Navy as Edwards in 1838 and since then this form of the surname has been continued by the family.

The loss of the 'on' from the suffix 'son' as mentioned earlier seems the fate of many names. While Richardson, Robertson and Johnson have survived, Edwardson, perhaps because it is less easy to say, has in nearly all cases become Edwards, or in Scotland Edward.

There are however examples of both Edward and Edwardson in the Shetlands and Orkneys. In the Commissariot of Orkney[3] there is a will of a Robert Edward of the parish of Orphir, proved 14 December 1665 and of a Thomas Edwardson, servitor to William Sinclair in Sandwick in South Ronaldsay, proved on 22 April 1625, and in the Shetland Commissariot[4] there is a James Edwardson in Udsta on the Isle of Fetlar, whose testament was proved on 20 July 1615, and a Marion Edwardsdochter (that is, Edward's daughter), spouse to William Jacobisone in Setter in the Isle of Yell, whose testament was proved on 10 August 1631.

When familes moved south to the mainland, their surnames usually became fixed at whatever stage the patronymic had then reached. There is a reference in the Exchequer Rolls of Scotland to a George Edwardson, customer of Dunbar, in 1447, and in 1451 to some tenements which he held in Dunbar, and to a William Edwardson, probably some relation, also a customer of Dunbar.[5]

At the end of the 15th century there is also a record of some Edwardsons in Edinburgh. One of them married Agnes Redshaw of the Edinburgh family of that name and their son, George Edwardson, is mentioned in a peremptory court order of October 1492.[6] But this name, which was possibly Scandinavian in origin and from Shetland or Orkney, seems to have died out in the 17th century. It probably became simply 'Edward'.

The use of patronymics naturally makes it difficult to trace ancestry, the lack of a surname to link each generation being very apparent. With Edward Donaldson, for instance, one has to look for a Donald . . . son, with little indication as to how to fill in the blank. One guide is the name pattern, which seems to have been followed fairly rigidly in the Shetlands and Orkneys. Thus one can look for an eldest son named after the father's father and so on (see Chapter V on naming customs). Nevertheless, the task is a very difficult one and the frequent gaps in the registers, which in any case do not start very early, the lack of wills among a community who mostly had no property to leave and consequently also do not appear in the sasines registers or in the retours of service of heirs, make this task even harder. Many Shetland and Orcadian families could recite their ancestry by heart, but unfortunately in few cases has this ancestry been committed to paper.

Foundlings

The possibility of a foundling ancestor should also be borne in mind. In Scotland as in England abandoned children were sometimes left in the church porch or near to the church. This frequently resulted in the surname having some connection with the church. Surnames such as 'Church' or 'Kirk' were often given to foundlings and these surnames and also the Christian names were usually the decision of the minister or session clerk. Only occasionally was there some note pinned to the baby's clothes asking that the child be given a particular Christian name. Otherwise it was often given the name of a saint, perhaps the name of the one on whose day the child was discovered or the name of the saint to whom the church was dedicated. Sometimes the saint's name might be given as the surname.

There were other variations and sources. In the baptismal register of Coupar Angus on 22 February 1745 there appears this entry, 'Allso ane Exposed infant found att Causyend Mundays night the 18th Current was baptized and is called Angus Coupar'. Probably descendants may have no idea that they owe their surname of Coupar or Cooper to this ingenious inversion of the name of the parish in which their foundling ancestor was discovered.

In Livingston, West Lothian, the name of the parish was also used, but this time in conjunction with the Christian name of the reigning sovereign. The following entry appears in the parish register in August 1800:

There was exposed at the door of John Tod, farmer, Longlivingstone, a Child found at 3 o'clock a.m. on the 4th August, 1800 – and baptized the 6th – after his present Majesty & the name of the parish – Livingston.

To the genealogist the discovery of a foundling ancestor must be a major disappointment. Even the baptism of a baseborn forbear will indicate, at any rate, the mother's name, but nearly always the foundling leaves the genealogist with a line beyond which it is not possible to penetrate.

The Most Common Surnames

The *Sixth Detailed Annual Report of the Registrar General of Births, Deaths and Marriages in Scotland* (1864) gives the fifty most common surnames in Scotland, based on the returns of 1861, and an estimate of the population holding those surnames in that year. The most common surname is Smith, which represented nearly 1½ per cent of the total entries and a population of 44,378. Smith is also the most common surname in England, but not quite so prevalent as in Scotland. The next most common in Scotland has a more Scottish flavour. This is Macdonald, with an estimated population of 37,572 bearing this name. The first twenty of the fifty most common surnames in Scotland and the estimated population bearing the name in 1861 are as follows:

	Surname	Est. No.		Surname	Est. No.
1.	Smith	44,378	11.	Mackenzie	23,272
2.	Macdonald	37,572	12.	Scott	22,342
3.	Brown	33,820	13.	Johnston	21,569
4.	Robertson	32,600	14.	Miller	21,318
5.	Thomson	32,560	15.	Reid	20,047
6.	Stewart	31,836	16.	Ross	18,254
7.	Campbell	31,555	17.	Paterson	18,048
8.	Wilson	29,741	18.	Fraser	18,013
9.	Anderson	28,300	19.	Murray	17,606
10.	Mackay	23,840	20.	Maclean	17,375

Christian Names

Scotland, like most other countries, has produced its share of Christian names peculiar to its boundaries or at any rate considerably more common there. Those which seem particularly linked with the Scots are Angus, Duncan (the name of the murdered king in *Macbeth*), Colin, Neil, Malcolm, Kenneth, Dugald, Lachlan and Murdoch. There are some rarer names which are also particularly Scottish and these include Evander, Gavin and Nicol.

The Registrar General for Scotland's report of 1864, besides giving the fifty most common surnames in Scotland, gave also a list showing the comparative frequency of Scottish Christian names, male and female, taken from the 1861 Index of Births. As of course Christian names do not occur as such in alphabetical order in the indexes the list has been made by taking the six most common surnames and examining in the case of the male names some 3,690 entries and compiling from these the number of entries of each Christian name. This showed John, as in England, the most common Christian name with 563 entries. This is followed by James, with 508 entries, not surprising when it is remembered that this was the Christian name of a succession of Scottish kings. Next comes William, then Alexander, followed by Robert and George, then David, Thomas, Andrew. The last mentioned might have been expected to be higher since it is the name of the patron saint of Scotland. The thirty most common male Christian names are given below, with the number found among the 3,690 entries.

	Name	No.			Name	No.
1.	John	563		15.	Donald	28
2.	James	508		17.	Walter	26
3.	William	473		18.	Joseph	24
4.	Alexander	318		19.	Colin	22
5.	Robert	225		20.	Samuel	19
6.	George	159		21.	Henry	18
7.	David	153		22.	Daniel	17
8.	Thomas	139		22.	Neil	17
9.	Andrew	102		24.	Malcolm	16
10.	Charles	65		25.	Francis	15
11.	Peter	64		26.	Matthew	11
12.	Hugh	49		26.	Roderick	11
12.	Archibald	49		28.	Richard	9
14.	Angus	40		28.	Allan	9
15.	Duncan	28		28.	Edward	9

The most common female names were calculated in a similar way, based in this case on the seven most common surnames in the Births Indexes for 1861 and relate to 3,689 entries. It is not surprising that Margaret comes out the most popular name for girls, since St Margaret, the 11th century Queen of Scotland was held in such veneration by the Scots. Mary comes next, followed by Elizabeth and then Ann.

Female Christian names which seem to have a particularly Scottish flavour are Christina, Grizel or Grisel, Geillis, Jeanie, Euphemia, Flora, Alexandrina, Clementina and Robertina, the last three illustrating the Scots' fondness for female forms of male names. The thirty most common

Christian names for girls, with the number of times they occur in the 3,689 entries examined, are given below:

Name	No.	Name	No.
1. Margaret	470	16. Grace	27
2. Mary	462	17. Eliza	25
3. Elizabeth	303	18. Betsy	21
4. Ann	271	19. Euphemia	18
5. Jane	262	20. Martha	17
6. Janet	213	21. Flora	14
7. Isabella	212	22. Charlotte	16
8. Agnes	193	22. Georgina	14
9. Catherine	166	22. Jemima	14
10. Helen	138	22. Susan	14
11. Christina (Christian)	107	22. Wilhelmina	14
12. Jessie	102	27. Alice	12
13. Marion	58	27. Joan	12
14. Jean (Jeanie)	48	29. Marjory	10
15. Barbara	32	30. Amelia	8

Some Shetland and Orcadian families could recite their ancestry by heart

V

NAMING CUSTOMS

I N MOST COUNTRIES parents have named their children after their own or their parents or grandparents or earlier forbears. Scotland, being a country appreciative of its traditions, had a highly developed system of naming children.

The general custom, to which there were some variations, was to name children as follows:

The eldest son after the paternal grandfather
The second son after the maternal grandfather
The third son after the father
The eldest daughter after the maternal grandmother
The second daughter after the paternal grandmother
The third daughter after the mother

Younger children would be named after earlier forbears, but the pattern in their case was less settled.

One variation from the above was for the eldest son to be named after the mother's father and the eldest daughter after the father's mother. In this case the second son would be named after the father's father and the second daughter after the mother's mother. Occasionally the second son and daughter would be named after the father and mother instead of the third son and daughter. Another variation was to call the third daughter after one of the great-grandmothers instead of after the mother. In such a case the fourth daughter would usually be called after the mother.

Variations were sometimes noticeable in particular localities. Mr J. F. Mitchell of Edinburgh has drawn my attention to the Isle of Bute, where he noticed the previously mentioned deviation in which the first daughter is called after the father's mother and the second daughter after the mother's mother. He kindly gave me a number of examples, mainly 18th century. It was observed from these that the variation applied generally only to the eldest and second daughters. The eldest son continued usually to be named after the father's father and the second son after the mother's father.

Certainly more research could profitably be made into this matter. It is not easy to get a sufficiently large sample of perfect examples, that is, of examples giving all lines to the great-grandparents in which it is known for certain there were no older or younger children whose Christian names are not known.

It will be appreciated that this conventional pattern of naming children, even with the variations, is of great value to the genealogist. From the names of the children, provided you know the orders of their birth, you can work out the probable Christian names of their grandparents and possibly get some idea of those further back. Then you can look out for ancestors of these names of the right period and perhaps substantiate such possible connections.

As indicated, the existence of earlier children who died young will affect the pattern. However, the third son being named after the father, whose name may be already known to you, will help you in that case to fix the position of earlier sons.

There were, as might be expected, factors which disturbed this name pattern. One of these would be the case of children of the third son. As he was normally named after the father his eldest son, being named after the grandfather, would have the same name as his father. Therefore the father's third son would not be given his name, as the eldest son already had this name, but would be given one of the earlier names in the family. A break in the pattern occurred also where the Christian names of, for instance, both the paternal and maternal grandparents were the same. You would not normally have two sons named the same. (When this is found it is an indication that the earlier son had died, as parents were usually anxious to perpetuate the family names.) This disturbance of the name pattern applies similarly in the naming of daughters, as when, for instance, both the paternal and maternal grandmothers had the same Christian name.

There were other factors which could cause variation in the pattern. A maternal grandfather, particularly if he was a man of importance, especially where his daughter was an heiress, might be given priority over the paternal grandfather, the eldest son being named after the former. Then there are cases where a son is named after a godfather or after his father's patron.

There were also customs which caused changes. One of these was the custom by which a child was named after a minister recently ordained to the parish, when the child's baptism was his first in the parish. The register of Abercorn records:

1791. baptism Decr 22 – George Hay in Crewstone & Elizth. Carlow his spouse had their fourth Child a Daughter born the 21st and bapd. 25th Do. named Hughina. N.B. The above being the first Baptism after Mr Meiklejohn's Ordination as Minr. of this Parish the Child took her name from his.

The minister, Hugh Meiklejohn, was ordained to this parish the very day of this baptism. The child, being a girl, was given a feminine form of the minister's Christian name.

Then again it was sometimes customary for a child to be given the Christian name or feminine equivalent of the doctor when it was the first birth at which he had attended.

In considering this name pattern it must be remembered that certain Christian names had different forms. The Gaelic Hamish, for instance, is the equivalent of James. Ian or Iain are Scottish forms of the Latin Johannes, which is the English John. Elspeth, with its diminutive Elspie, Isobel and Isabel are forms of Elizabeth. Daniel is the equivalent of Donald.

The pedigree given on pages 74–5 of a Johnstone family of Ayrshire, which was settled in Old Cumnock parish in the 18th century, will help to illustrate the name pattern. Examining the children of Alexander Johnstone and Helen Sutherland, it will be seen that James, the eldest son, is named after the paternal grandfather, Daniel the second son should be named after his mother's father. Unfortunately the Old Cumnock baptisms begin only in 1704 and there is a gap in them from the latter part of 1706 until 1718, and Helen Sutherland's baptism has not been found, nor has her parentage so far been discovered from other sources. There are good reasons for thinking her to be the daughter of Daniel Sutherland and Janet Rankin, these being the only couple of the name of Sutherland having children baptized in Old Cumnock parish during the period. Certainly this would account for her second son being called Daniel and also for Janet, the eldest daughter, being called that name after her mother's mother.

The third son in this generation, Alexander baptized in 1728, is named after his father. The fourth son, William, and the fifth son, George, are no doubt named after earlier forbears. It will be noticed that both the first daughter named Janet and the first son named George must have died young, as in each case there is a younger child of the same name.

F

J O H N S T O N E   O F

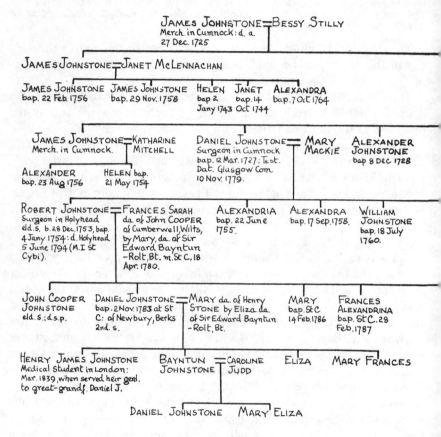

1 JOHNSTONE OF OLD CUMNOCK

OLD CUMNOCK

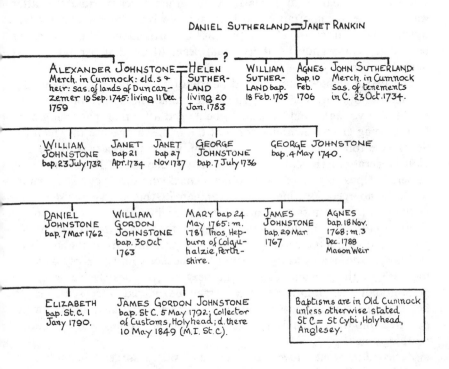

DANIEL SUTHERLAND ⚭ JANET RANKIN

?

ALEXANDER JOHNSTONE ⚭ HELEN
Merch. in Cumnock: eld. s &
heir: sas. of lands of Duncan-
zemer 19 Sep. 1745: living 11 Dec.
1759

HELEN
SUTHER-
LAND
living 20
Jan. 1783

WILLIAM
SUTHER-
LAND bap.
18 Feb. 1705

AGNES
bap. 10
Feb.
1706

JOHN SUTHERLAND
Merch. in Cumnock
Sas. of tenements
in C. 23 Oct. 1734.

WILLIAM
JOHNSTONE
bap. 23 July 1732

JANET
bap 21
Apr. 1734

JANET
bap 27
Nov 1737

GEORGE
JOHNSTONE
bap. 7 July 1736

GEORGE JOHNSTONE
bap. 4 May 1740.

DANIEL
JOHNSTONE
bap. 7 Mar 1762

WILLIAM
GORDON
JOHNSTONE
bap. 30 Oct
1763

MARY bap 24
May 1765: m.
1781 Thos. Hep-
burn of Colqu-
halzie, Perth-
shire.

JAMES
JOHNSTONE
bap. 29 Mar
1767

AGNES
bap. 18 Nov.
1768: m. 3
Dec. 1788
Mason Weir

ELIZABETH
bap. St. C. 1
Jany 1790.

JAMES GORDON JOHNSTONE
bap. St C. 5 May 1792.; Collector
of Customs, Holyhead; d. there
10 May 1849 (M.I. St. C).

Baptisms are in Old Cumnock
unless otherwise stated
St C = St Cybi, Holyhead,
Anglesey.

In the next generation, among the children of Daniel Johnstone and Mary Mackie, we have Robert Johnstone established as the eldest son in a service of heirs dated 19 March 1839. The eldest son should have been called Alexander and it is possible that there was an elder son of this name who died young. Alternatively, this may be a case where the eldest son was named after his maternal grandfather because the latter was someone of importance and the parents wished to compliment him by naming their eldest son after him. Unfortunately, Mary Mackie's parentage is not known but it would seem likely that her father was named Robert.

The two daughters, one named Alexandria and the other Alexandra (probably both intended to be the same name, the earlier of whom no doubt died young), would appear to be named after their paternal grandfather, being given a feminine form of the name, a practice of which the Scots were fond. The next son is William, which name exists in the previous generation. He should normally have been called Daniel after the father, but possibly there was another Daniel who died young, of whom we have no record owing to another gap in this parish register. The next eldest son is, in fact, named Daniel after his father and then comes William Gordon Johnstone, which suggests that the earlier William died young. No doubt Gordon is a surname, probably from the mother's forbears. Then comes Mary, bearing her mother's and possibly also her mother's mother's name. James, the next son, carries the name of the great-grandfather Johnstone. Agnes may be named after someone on her mother's side, or possibly after the Agnes Sutherland shown in the pedigree who was probably a sister of the younger Agnes' paternal grandmother, Helen.

Robert Johnstone moved to Wales and was a surgeon in Holyhead, marrying an Englishwoman. This naturally influenced the name pattern but it is interesting to see how the Scottish influence persisted. Robert Johnstone married Frances Sarah, daughter of John Cooper of Cumberwell, a well-connected landowner of Wiltshire. Their eldest son is called, in consequence, John Cooper Johnstone after his mother's father, being given both his Christian and surname, a custom which was spreading at this period, when people were beginning to be given more than one Christian name. It is the second son this time who is named after the father's father. Mary, the eldest daughter, is in accordance with custom named after her mother's mother. As Mary happens to be the Christian name of her father's mother also, the next daughter is named after the mother Frances, but given the name Alexandrina as well, which comes from her aunt baptized Alexandra. It is uncertain after whom Elizabeth is named, but James Gordon Johnstone continues the name James and also the surname Gordon, which is obviously an important connection in the family.

The children of Daniel Johnstone and Mary Stone in the next generation, though departing somewhat from the Scottish pattern, being now perhaps thoroughly anglicized, nevertheless still show consideration for it. Henry James Johnstone, the eldest son, is clearly named after his maternal grandfather Henry and also continues the name James. The second son, Bayntun Johnstone, takes his Christian name from his maternal grandmother's maiden name. Eliza is named after her mother's mother in accordance with the Scottish custom and Mary Frances takes her first Christian name from her mother and her second Christian name from her father's mother. With Bayntun and Caroline Johnstone's two known children, Daniel is quite correctly named after his father's father and Mary Eliza carries the Christian names of her paternal grandmother and her paternal grandmother's mother, although either or both of these names may also be the Christian names of Caroline's mother, whose names are not known.

Mr Lawson Edwards has kindly provided me with a pedigree of his mother's family which is both more modern and more perfect in its name pattern, and interesting in showing how a Scottish family continued to name its children in accordance with established custom even into the 20th century. This pedigree will be seen on page 79.

Examining the last generation shown, it will be seen that Jane Moffat, the eldest daughter of William Lawson, is named correctly after her mother's mother. Margaret Gillies, the next daughter, is named equally correctly after her father's mother. Martha is named after her maternal grandmother's mother rather than after her own mother. This is one of the variations previously mentioned. The next daughter, Helen is named, after her mother.

Of the sons, William, born 1899, is named after his father's father, this also being his father's name, the father not being the eldest son. The second son, Joseph Hope, is named Joseph after the mother's father in accordance with the usual custom but is given also this grandfather's surname in accordance with a custom by this date becoming common. It will be noted that the two eldest daughters, Jane and Margaret, had both been given the surnames as well as the Christian names of the grandmothers after whom they were respectively named. The third son is not, of course, given the father's name of William, as there is already a son so named. The third son's name comes from his father's mother's father.

Mr Lawson Edwards informs me that there are several other ancestors of this West Scotland family, both direct and collateral, whose naming shows an adherence to the Scottish naming system.

Multiple Christian Names
Before the middle of the 18th century it was very rare to find more than one Christian name, but after that time the gradual introduction of a second Christian name naturally affected the name pattern.

Dr Maitland Thomson gives some interesting information on the matter of multiple Christian names. In the year 1760 in Edinburgh he found that only about 1 per cent of children baptized had two Christian names. By 1790 this had risen to 7 per cent and by 1820 it was nearly 25 per cent.

More than one Christian name for working-class families is very seldom found until the 19th century and even then it is rare to get more than two names. In the upper and professional classes, however, more than one Christian name begins to be more general from the beginning of the 19th century.

This second Christian name was sometimes the name of a godfather or godmother or of some patron. An example of the last-mentioned is found in the Morison family of Lewis. Daniel Morison had served in the Dumfriesshire Militia, the commanding officer of which had been Charles William Montague Scott, Earl of Dalkeith and later 4th Duke of Buccleuch. The entry, which is from Glasgow City register, reads:

August 1809. Daniel Morison, Comptroller of the Customs & Margaret Hall a L[awful] Son, Charles William Montague Scott, bo. 14th Witn. William & Murdoch Morison.

Lord Dalkeith had obtained for Daniel the post of Controller of Customs in Glasgow. An earlier son, baptized in the same parish and born 27 April 1807, was named Henry Montague Morison, his second name being given, no doubt for the same reason.

The developing custom of giving more than one Christian name brought with it the custom of including a surname from the mother's side of the family. Thus a second son, instead of being named after the Christian name of the mother's father, was sometimes given both the Christian and surname, as we have seen in the Johnstone pedigree in the case of John Cooper Johnstone and in the Lawson pedigree in the case of Joseph Hope

LAWSON OF DENNY, STIRLINGSHIRE

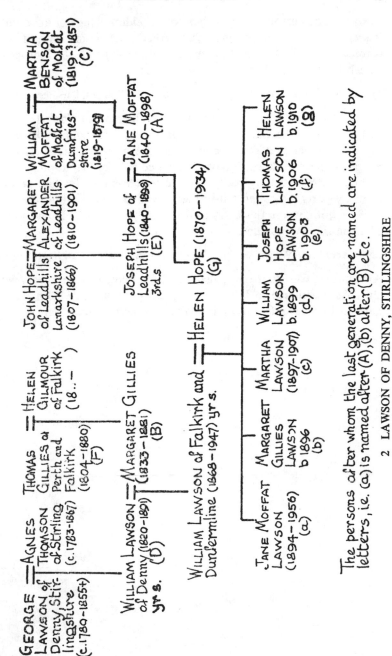

The persons after whom the last generation are named are indicated by letters, i.e. (a) is named after (A), (b) after (B) etc.

2 LAWSON OF DENNY, STIRLINGSHIRE

Lawson. The custom applied also to the eldest daughter of families, as is seen in the Lawson pedigree. An earlier example of a variation of this is found in the Kelly family in Inch, Wigtownshire. In the register of that parish for the 1798 baptisms is this entry:

June 22 Born Teckla Hamilton Dau. to Alexr. Kelly Tennant, Barsolus.

Teckla Hamilton Kelly was the first daughter of an elder daughter and had been given the Christian name of her maternal grandmother and the surname of her maternal grandfather, the grandmother Teckla (whose maiden name is unknown) having married a John Hamilton.

Inch is a particularly badly kept register even at this late period, and in many parts it is almost illegible. It will be noticed that the mother's name is not given in this entry and was only discovered from the baptism of a son three years later, namely:

1801 – April 27th. William Kelly Lawful son to Alexr. Kelly & Cathrie Hall in Barsolus.

An unusual Christian name, as Teckla is here, can be a very valuable clue. As mentioned in the first chapter, some unusual Christian names have in fact become almost hereditary in certain families.

VI

TESTAMENTS

SCOTTISH TESTAMENTS, like the wills and administrations in England and Wales, were, from earliest known times, in the hands of the Church authorities. In Scotland, before the Reformation they were controlled by the Church courts, the officials of which had the duty of seeing if there were any legacies for pious purposes and also that a suitable sum should be spent on prayers for the soul of the deceased. There were also dues to be paid, the 'quota', in Scotland often called the 'quot'.

At the Reformation the Church courts were abolished, but in 1564 the commissary courts were set up in their place for the purpose of confirming wills, and they also dealt with matrimonial and slander cases. In addition they were a court of records.

The commissariots were abolished in 1876 when their duties relating to the confirmation of wills were passed over to the sheriff courts. Their jurisdiction in consistory cases had been, at an earlier date, transferred to the court of session and their registering of deeds had been abolished some time before.

The commissariot districts were made to coincide more or less with the dioceses of the bishops, though some of these were sub-divided. There were thirteen of them, but a fourteenth (for Edinburgh) was set up by King Charles I. In the days of Roman Catholicism there had been fifteen operating districts, because St Andrews and Glasgow dioceses had been divided into two archdeaconries. Later on, the commissariot districts were increased to twenty-two. During the time of the Protestant episcopacy the commissaries came again under the bishops.

The records of only three commissariots go back before the time of the Reformation and in none of the commissariots are the records complete. It is particularly regrettable that in 1721 a fire destroyed the early commissary records of Aberdeen, because that burgh and diocese had a reputation for accurate and carefully kept records.

Prior to the Reformation wills had been written in Latin but after it they are in English. The register of testaments gives the names of the executors, the inventory of the moveable estate, normally the date of death – which may be only the month, and if there was a will, it gives a copy of the will.

The Scottish Record Society has indexed all the commissariot records up to 1800, the indexing having been carried out mainly under the editorship of that devoted genealogist, Sir Francis Grant, a former Lyon King of Arms. This makes the testaments of Scotland far more accessible than those of England and for that reason they are among the most frequently consulted records.

The Edinburgh commissariot covered testaments from all parts of Scotland and of those who died abroad. It was in this respect comparable to the prerogative court of Canterbury in England. The other commissariots include only those within the jurisdiction covered by them.

It is important to remember that in Scotland only moveable property could be left by a testament. Landed property descended according to certain fixed laws. This accounts for the situation in which a person leaving considerable property has his estate entered as in debit rather than in credit, 'debita excedunt Bona' ('debts exceeding the assets').

When a widow and children survived, the moveable estate would be divided into three. One third (or terce) would go to the relict; one third to the children and the remaining third could be left by the deceased to whomever he wished. When the husband or wife was deceased the property would be divided into two parts, one part going to the children and the other according to the wishes of the testator.

The existence of the inventory with the testament is particularly valuable, throwing as it does light on the occupation and social position of the testator. In cases where the person left a testament and named the executors the confirmation is known as a testament testamentar but when the deceased left no testament, in other words died intestate, and the executor was in consequence appointed by the court, it was called a testament dative. However, this latter document is far more informative than the administration of an intestate in England and Wales. The executorship of a deceased man may be given to his widow and his surviving children and these may all be mentioned by name. Where someone dies greatly in debt the executorship may be granted to a creditor.

Where a testament testamentar or 'latter will' was proved, the language was frequently colloquial, for example, 'To James Stewart my sone and the bairnes Laullie to be gotten of his awen bodie'.[1] These testaments

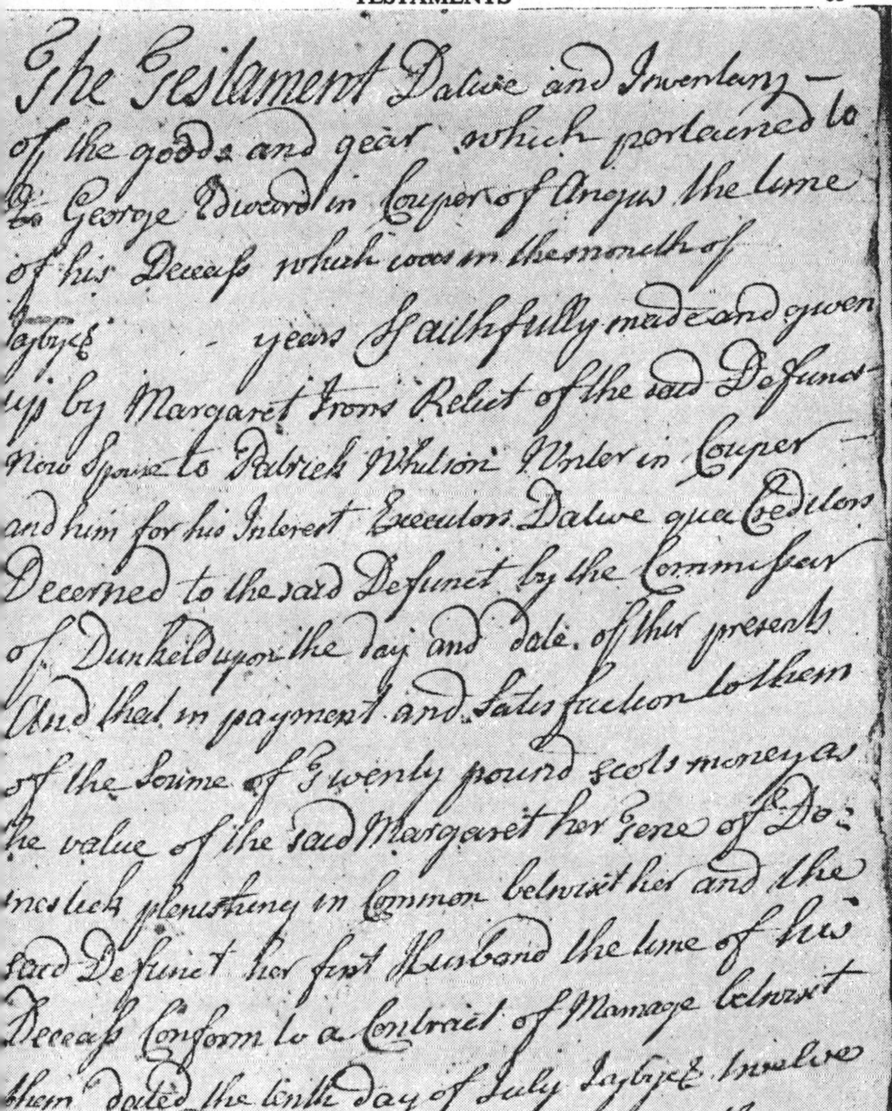

The Testament Dative and Inventary —
of the goods and gear which pertained to
George Edward in Couper of Angus the tyme
of his Deceass which was in the moneth of
[   ]   yeirs Ffaithfully made and gwen
up by Margaret Irons Relict of the said Defunct
now Spouse to Patrick Whitson Writer in Couper
and him for his Interest Executors Dative qua Creditors
Decerned to the said Defunct by the Commissar
of Dunkeld upon the day and date off thir presents
And that in payment and Satisfaction to them
of the Soume of Twenty pound scots money as
the value of the said Margaret her Terce off Do=
=mestick plenishing in Common betwixt her and the
said Defunct her first Husband the tyme of his
Deceass Conform to a Contract of Marriage betwixt
them dated the tenth day of July [   ] twelve
years And Alse in payment to them —
of the Soume of Ffifty two pound three shilling
four pennies money forsaid off Ffunerall Expence
Expended by them upon the said Defuncts Generalls

FIG. 3

Testament Dative of the George Edward in Coupar Angus in the pedigree on pages
106–7. It will be noticed that the widow's terce is mentioned and also a contract of
marriage, including its date. It is also seen that Margaret Irons, the widow, is now
married again, her second husband being a writer called Patrick Whitson. *Reproduced
with the approval of the Keeper of the Records of Scotland* [Scottish Record Office
ref. CC7/5/4].

often throw light on a number of matters, such as the status of the family, 'My body to be honestly buried according to my station' or on the kindness or otherwise of relatives during sickness, 'oyre my sisters and nearest of Kin' are debarred from any part of the estate 'insofar as they Disowned me in my sickness and Distress And this my Letterwill to all to whom it effects I notify and make known'.[2]

Because the laws of Scotland governed the descent of landed property the necessity for making a will was less urgently felt, as this only affected moveable property. In consequence, many of the testaments listed in the various commissariots will be found to be testaments dative.

It also seems that there must have been many cases, particularly in remote areas, where the testament was never handed in or confirmed. The property was probably just divided up amicably among those to whom it was bequeathed or, where there was no will, according to the inheritance customs and laws.

The commissariot had its own register of deeds, which was mainly concerned with jurisdiction over small debts. Another series of commissariot records were concerned with consistorial jurisdiction, that is the jurisdiction in matrimonial cases and cases of legitimacy and slander. These may reveal a considerable amount of personal and often unpleasant detail. Under canon law marriage was indissoluble. In pre-Reformation times the only way married people could be free of each other was by proving that the marriage from its beginning had been invalid under canon law. This invoked all the ingenuity of the ecclesiastical lawyers. Under the reformed system divorce was granted for misconduct and as a result the commissary court records from the Reformation onwards provide much scandalous material.

Another branch of the consistory court covered cases of slander, and the indelicacy which is revealed in such cases is often amazing. The Scottish Record Society have published an index to the consistorial cases in the Edinburgh commissariot from 1658 to 1800.[3]

The Act of 1609 allowed appeals from the inferior commissaries to the Edinburgh commissary court and ultimately to the court of session. Later on it became the practice to appeal direct from all the commissary courts to the court of session.

In 1823 the boundaries of the commissariots other than Edinburgh were made to coincide with the boundaries of the sheriffdoms, and the sheriff was given the office of commissary and the sheriff's clerk became the commissary clerk. In 1876 the commissary courts were abolished altogether, although for practical convenience the terms 'commissariot' and 'commissary records' are still in use. The office of commissary clerk of Edinburgh was still retained and the sheriff court there continued to hold the power of granting confirmation of testaments for the estates of persons dying outside the kingdom and possessing moveable estate.

The commissariot records up to 1823 are now held in the Scottish Record Office, Edinburgh, but those registered after that date are in some cases still in the custody of the sheriff clerks. There are MS. indexes of these records from 1810 to 1823 in the Record Office. Testaments since 1876, which are fully indexed, are held in the main office dealing with present-day confirmations on the ground floor of the Register House.

Below are given the commissariots with the date of the earliest testaments held by them. Fuller details of these commissariots will be found in the introductory pages of the indexes to the commissariots published by the Scottish Record Society and also in Anthony J. Camp's *Wills and their Whereabouts* (1963), pages 104–111.

Commissariots with Date of Earliest Will and Jurisdiction

EDINBURGH 1514
Jurisdiction: The whole of Scotland and abroad.

ABERDEEN 1661
Jurisdiction: Aberdeenshire, except for the parishes of Gartly, Glass and Rhynie, Banffshire, except for the parishes of Aberlour, Botriphnie, Grange, Inveravon, Inverkeithny, Keith, Kirkmichael, Marnoch and Rothiemay.

ARGYLL 1674
Jurisdiction: parishes in Argyllshire (mainland) and parishes of Glenelg, Kilmallie and Kilmonivaig in Inverness-shire.

BRECHIN 1576
Jurisdiction: parishes of Brechin, Carmyllie, Careston, Cortachy and Clova, Dundee, Dunnichen, Farnell, Glenisla, Guthrie, Kingoldrum, Lethnot and Navar, Lochlee, Maryton, Monikie, Montrose, Oathlaw, Panbryde, and Stracathro in Angus; Glenbervie and Strachan in Kincardineshire.

CAITHNESS 1622
Jurisdiction: the counties of Caithness and Sutherland.

DUMFRIES 1624
Jurisdiction: Dumfriesshire and parishes of Colvend, Kirkbean, Kirkpatrick-Durham, Kirkpatrick-Irongray, Lochrutton, New Abbey, Terregles and Troqueer in the Stewartry of Kirkcudbright.

DUNBLANE 1539
Jurisdiction: parishes of Aberfoyle, Abernethy, Auchterarder, Balquhidder, Blackford, Callander, Comrie, Culross, Dron, Dunblane, Dunning, Findo-Gask, Fowlis Wester, Glendevon, Kilmadock, Kincardine, part of Kippen, part of Lecropt, Logie, Monzie, Monzievaird, Muthill, Port of Menteith, St Madoes, Trinity-Gask, and Tulliallan in Perthshire; Tillicoultry in Clackmannan; Fossoway in Kinross.

DUNKELD 1682
Jurisdiction: parishes of Aberdalgie, Abernyte, Alyth, Auchtergaven, Blair-Atholl, Caputh, Cargill, Cluny, Coupar-Angus, Crieff, Dowally, Dull, Little Dunkeld, Forgandenny, Fortingall, Kenmore, Killin, Kinclaven, Kinloch, Kirkmichael, Lethendy, Logierait, Madderty, Meigle, Moneydie, Moulin, Redgorton, St Martins, Tibbermore, Weem and part of Arngask in Perthshire; Aberdour, Leslie and Strathmiglio in Fife; Abercorn in West Lothian; Aberlady in East Lothian; Auchterhouse, Fearn, Ruthven and Tealing in Angus.

GLASGOW   **1547**
Jurisdiction: Ayrshire, Dunbartonshire (except part of parish of Cardross), Renfrewshire (except parish of Renfrew and part of parish of Cathcart); parishes of Avondale, Barony, Blantyre, Bothwell, Cadder, Cambuslang, Cambusnethan, Carmunnock, Dalziel, Glasgow City, Glassford, Rutherglen and Stonehouse in Lanarkshire; Balfron, Baldernock, part of Campsie, Drymen, Fintry, Killearn, Kilsyth and Strathblane in Stirlingshire.

HAMILTON AND CAMPSIE   **1564**
Jurisdiction: parishes of Hamilton, Cadder, part of Cathcart, Govan, Gorbals, Old Monkland, New Monkland, Dalserf, East Kilbride and Shotts in Lanarkshire; Cardross in Dunbartonshire; Campsie and Baldernock in Stirlingshire and Renfrew in Renfrewshire.

INVERNESS   **1630**
Jurisdiction: Inverness-shire.

THE ISLES   **1661**
Jurisdiction: county of Bute and the Western Isles.

KIRKCUDBRIGHT   **1809**
(Executory papers exist 1663–1800).

LANARK   **1595**
Jurisdiction: parishes of Biggar, Carluke, Carmichael, Carnwath, Carstairs, Covington, Crawford, Crawfordjohn, Culter, Dolphinton, Douglas, Dunsyre, Lanark, Lesmahagow, Libberton, Pettinain, Roberton, Symyngton, Walston, Wandell and Wiston.

LAUDER   **1561**
Jurisdiction: Berwickshire.

MORAY   **1684**
Jurisdiction: counties of Moray and Nairn; parishes of Aberlour, Botriphnie, Grange, Inveravon, Inverkeithny, Keith, Kirkmichael, Marnoch, and Rothiemay in Banffshire; Gartly, Glass and Rhynie in Aberdeenshire; Petty in Inverness-shire.

ORKNEY AND SHETLAND   **1611**
Jurisdiction: counties of Orkney and Shetland.

PEEBLES   **1681**
Jurisdiction: counties of Peebles, Roxburgh and Selkirk.

ROSS   **1802**
Jurisdiction: county of Ross.

ST ANDREWS   **1549**
Jurisdiction: county of Fife (except possibly the parishes of Carnock, Saline, Culross and Tulliallan); county of Kinross (except Fossoway); parishes of Aberlemno, Airlie, Arbirlot, Arbroath, Barry, Craig, Dun, Eassie, Edzell, Forfar, Glamis, Inverarity, Inverkeillor, Kettins, Kingoldrum, Kinnell, Kinnettles, Kirkden, Kirriemuir, Liff and Benvie, Lintrathen, Logie-Pert, Lunan, Lundie, Mains and Strathmartin, Monifieth, Murroes, Newtyle, Rescobie, St. Vigeans, and Tannadice in Angus; Arbuthnot Benholm, Bervie, Dunnottar, Durris, Fettercairn, Fetteresso, Fordoun, Garvock, Kinneff, Laurencekirk, Marykirk, Nigg and St Cyrus in Kincardineshire; Bendochy, Blairgowrie, Collace Dunbarnie, Errol, Forteviot, Fowlis Easter, Inchture, Kilspindie, Kinfauns, Kinnaird, Kinnoull, Longforgan, Methven, Muckart, Perth, Rhynd and Scone in Perthshire.

STIRLING   **1607**
Jurisdiction: parishes of Airth, Bothkennar, Denny, Dunipace, Falkirk, Gargunnock, Kilsyth, Larbert, part of Lecropt, part of Logie, Muiravonside, Polmont, St Ninian's, Slamannan and Stirling in Stirlingshire; Alloa, Alva, Clackmannan and Dollar in Clackmannanshire; Muckhart in Perthshire; Carnock, Saline and Torryburn in Fife. Testaments of the time of the Commonwealth for the parishes of Baldernock, Buchanan, Killearn, New Kilpatrick and Campsie are also found here.

WIGTOWN   **1700**
Jurisdiction: county of Wigtown and parish of Minnigaff in the Stewartry of Kirkcudbright.

In addition to the indexes of all commissariots published by the Scottish Record Society down to 1800 there are the following indexes in the Scottish Record Office:

Index to Miscellaneous Executry Papers 1481–1740 (Scottish Record Office) with MS. additions to 1882;
Index (TSS) to Register of Testaments for the Various Commissariots 1801–1823 – this covers the period after the Scottish Record Society indexes cease up to the time when the commissariots (except Edinburgh) were transferred to the sheriff courts;
Index to Personal Estates of Defuncts – Edinburgh (including Haddington and Linlithgow) 1827–1865; Other Commissariots 1846–1867 (printed) 6 vols. H.M.S.O.

Testamentary deeds were, quite frequently, especially from the 18th century onwards, registered in the register of deeds during the testator's lifetime. For further details of this custom reference should be made to Chapter IX.

The location of sheriff court confirmations since 1823 varies. Those of Edinburgh and a certain number of other sheriff courts have been transmitted to the Scottish Record Office. Others are in the hands of the sheriff clerks.

Since 1876 a calendar of all the confirmations granted and inventories lodged is issued annually by the commissary clerk of Edinburgh. This covers all testaments proved in the sheriffdoms.

Appendix D at the end of this book gives an alphabetical list of the parishes as existing in 1855, showing in which commissariots they were situated.

Just divided up amicably

VII

THE SASINE REGISTER

L AND REGISTRATION in Scotland derives from the existence of the notary public, an office having its origins in Roman Law. Both the Pope and the Emperor, claiming respectively spiritual and temporal sovereignty of the world, appointed notaries public. In France their use developed rapidly and people would come before this official, possibly sitting in some shop locally, and record their deeds before him and before witnesses. Thus from the second half of the 12th century onwards and throughout the Middle Ages in the south of France the notaries were responsible for framing the majority of private deeds. Many of their registers have survived and form an immense source of historical information of every sort. England, which had early built up its own system of law, was not influenced by Roman Law and did not accept the imperial notaries, on the grounds that England was not part of the empire; the only notaries who existed in England were the apostolic notaries, but the latter's actions were only accepted in ecclesiastic courts, the king's courts refusing to accept their authority, regarding them as witnesses on the same plane as any others.

Scotland was influenced by Roman Law and both imperial and papal notaries are heard of in early times. One of the earliest notarial instruments is that of 1291, mentioned by Maitland Thomson, on the settlement of a dispute between the monks of Melrose and the parson of Dunbar before the notary public Nicholas, called Campion, appointed by imperial authority. Maitland also mentions an instrument made in 1298 regarding the injury to the muniments of Scone Abbey at the time of the war, the notary being Robert Garwald, appointed notary public by apostolic authority.

There was no great increase in the number of notaries during the 14th century in Scotland, but in the next century the notarial instruments begin to be numerous. Their scope was most varied. There were instruments on leases, indentures, personal obligations, marriage celebrations, institution to benefices, parish clerkships or on the result of a lawsuit.

Undoubtedly, the most important class of notarial instrument is the sasine. The idea that the sasine of land should be provable by a notarial instrument grew in Scotland, and this constitutes a registration of land which is of the greatest value to the genealogist and historian. The system increased in the 15th century and the instrument of sasine recorded transactions which took place on the grounds of the lands concerned and not in a court-house. The notary's record of these proceedings was preserved in a book. It thus became a rule that the sasine must be proved by writing and the notary and his instrument became the necessary means of doing this.

It has been pointed out that there were originally both imperial and papal notaries, but in 1469 an Act of Parliament forbade the imperial notaries to practise in Scotland in future unless they had been accepted and approved by the King.

The registers in which the notaries public recorded their actions are known as protocol books. The earliest of these books in the Scottish Record Office are two which begin in the 15th century and a great number of these protocol books have now found their way into the record office. From 1503 onwards there were attempts to make the sheriff court books the record for the sasine of lands within the sheriffdom, but this proved ineffectual, the sheriff court records being frequently ill-preserved. Far better was the Act of 1587, repeated in 1617, requiring protocol books to be brought in to the clerk register for custody.

The Act of 1587 had also required notaries' protocol books to be handed in, in the case of burghs, to the provost and bailies, and this in some cases appears to have been carried out effectually, since the series of protocol books in the custody of some burghs is nearly complete. The clerk register, on the other hand, was never successful in enforcing the acts which required the protocol books to be handed in to him. Nevertheless today the Scottish Record Office hold over 200, mainly of the 17th century. The City of Edinburgh on its own has about the same number.

In 1599 the register of sasines and reversions (redemptions of mortgage lands) was established under the Secretary of State, Scotland being divided into seventeen districts. In only seven of these districts does any part of this register survive and the register itself was abolished in 1609 as unnecessary.

The secretary of this register during its whole existence had been Lord Balmerino, who had probably been influential in its establishment. At the time it was abolished he was in disgrace on account of an imprudent letter for which he was deemed officially responsible. The King is said to have been influenced in his decision to abolish the register by George Home, Earl of Dunbar, but it is not known whether its abolition was with the object of discrediting Lord Balmerino or in accord with the wishes of certain powerful people who felt the existence of the register was not in their interest.

However, only eight years later the Act of 1617 instituted the general and particular registers of sasines. The general register was available for sasine of land in any part of Scotland and the particular register only for lands belonging to the district which it served. Thus we see established the land registration system which exists today. These new registers were put under the control of the Lord Clerk Register; all the register volumes had to be issued by him and on their conclusion returned to him for permanent custody. They form therefore a fairly complete registration of all land in Scotland from that date to the present time, and their existence is of great value to genealogists. By this means it should be possible to trace the ownership of land, even of small extent (apart from that in royal burghs which have their own registers of sasines) from that time to the present day. As land frequently descended to relatives and as details of relationship are so genealogically valuable, their outstanding worth will be appreciated.

In the course of time there were modifications to the sasine registers. In 1681 an Act required the royal burghs to keep sasine registers of their own, since they had been exempted from the operation of the earlier acts. These registers are therefore not under the control of the Lord Clerk Register but of the burgh magistrates. For many years before the date of this Act the royal burghs had preserved the protocol books of the burgh notaries and the Act of 1681 merely extended the practice by requiring them to maintain a register. The survival of these records varies. Some burghs have cared for and preserved them: others have been careless about their disposal.

From the earliest time the act of taking sasine of land was accompanied by the ceremony of handing over earth and stone or other symbols, according to the nature of the matter transferred, on the land itself. This continued until 1845. There existed from 1617 onwards the option of registering the lands in the particular register applicable or in the general register in Edinburgh.

In 1857 the registration of long leases was introduced and the register thenceforth ceased to be only a register of feudal rights. Today the registration of feudal titles is compulsory but the registration of non-feudal titles is voluntary. In 1863 the introduction of 'search sheets' was instituted to assist searchers in ascertaining what encumbrances, if any, existed on a property.

The registers with which the genealogist is mainly concerned are those instituted in 1617 and continued up to the middle of the 19th century. These consist of:

(i) *The Old General Register of Sasines*, 1617–1868, contained in 3,779 volumes. There are also minute books which are a kind of digest or abstract, and thus the best way of searching the parts of the register unindexed.

(ii) *The Particular Registers of Sasines* for the various counties, which run parallel with the general register.

What is known as the *Secretary's Register* covers the short period 1599–1609.

The modern register, known as the *New General Register*, which begins in 1869 and continues today, is kept in county divisions. By 1928 this register had reached 36,000 volumes and increases by about 500 folio volumes a year.

The Scottish Record Office has been indexing gradually both the general register and the various particular registers. Below is given a list of the counties, bailiaries and stewartries for which there are printed or MS. indexes prior to 1781. Registers of dates prior to 1617 are the secretary's registers. The Record Office index volume number is shown against the entries. All MS. indexes are in the Record Office.

County, Bailiary or Stewartry		Printed Index No.	MS. Index
General Register	1701–1720	3	1607–1700
Aberdeen	1599–1609	7	
	1617–1629	7	
	1630–1660	15	
Argyle, Dunbarton, Bute, Arran and Tarbet	1617–1780	9	
Ayr, Kyle, Carrick	1599–1609	23	
	1617–1660	29, 31	
Banff	1600–1609 ⎫ 1617–1780 ⎭	18	
Berwick and Lauderdale	1617–1780	12, 13	
Caithness	1646–1780	33	
Dumfries, Kirkcudbright and Annandale	1617–1780	21, 25, 27, 49, 51	
Edinburgh, Haddington, Linlithgow and Bathgate	1599–1609 1617–1660	47 36, 38, 40, 42, 44, 46	
Elgin, Forres and Nairn	1617–1700	53	

County, Bailiary or Stewartry		Printed Index No.	MS. Index
Fife and Kinross	1603–1609	55	
	1617–1660	57	
Forfar	1620–1700	59	
Inverness, Ross, Cromarty and	1606–1608	61, 63, 64	
Sutherland	1617–1780		
Kincardine	1600–1608 ⎫	16	
	1617–1657 ⎭		
Perth			1601–1609
West Lothian			1701–1760

After 1780 the genealogist's task is considerably lightened. From 1781 onwards there are printed abridgements to the sasines, both general and particular. These though greatly reduced in length in comparison with the original documents, give most if not all of the information the genealogist is likely to want. So it is often unnecessary to consult the original document, though this is advisable in cases of importance. Sometimes hidden away in the original there is some significant item. For instance, a person may be described in the abridgement as of such-and-such a place, whereas in the original he may be termed 'merchant' of such-and-such a place and this piece of information will be of course extremely valuable.

The abridgements have been indexed in MS. from their beginning, both for persons and (except for 1830–68) for places. These MS. indexes are in the Scottish Record Office.

An example of a sasine is given below. There is much repetition and legal verbiage but genealogists will quickly pick out the parts which give valuable information. This is a sasine which relates to the Johnstone pedigree given on pages 74–5 and discussed in Chapter V.

At Ayr the first day of August mvii^c [1700] year
The seasine following presented Be James Tailyeor in Sandbed of Killmarnock is regrat in the sixt Book of the new register of Seasins Within the Shiriffdome of Air Conforme to the act of Parliament quherof the tenore is as Follows In the name of god amen Be it knoun to all men by this present publique Instrument that upon the nynth day of the moneth of july and year of the incarnatione of our Lord an thousand and Seven hundreth year & of the reigne of our most dread Sovereigne William By the Grace of God King of Great Brittain france & Ireland defender of the faith the Eleventh year in presence of me nottar publique and witnesses under subscryveing Compeared personallie ane descreat man James Johnstoune merchd in Cumnock wt Bessie Stillie his spouse wt Allexd Johnstoune ther eldest son & past wt William Patersone in Wodsyd Bailyie in that pairt speciallie constitute Be the precept of Seasine after insert to the Ground of the tenement of houses yeards and pertinents after specifeit and that the sd James Johnstoune haveing and holding in his hands ane certaine Letter of heretable allienationne and dispositione made and Granted Be James Riddock Bailyie of the regality of Cumnock for himself & wt the speciall advyce Consent & assent of Hugh Jamiesone massone & wright in Cumnock and the sd hugh for himself and each of them for ther severall & respective ryts and interests To and In favors of the sd James Johnstoune and Bessie Stillie spouses and Allexd Johnstoune ther eldest son dated the eight day of december mvi^c fourscore eighteen years [1698] quherby and for the soume of four hundreth and fyftie merks money of Scotland therin specifeit advanced and payed be the sd James Johnstoune to the sd James Riddock & huge Jamiesone as being

the full worth and pryce of the tenements houses yeards and pertinents aftermentionat
Therefor the sd James Riddick and huge Jamiesone for ther severall and respective
ryts and interests both wt an joynt mynd Consent and assent sold anailyied and heretabillie simpliciter disponed from them and each of them ther aires and successors
To and In favors of ther saids James Johnstoune and Bessie Styllie Spouses and Longest
Liver of them two in Liferent and Conjunct fie and to the sd Allexd Johnstoune ther
eldest son his aires and assigneys quwhatsomever in fie heretabillie and irredeamablie
wtout any maner of reversione redemption Bond promise or Conditione of reversione
or reagress quhatsoever All and Haill that tenement of houses Back and fore yeard
middingstead wt the pertinents formerly possest Be umqll John Campbell in woodsyd
& John Stillie officer in Cumnock therafter Be Wm Mcrevall & patrick parkhill therafter
Bye jean Johnstoune & umqll John Murdoch ther husband and then be the said huge
Jamiesone Lying Within the burgh of Cumnock Kinkskyle & Shereffdome of Air on
that pairt therof called the Craighead Betwixt the water of Glasnoch on the South the
tenement possest be James Stillie on the east the tenement pertaining to Mr Wm
Crauford of dalegles on the north the house pertaining to Martine Stillie wt the mercat
place on the west pairts together wt the yeard on the west pairt of the tennement
sometyme possest be Wm Campbell therafter Be John McLellane the yeard possest be
the sd James Stillie on the South the yeard sometyme possest Be James Reid on the
west and the yeard pertaining to henry Tennent on the north pairts together also wt the
middinestead Lying on the west end of the rig of Kirkland now pertaining to the sd
James Riddoch together wt all heretable rycht other rycht or title quhich they or aither
of them could ask claim or pretend therunto or to the maills and dewtys thereof or
possessione of the same in all tyme therafter in the quhich tenement of houses yeards
and pertinents the sd James Riddoch Bund and obleidged him and his forsaids dewly
validly and sufficiently with all convenient dilligence to infeft and sease the sd James
Johnstoune and Bessy Stilly Spouses and Longest Liver of them in Lyferent and the
sd Allexd Johnstoune ther eldest Lawll son & his forsaids in fie heretablie and irredeamablie as said is and that be to severall charters and Infeftments to be holden wt absolute
warrandice in maner mentionat in the disposition as in the samen Containing a precept
of seasine in the end therof wt diverse others obleisments and Clauses of the date above
specifeit att more Lenth bears which dispositione the sd James Johnstoune for himself
and in name and Behalf of his sd Spouse and sone reverently as became presented and
delyvered to the sd Wm patersone Bailyie in that pairt forsaid therby speciallie Constitute
humbly desyring and requyreing him to put the precept of seasine therin Contained to
all dew executione quhich the sd Bailyie receaved in his hands & did give and delyver
the same to me nottar publique under subscryveing to be red & published quhich I did
of the quhich precept of seasine the tenor follows ATTOUR to the effect the sd spouses
& ther sd son may be infeft and seased in the forsd tenement of houses yeards and
pertinents therof above disponed witt ye us for our severall and respective rychts &
Interests to have made Constitute & ordained Lyke as we Be the tenore hearof make
Constitute and ordain William patersone in Wodsyde and Ilk ane of yow our Bailyies
in that pairt conjunctlie and severallie speciallie Constitute greeting By this our precept
It is our will and we Charge you that incontinent this precept seen ye pass to the Ground
of the Forsd tenement of houses Back and foreyeard middinestead wt the pertinents
Lying and Bounded and now possest be me the said huge Jamiesone & give and delyver
herctable state and of Seasine wt reall actuall corporall and peaceable possessione all &
haill that tenement of houses Back & fore middinstead wt the pertinents Bounded and
possessed as sd is lying wtin the toune of Cumnock on that pairt yrof Called the Craighead to the sds James Johnstone & Bessy Stillie Spouses and Longest liver of them two
in Conjunct Fee and Lyferent and to the sd Allexd Johnstoune ther son in fie Be delyverance to them or to ther Certane acturney in ther names of earth & Stone of the Ground
of the sd tenement as the manor is to be holden in maner above written and this on noe
wayes ye Leave undone the whilk to doe we Committ to you & each of you conjunctlie
& severallie our Bailyies in that pairt Forsaid our full & irrevocable power and warrand
Be this our precept and for the mair security we wt Consent and Consents these presents
Be insert and registrat in the bookes of Councill and Sessione or any uther inferior
Court Books Competent to have the strenth of ane decreit of any of the judges therof
and ther authority interponed therto that all Letters and executiorells necessar may pass
hearupon on six days warning And Constitute [blank] our procurators in witnes

quherof written Be john Fergussone wryter in Cumnock we have subscribed thir presents wt our hands att Cumnock the Eight day of december mvic and fourscore Eighteen years [1698] Before thir witnesses John Campbell of Horsecleugh younger Wm Reid mercht in Cumnock & the sd John Fergussone *sic subscribitur* Ja Riddock huge Jamiesone John Campbell witness Wm Reid witness John Fergussone witness After the reading & publishing of the quhich dispositione and precept of seasine above insert the said William patersone Bailyie in that pairt forsaid therby speciallie Constitute By virtue of his office of Baillyierie therby Committed to him did Give and delyver heretabill state & seasine wt reall actuall corporall & peaceable possession to the saids James Johnstoune & Bessie Stillie Spouses & Longest Liver of them two In Conjunct fie & Lyferent and to the sd Allexd Johnstoune ther son in Fie of all and haill the sd tenement of houses Back and fore yeard middinestead and pertinents Lying bounded and possest in maner above written By delyverance to the sd Spouses and ther sd son of earth and stone of the ground of the sd tenement yeard & middingstead successive they being all personally present & accepting the same to be holden in maner Contained in the forsd dispositione after the forme & tenore therof and precept above insert in all poynts wherupon and upon all and sundrie the premisses the sd James Johnstoune and his sd Spouse & ther son asked & requyred instruments ane or mae in the hands of me nottar publique under subscryving ther things were done upon the Ground of the tenement yeard & middinestead betwixt nyne & ten houres Before noon day moneth year of God & of our soverane Lords Reigne above written in presence of john Harvie merchant in Cumnock Charles Willsone son to William Willsone merchant ther Charles Logan son to umquhill Allane Logane wryter in Edinbz and James Laurie son to Mr John Laurie minister at Auchinleck witnesses Called and requyred to the premisses *sic subscribitur* Et ego viro Joannes Fergussone Clericus Glasguensis diocesis authoritate regale ac per dominos concilii secundum tenorem acti parliamenti admissus et probatus quia praemissis omnibus et Singulis dum sic ut praemittitur dicerentur agrentur et fierent una cum praenominatis testibus presen personaliter interfui eaque omnia et singula praemissa sic fieri vidi scivi et audivi ac in notam caepi ideoque hoc presens publicum instrumentum manu mea fideliter scriptum exinde confeci et in hanc publici instrumenti formam redegi signo nomine et cognomine meis solitis et consuetis signavi et subscripsi in fidem robur et testimonium veritatis omnium et Singulorum praemissorum rogatus et requisitus nec vi nec metu coactus Joannes Fergussone N.P. Charles Logane witnes Charles Willsone witnes James Laurie witnes John Harvie witnes.[1]

This example will give some idea of the style of a sasine and also of its length, though this is not an unduly long one.

Very often the abstracts in the minute books, or after 1780 the printed abridgements, may give all the information which the genealogist requires. But as previously mentioned this is not always so, and for an important sasine in the family genealogy it is always desirable to look at the full sasine. Apart from more detailed descriptions of persons the description of the property, as will be seen in the example, normally mentions the owners of the adjacent properties and sometimes their parentage, or the previous owners.

As there is no index of sasines for a number of sheriffdoms prior to the MS. indexes to the abstracts, from 1781 onwards, it is sometimes possible to find an earlier reference to a sasine of the property, or to other deeds prior to 1781 by searching the place indexes to the abstracts from 1781 and then by examining the full sasine of this later date to find reference to previous sasines with the dates and details of their recording. The earlier sasines can then be found comparatively easily, thus saving hunting through many years of the minute books.

There may also be reference to other deeds and their place of registration. This was the case in another sasine referring to the same family of Johnstone of Old Cumnock. In this case a sasine was found of 20 June 1783 in the particular register of sasines for Ayr[2] for Alexander Johnstone, son to James Johnstone, merchant in Cumnock. This referred to 'an Extract Trust right and disposition' of 8 January 1762 'registrate in the Sheriff Court Books of Ayr upon the Eight day of February 1779 years granted by the deceased Alexr. Johnston, merchant in Cumnock' made in favour of 'the said James Johnston merchant in Cumnock his oldest son and Daniel Johnston Surgeon in Cumnock now deceast his second son or the survivor of them or their or his assignees and that in trust for the behoof of the persons therein named'.

The property referred to was the tenement of houses in the town of Cumnock which had featured in the earlier sasine quoted and there was a reference to 'also another disposition of date 20th June 1783 & granted by the said James Johnston the surviving Trustee whereby for the Causes therein mentd. he dissigned disponed To and in favour of the said Alexander Johnston his son his heirs and assignees' the said tenement of houses 'sometime possessed by the said deceased Alexander Johnston now by his relict'.

This kind of sasine can link up with other documents of value to the genealogist, and can itself provide much information. From the above extracts, for instance, it will be noticed that the elder Alexander Johnstone's relict, who we know from other sources was Helen Sutherland, was still living in June 1783, and that James, the eldest son was living, but Daniel, the second son, was deceased at this time.

VIII

SERVICE OF HEIRS

W HEN LANDS WERE handed over to an heir rather than to a grantee the procedure was for a brieve, similar to the English brieve of mortancestry, to be issued from Chancery. This instructed the sheriff of the county concerned to empanel a jury which had the duty of discovering what lands the ancestor possessed at his death, whether the person claiming them was the true heir and certain other matters.

The verdict of this jury was sent back or 'retoured' to Chancery, whereupon in the case of lands held of the Crown in chief a precept of sasine, known technically as a precept of clare constat, was issued to the sheriff instructing him to grant possession. There was usually some fee payable to the Crown and the sheriff had to collect this and enter it in a register called the respond book, which was preserved in Chancery. This record goes back to 1515 and there is also a minute book going back even further – to 1437. These together form a valuable record of lands held directly from the Crown for the period before which the record of retours survives.

The jury's verdict on the brieves of mortancestry were entered in this record of retours which was preserved in Chancery and is now in the Scottish Record Office. Where a retour survives it gives a complete account of the inheritance of those who died with feudal possessions and of their heirs and the date of the ancestor's death, the value of the lands as retoured, which may bear very little relation to their real value, and the names of the superiors from whom they were held.

Very often a relative served on the inquest who was in a position to confirm the relationship of the petitioner to his ancestor. Therefore, when a namesake is listed among the jurors there is always a likelihood of his being of the same blood.

It will be obvious that such records are of great value to the genealogist. The correctness of the descent, however, particularly in the case of a descent from a remote ancestor, must be accepted with caution. There are abridgements published by the Record Commissioners but these do not give the superiors from whom the lands were held, nor the date of the ancestor's death.

Except for one gap of a few years these records are complete from 1600. Prior to that date they are very incomplete. Abstracts of the earliest services, which exist from 1544, have been published in three folio volumes, under the title *Inquisitionum ad Capellam Regis retornatarum Abbreviatio*, edited by T. Thomson, 1811–16. They are well indexed for both names and places. These cover the period from the earliest recorded services until 1699. From 1700 onwards there are decennial indexes, which though much abbreviated, give the relationships and often a great deal of the information required by the genealogical researcher. These abridgements continue by ten-yearly periods down to 1860, after which they are annual. They were printed for use in the Register House and though those down to 1860 were nominally on sale, few copies have been acquired by libraries, though the largest, such as the British Museum and the university libraries of Oxford and Cambridge, hold sets, as does the Scottish Library in the Edinburgh Public Library.

The special services relate to land and the general services to other property. The latter are particularly valuable since there is no sasine record to supplement it as there is in the case of a special service, when the sasine of the lands follow the settlement of the heirship and will be found in the register of sasines in the usual way.

Sometimes a service may reveal several generations. This is so in one of the early services, dated 9 May 1620, when Thomas Blair of Balthyok (Balthayock) was served heir to his great-great-grandfather (abavus) in certain lands between Mugdrum and Heidis of Streathern.[1]

A much later service to a great-grandfather throws considerable light on the family of Johnstone of Old Cumnock, whose pedigree is illustrated in Chapter V.

The abstract of this service in the decennial index for 1830–39 gives the following information:

JOHNSTONE – Henry James, London, to his Great-Grandfather Daniel Johnstone, Surgeon, Old Cumnock – Hr. of Line and Conqt Gl. – 11th March 1839 (Recorded) 1839, Mar. 19 (Monthly No.) 37.

The full service is given below. As will be seen, full details of the descent of the petitioner from his great-grandfather are given, and this reveals among other facts that the petitioner's father's elder brother had died without issue. The service is given in translation, the original being in Latin.

March 19th 1839.

This Inquisition was made in the Court of the Royal Burgh of the Canongate the eleventh day of March in the year of our Lord one thousand eight hundred and thirty nine before the honourable man William Arthur esquire one of the bailies of the said burgh and before these worthy and faithful men of the district, namely James Martin and James Morgan esquires solicitors before the Supreme Court of Scotland Robert Hall William Fraser and James Crawford junior esquires writers to the royal signet David Mackenzie Daniel Taylor William George Bell and Robert Oliphant writers in Edinburgh James Jaap professor of music there William Lothian merchant there Richard Miller watchmaker in the same place Thomas Raitt resident in Rose Street there Alexander Listow and John Gordon residents in the Canongate who having taken the great oath said that a former Daniel Johnstone surgeon in Old Cumnock in the sheriffdom of Ayr great-grandfather of Henry James Johnstone medical student in London eldest lawful son of Daniel Johnstone formerly of Newbury in the county of Berkshire who was second lawful son of Robert Johnstone formerly surgeon in Holyhead (John Cooper Johnstone eldest lawful son of the said Robert Johnstone having died without offspring) which Robert Johnstone was eldest lawful son of the said former Daniel Johnstone died at the faith and peace of the Queen And that the said Henry James Johnstone bearer of these presents is nearest and legitimate heir of line and conquest in general of the said Daniel Johnstone his great-grandfather and that he is of lawful age In testimony whereof the seals of certain of the said jurymen with the signature of the clerk of the burgh under cover of the seal of the said bailie with the royal brief included are subscribed the place day month and year above written (thus subscribed) William Fraser Jr. Clerk.

Where the heirs are heirs portioners, that is females or their issue succeeding jointly, useful information may be gleaned of collateral relatives. As an example, in the indexes for the period 1810–19 are found the following:

MORISON – Delvina Mackenzie (or Miller), Wife of J. Miller of Milton, to her cousin William Morison, Writer, Edinr. – Heir Port. Genl c.b. Invent. – 9th May 1810. [Recorded] 28 June 1810.

MORISON – Janet – (or Wilson) Wife of The Rev. J. Wilson, Abernite, to her cousin William Morison, Writer, Edinr. etc (*details as before*).

MORISON, Margaret – (or Blair) Wife of John Blair, Dunkeld, to her cousin William Morison, Writer, Edinr. etc (*details as before*).

The full service reveals that William Morison, writer in Edinburgh was a cousin on the father's side (patruelis) of the three petitioners and that they were daughters of the Reverend John Morison, minister of Petty, deceased, who was brother-german of the late Norman Morison, minister at Uig in the Isle of Lewis, the father of William.

A series of services to various relatives may also provide much information even from the indexes alone, Thus 'John Blair, Surgeon in Edinr.' was served heir general on 2 April 1747 to his grandfather 'Patrick Blair writer there', and on 15 October 1750 heir general to his father John Blair 'Surg. Apothecary there', and on 26 June 1751 heir special in '¼ part of Lands of Bellita, with Manor Place, etc. pa. of Gordon, Berwickshire' to his mother 'Elizabeth Fullerton (Wife of John Blair, Surgeon in Edinr.) who d. 2d Feb. 1738'.

In the early service of heirs evidence was no doubt given as to the identity of the petitioner but either this was not recorded or the documents have not survived. In the 19th century, however, there is often valuable information in the depositions made by witnesses as to the identity of the petitioner.

In a service, for instance, of John Morison to his father Donald Morison, a shipmaster in Greenock, on 1 November 1865, Mrs Eliza Thomson or Robertson of 21 Brougham Street, Greenock, widow of John Robertson, bank accountant, stated that she 'knew the late Donald Morison, the father of the petitioner,' that the said Donald Morison had died at Greenock of cholera about July 1832 and that the petitioner was his eldest lawful son by Jessie Fish or Morison, his wife, the deponent also stating that she was a cousin of the petitioner. Another deposition was made by Eliza Fish or Thomson, of 25 Brougham Street, Greenock, widow of Neil Thomson, shipmaster in Greenock, in which she stated that she was seventy-four years of age, mother of the preceding witness and aunt of the petitioner. A third witness was Donald Morison, residing at Gages near Ashburton, Devonshire, who stated that he was upwards of forty-four years of age and a son of the late Donald Morison, shipmaster in Greenock and of Jessie Fish or Morison, his wife, and that the petitioner was the eldest son of the said Donald Morison and brother of the deponent.

Similarly, in a petition recorded 9 May 1862 by a Mrs Henrietta Elizabeth Morison or Walton, the wife of the Reverend Stanley Walton, vicar of Fenstanton in the county of Huntingdon, and her sister Maria Frances Morison to be served heirs to their brother, James Mitford Morison, a solicitor of the Supreme Court, David Ramsay, guild accountant, deponed that he knew the deceased James Mitford Morison who was only once married and that to Elizabeth Rodger, daughter of — Rodger Esq., writer in Paisley, 'who survived him but there was never any lawful issue of the marriage', and that the said deceased never had any brothers. James MacArthur, merchant in Glasgow, concurred in the above statement.

IX

REGISTERS OF DEEDS

FOR THE GENEALOGIST the register of deeds is one of the most valuable of Scottish records. This vast register contains all the deeds which have a clause consenting to their registration for preservation and execution. Almost anything may be recorded in this great register, and it can contain information of the highest value to the genealogist. J. Maitland Thomson has described it as 'an inexhaustible store of information about the private life of our forefathers'.[1]

This register is a branch of the register of the court of session, which was kept by the clerks of session as nominees of the court until 1821, when the appointment of a keeper in that year handed over control to the Lord Clerk Register. Even so, the register is still frequently cited as 'the Books of Council and Session'.

Like the sasine register there are three series. The first, in 621 volumes, covers the period from 1554 to 1657. The second series is subdivided into three, which run parallel with each other chronologically. These three divisions correspond to the three clerkships of session, and this means that searchers have to hunt through three records instead of one for any special information. This system continued until 1811. The three series are known by the names of the clerks – Dalrymple, Durie and Mackenzie. There are 313 volumes in Dalrymple's office, 296 in Mackenzie's and 350 in the apparently overworked Durie's.

The modern series from 1812 onwards is numbered consecutively and there is a MS. index for it. The Scottish Record Office is printing indexes for the period from 1661 and has reached 1695. In the Record Office itself there are MS. indexes for the years 1750–54, and then continuous MS. indexes from 1770 onwards. All these indexes are for persons only.

The practice of entering bonds in the books of the court of session grew gradually and in time became more uniform. At the beginning of the reign of Mary, Queen of Scots, some of the volumes of the registers consisted almost entirely of deeds and, in consequence, in 1554 the clerks began to enter deeds in separate registers. Registration in the Register of Deeds was never compulsory, but the business community soon recognized its value, as is shown by its growth.

The variety of matters contained in the register is extraordinary. Thomson mentions the possibility of finding the contract for building some bridge or castle; the setting up of a parish school, including details of the salary to be paid to the schoolmaster; the contract for the building of a church or the purchase of a peal of bells; accounts of arrangements made between the patron of a living and his presentee; the agreement between neighbours regarding the draining of a bog or even the contract for raising a regiment of Scotsmen for service to some foreign country. Quite a number of deeds refer to trade, particularly the grain trade, and to apprenticeships with all kinds of curious conditions attached to them. Among the commonest of such registered deeds are marriage contracts and testamentary settlements, which are rich food for the genealogist.

From 1698 onwards an addition was made to the type of deed registered, when what is known as the registration of probative writs for preservation was introduced. These are writs which, though correct in form, do not contain any clause consenting to registration.

An example of the kind of information which may be disclosed in this register is that contained in a series of letters which the author discovered in his own family. These were four letters ranging from 1746 to 1753, written by a direct ancestor, John Edward.[2] This may have been a particularly fortunate discovery, but there must be numbers of such documents relating to other families.

These letters have been preserved as 'probative letters'. The first was dated 18 August 1746 and was written, as were all four letters, by John Edward or Edwards to his brother Thomas (about this time both John and his brother seem to have added an 's' to their surname). It is mainly concerned with the possible agreement between the two brothers and George Young about some money they owed him. There are various human and revealing passages about the family, and genealogically the letter reveals various relationships which were previously unknown.

My Ant Mary wants a Glass for a Chimney about 4 foot three inches in glass length with a plain wooden frame & fashionable . . . direct it for Mr Richard Dick Master of the Grammar School of St Andrews . . . My Service to my Cousin Mr Robert Ogilvy & tell him I shall be glad to have an answer to the Letter I wrote him.

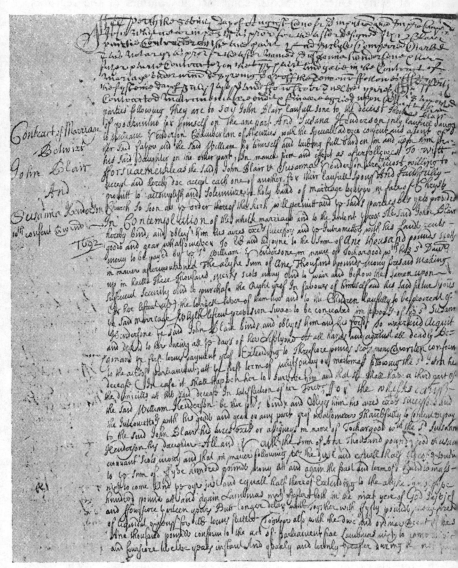

It was not difficult to discover from other sources that this Aunt Mary was married to Richard Dick, rector of the Grammar School at St Andrews and later Professor of Civil History in St Andrews University; that her maiden name was Irons and that she was therefore a sister of Margaret Irons who had married George Edward, the father of John and Thomas. The confirmation of her testament was found in St Andrew's commissariot, and this indicated a disposition and settlement by her, recorded 27 November 1779, also in the register of deeds.[3] This mentioned her sister, Ann, and a number of her nieces.

The second of John Edwards' letters is dated from Dundee, 13 September 1746. It appears that John had been four weeks at St Andrews, probably staying there with his uncle and aunt, and was now at Dundee on the road to his home in Coupar Angus, where he expected to arrive the next day.

There are further references to relatives: 'My kind Compliments to my dear Uncle Alexander Irons in your letter, and tell him that all our Ants thought he was dead as he never wrote to my Ant Mary . . . My service to my Cousin George Freer'. The last mentioned was evidently the cousin at whose book-bindery the letters for John's brother Thomas were to be left, for they are addressed, 'Mr Thomas Edwards to be left at Mr George Friers bookbinder at the sign of the Bible in Bell Yard near Temple Barr London'.

The author was fortunate in discovering a pedigree of this family of Freer, published in *Miscellanea Genealogica et Heraldica*.[4] This showed that George was the fifth son of George Freer, minister of Lethendy and Kinloch who had married in December 1699 Helen Blair described as 'of a good family in Perthshire'.

The Lethendy registers give the baptism of George Freer on 11 November 1711 and those of three brothers and two sisters between 1700 and 1708. The minister's marriage was also recorded on 26 December 1699 but the father of his bride was not mentioned. As, however, he was the minister it was thought the kirk session records might give fuller information and this proved to be so. These recorded, 'Decbr ye 10th 1699 . . . This day Mr George Freer min[r] was proclaimed wt. Helen Blair daughter to Thomas Blair of pockmilne for present in ye paroch of Rattray.'

This information, incidentally, corrected an error in the *Fasti* which stated that Helen was a daughter of James Blair of Ardblair.

John's next letter is dated from Spithead, 22 January 1746/7. This is a short letter which contains less genealogical information but is interesting because it mentions that they were sailing, presumably in convoy, with

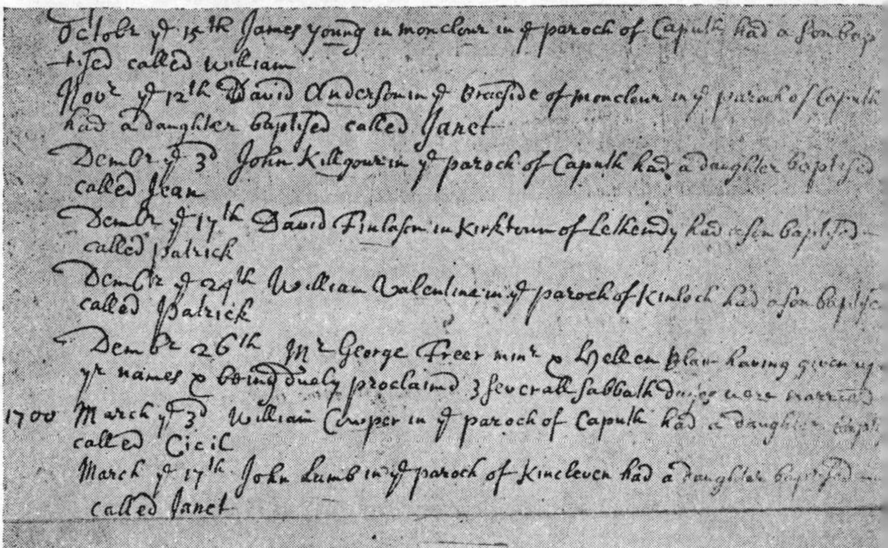

Octobr ye 15th James Young in Monclour in ye paroch of Caputh had a son bap-
-tised called William
Novr ye 12th David Anderson in ye Braeside of Monclour in ye paroch of Caputh
had a daughter baptised called Janet
Decmbr ye 3d John Killgour in ye paroch of Caputh had a daughter baptised
called Jean
Decmbr ye 17th David Finlason in Kirktoun of Lethendy had a son baptised
called Patrick
Decmbr ye 24th William Valentine in ye paroch of Kinloch had a son baptised
called Patrick
Decmbr 26th Mr George Freer minr & Hellen Blair having given up
yr names & being dualy proclaimd 3 severall Sabbath dayes were married
1700 March ye 3d William Cowper in ye paroch of Caputh had a daughter bapti
called Cicil
March ye 17th John Lamb in ye paroch of Kinclevin had a daughter baptised
called Janet

Fig. 5

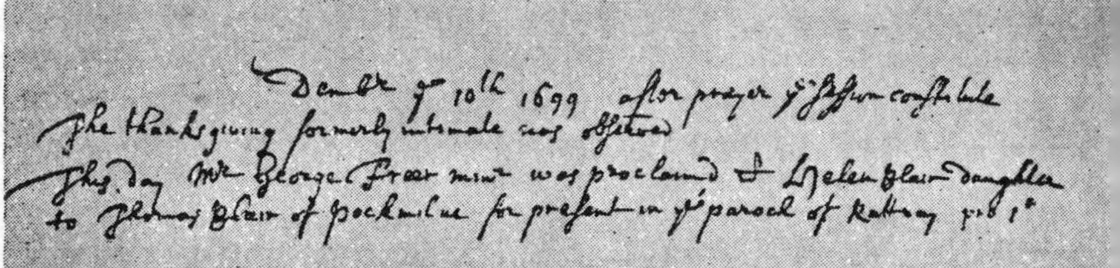

Decmbr ye 10th 1699 after prayer ye Session constitute
The thanksgiving formerly intimate was observed
This day Mr George Freer minr was proclaimd & Hellen Blair daughter
to Thomas Blair of Pockmilne for present in ye paroch of Rattray pro 1o

Fig. 6

FIGS. 5 and 6

(Fig. 5) Part of the parish register of Lethendy of 1699 including the entry on December 26th of the marriage of George Freer, the minister, and Helen Blair mentioned on p. 103 and shown in the pedigree on pp. 106–7, and (Fig. 6) the reference to this proclamation of marriage in the Lethendy Kirk Session Minutes of 10 December the same year. It will be noticed that the latter entry gives the valuable additional information that Helen Blair is a daughter of Thomas Blair of Pockmyln. *Reproduced by courtesy of the Church of Scotland and the Registrar General for Scotland* [R. G. ref. no. OPR/372/1].

Admiral Byng. This was the admiral who was executed for neglect of duty in 1757, when he was shot on the quarterdeck of his own ship, an action which has since been a matter of much controversy and condemnation.

John Edwards had entered the service of the East India Company, going out first as a seafaring person, later becoming a free merchant and sea-captain. The last of the four letters is dated from the Downs, 27 January 1753, and written from the ship *Egmont*. John's recent petition to be allowed to proceed to India as a free merchant had been successful and meanwhile he had been married at the Mayfair Chapel on 11 November of the previous year to a Mrs Henrietta Moore, a widow, described as 'of St James's, Westminster'. He mentions in this letter that his wife joins with him in sending compliments 'to you, your spouse and all friends', which shows that his brother Thomas was also by this time married.

There is no other genealogical information in this letter, but many of the little touches of human feeling which are so valuable in building up a picture for us of our ancestors, such as the little note which he included for his mother.

Dear Mother – I hope you will not be cast down on Account I am agoing abroad, for be asured I shall write you every opportunity, and I trust in God in a little time to come home with a fortune that will make us all live genteely. May the omnipotent God send us a happy meeting. Long live healthy & happiness is the earnest prayer of your dutyfull son untill death – John Edwards – Ship Egmont Capt. Tolson Commdr. – Saturday morning: – [Addressed] Mr Thomas Edwards in Coupar of Angus Scotland.

In expressing the hope that he would come home with a fortune he was echoing the hopeful longings of most men who entered the service of the East India Company. Some did return with great fortunes, but many more perished out there in their efforts to achieve them at a time when the standards of hygiene were extremely low and dangers from shipwreck and enemy action abounded. The author's ancestor died there, described as 'having been lost in the East Indies' some ten years after writing this letter. During those years he had succeeded in amassing a fortune, which in due course was dissipated by his only son and heir, an occurrence which was not unusual in families of that period of extravagance and high living.

The pedigree on pages 106-7 shows the extent of relationships and information discovered through these four letters of an adventurous ancestor.

When the Scottish Record Office concludes its survey of sheriff court, royal burgh and other local records, which it is at present making, a great deal more will be known about them. The committee appointed by the Secretary of State for Scotland to enquire into local records has in broad

A PEDIGREE MAINLY

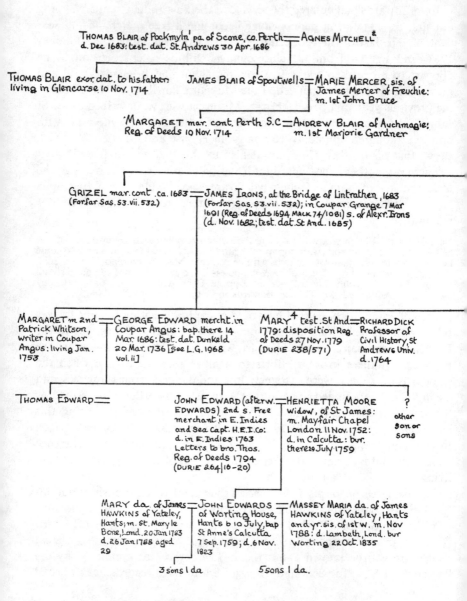

THOMAS BLAIR of Pockmyln' pa. of Scone, co. Perth══AGNES MITCHELL[2]
d. Dec 1683: test. dat. St. Andrews 30 Apr. 1686

THOMAS BLAIR exor. dat. to his father:
living in Glencarse 10 Nov. 1714

JAMES BLAIR of Spoutwells══MARIE MERCER, sis. of
                                          James Mercer of Freuchie:
                                          m. 1st John Bruce

MARGARET mar. cont. Perth S.C══ANDREW BLAIR of Auchmagie:
Reg. of Deeds 10 Nov. 1714   m. 1st Marjorie Gardner

GRIZEL mar. cont. ca. 1683══JAMES IRONS, at the Bridge of Lintrathen, 1683
(Forfar Sas. 53.vii. 532)   (Forfar Sas. 53.vii. 532); in Coupar Grange 7 Mar
                                          1691 (Reg. of Deeds 1694 MACK 74/1081) s. of Alexr. Irons
                                          (d. Nov. 1682; test. dat. St. And. 1685)

MARGARET m. 2nd══GEORGE EDWARD mercht. in   MARY[4] test. St. And══RICHARD DICK
Patrick Whitson,   Coupar Angus: bap. there 14   1779: disposition Reg.   Professor of
writer in Coupar   Mar 1686: test. dat. Dunkeld   of Deeds 27 Nov. 1779   Civil History, St
Angus: living Jan.   20 Mar. 1736 [see L.G. 1968   (DURIE 238/571)   Andrews Univ.
1753   vol. ii]   d. 1764

THOMAS EDWARD══   JOHN EDWARD (afterw.══HENRIETTA MOORE   ?
                                EDWARDS) 2nd s. Free   widow, of St James: other
                                merchant in E. Indies   m. Mayfair Chapel   son or
                                and Sea Capt. H.E.I.Co: London 11 Nov. 1752:   sons
                                d. in E. Indies 1763   d. in Calcutta: bur.
                                Letters to bro. Thos.   there 19 July 1759
                                Reg. of Deeds 1794
                                (DURIE 264/16-20)

MARY da. of James══JOHN EDWARDS══MASSEY MARIA da. of James
HAWKINS of Yateley,   of Worting House,   HAWKINS of Yateley, Hants
Hants; m. St. Mary le   Hants b 10 July, bap   and yr. sis. of 1st w. m. Nov
Bone, Lond. 20 Jan 1783   St Anne's Calcutta   1788: d. Lambeth, Lond. bur
d. 26 Jan 1788 aged   7 Sep. 1759; d. 6 Nov.   Worting 22 Oct. 1835
29   1823

3 sons 1 da.   5 sons 1 da.

A PEDIGREE MAINLY FROM REGISTERS OF DEEDS

FROM REGISTERS OF DEEDS

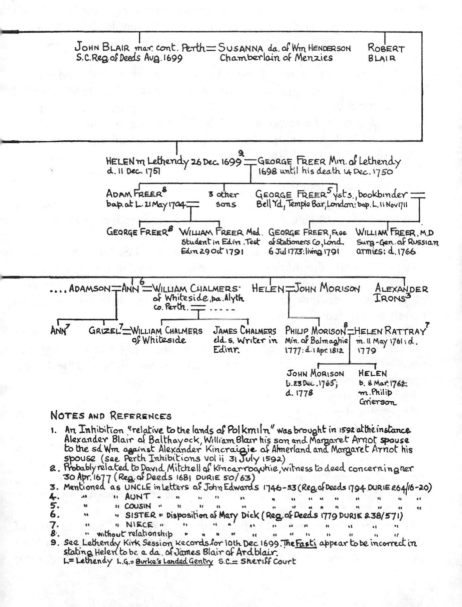

JOHN BLAIR mar. cont. Perth ═ SUSANNA da. of Wm HENDERSON   ROBERT
S.C.Reg. of Deeds Aug. 1699   Chamberlain of Menzies   BLAIR

HELEN m Lethendy 26 Dec. 1699 ═ GEORGE FREER Min. of Lethendy
d. 11 Dec. 1751   [2]   1698 until his death 14 Dec. 1750

ADAM FREER[8]   3 other   GEORGE FREER[5] yst s., bookbinder ═
bap. at L. 21 May 1704 ═   sons   Bell Yd, Temple Bar, London: bap. L. 11 Nov 1711

GEORGE FREER[8] WILLIAM FREER Med.   GEORGE FREER, Free   WILLIAM FREER, M.D
             Student in Edin. Test   of Stationers Co, Lond. Surg.-Gen. of Russian
             Edin 29 Oct 1791   6 Jul 1773: living 1791   armies: d. 1766

.... ADAMSON ═ ANN ═ WILLIAM CHALMERS·   HELEN ═ JOHN MORISON   ALEXANDER
              [6]   of Whiteside, pa. Alyth   IRONS[3]
                    co. Perth ═ .....

ANN[7]   GRIZEL[7] ═ WILLIAM CHALMERS   JAMES CHALMERS   PHILIP MORISON[8] ═ HELEN RATTRAY[7]
                    of Whiteside   eld. s. Writer in   Min. of Balmaghie   m. 11 May 1761; d.
                                        Edinr.   1777: d. 1 Apr. 1812   1779

                                                          JOHN MORISON   HELEN
                                                          b. 23 Dec. 1765;   b. 8 Mar. 1762:
                                                          d. 1778   m. Philip
                                                                             Grierson

NOTES AND REFERENCES

1. An Inhibition "relative to the lands of Polkmiln" was brought in 1592 at the instance
   Alexander Blair of Balthayock, William Blair his son and Margaret Arnot spouse
   to the sd Wm against Alexander Kincraigie of Ahmerland and Margaret Arnot his
   spouse (see Perth Inhibitions vol ii 31 July 1592)
2. Probably related to David Mitchell of Kincarroquhie, witness to deed concerning ner
   30 Apr. 1677 (Reg. of Deeds 1681 DURIE 50/63)
3. Mentioned as UNCLE in Letters of John Edwards 1746-53 (Reg. of Deeds 1794 DURIE 264/16-20)
4.   "   " AUNT "   "   "   "   "   "   "   "   "   "
5.   "   " COUSIN "   "   "   "   "   "   "   "   "   "
6.   "   " SISTER " Disposition of Mary Dick (Reg. of Deeds 1779 DURIE 238/571)
7.   "   " NIECE "   "   "   "   "   "   "   "   "   "
8.   "   " without relationship "   "   "   "   "   "   "   "   "
9. See Lethendy Kirk Session Records for 10th Dec 1699. The Fasti appear to be incorrect in
   stating Helen to be a da. of James Blair of Ardblair.
   L = Lethendy L.G. = Burke's Landed Gentry S.C. = Sheriff Court

terms recommended that the local authority records deemed worthy of preservation shall be formally transmitted to the Keeper of the Records of Scotland as soon as possible after they pass out of current use and that the Keeper should place these records in the nearest local repository suitable for them; that they should be available to the public in these depositories; that the Keeper should exercise a supervision over these records and their custody, and that where no local accommodation is available these records may be kept temporarily in a central repository of the Scottish Record Office.[5]

In the same year a report by another committee appointed by the Secretary of State to enquire into the sheriff court records recommended that the sheriff court records prior to 1860 should be kept entire, and that the sheriff should be responsible only for the preservation of current records and that those more than twenty-five years old should be transmitted to the Keeper of Records, who may place them in suitable local repositories under his control and inspection, or he may retain them centrally if found desirable.[6]

Certain categories of these post-1860 records are recommended for destruction after varying periods and some categories for weeding by the Record Office.

The Scottish Record Office has recently acquired St George's Church, Charlotte Square, Edinburgh, which is being converted into a depository for records and this will allow a great number of local records to be held temporarily while they are being sorted out and their final place of deposition decided.

The manuscript material in the sheriff courts which is most likely to interest genealogists is the register of deeds. The register of hornings and recorded protests are other documents which contain genealogical material.

From early times sheriff courts registered deeds. Their survival varies in different sheriff courts, but where they have been well preserved they may go back a considerable way. Prior to about 1808 these registers are not indexed and this of course restricts their value considerably, but there were minute books and where these survive they will prove the easiest way of searching the registers. Where the date of the deed or suspected deed is known fairly closely a search in these minute books may prove profitable and not too lengthy.

The earliest existing book of records of any sheriffdom is that of Aberdeen, which begins in 1503. Down to 1660 these court records have been edited in abstract by Dr David Littlejohn in the New Spalding Club series and this book is valuable as a source of information regarding sheriff court procedure.[7] The Stair Society has published a list of extant sheriff court records in their *Sources and Literature of Scots Law*, vol. 1 (1935).

Other courts which registered deeds were the royal burghs, the commissary courts (as previously mentioned) and, up to 1747, the courts of regality, these last mentioned ceasing when the heritable jurisdictions were abolished.

It is obvious that a great deal of genealogical information is lodged in these registers of deeds; in particular, a great number of marriage contracts which are not to be found in the general register of deeds are no doubt recorded in sheriff court or other local registers of deeds. It is to be hoped that when their disposal has been settled a start may be made in indexing these records so that their great value may be more accessible to genealogists and local historians.

As in the general register of deeds, the sheriff court registers of deeds and probative writs contain many personal letters, recorded probably as evidences of relationship or of the testamentary wishes of the writers. Such a letter is that recorded in the Argyllshire sheriff court register on 10 February 1810 by a Daniel Morison to his father John Morison. Daniel appears to have been a shipmaster trading for ship owners. This letter is dated from Greenock, 29 November 1808, and reads as follows:

Dear and honoured Father,
My being so long hear and not having the pleasure of seeing you is much against me as am afraid youll think that I might go that leanth was Inclind – But Father you must consider – am not arivd at that pitch as to go when I wish for but must go by my owners orders am still in hopes to see You by the Month of May as am determint to tak a Start to the Highland in Summer I had a letter from Neill he and family are well he being the only one now we expect to hear from – in case any thing happening me anexed you have a list of all the money that am worth which is as follows Vizt:

Messrs Henderson Wood & Co	£1,000
Messrs David Hynd & Co	200
Messrs Stevenson & McLachlan	100
Messrs Patrick Moric & Co	70
Mr Robert Buchanan	58.12
Mr William Kerr	100
	£1,528.12

Say One thousand five hundred and twenty eight pounds Sterling – there is also Seven hundred pounds Sterling which I left in Handuy which I left with Mr James Hyde to purchase Bills and expect it everyday – Shoud any misfortune happen me it is my request you will keep the thousand pound where it is, and use the Interest of it, which is fifty pounds yearly and divide the rest agreeable to my Will and Testament which was made two years ago only to give Neill what his two Brothers should get – Dear Father, altho I left you this Statement am in hopes to use it all myself. But am in hopes you'll oblige me so far as to keep Yourself in good Boarding and Cloathing as I should feel much hurt that any person say that you would want any thing while I have. I remain, Dear Father, your affectionate Son (signed) Daniel Morison (addressed) Mr John Morison Kildurgland near Lochgilphead.[8]

These simple, sometimes naive and often ungrammatical and ill-spelt letters, besides giving information on relationships and occupations, often throw interesting and even fascinating light on their writers' feelings and ambitions and on their social and economic circumstances.

Some did return with great fortunes

X

OTHER COURT REGISTERS

A LMOST ANY DOCUMENT belonging to the past may by chance throw light on a particular individual and in this way all historical documents may have genealogical value. In the preceding chapters attention has been given to those records which are particularly useful to genealogists. In this chapter some records will be mentioned which, though generally of less value to searchers, nevertheless sometimes reveal information which may in a few cases be surprisingly extensive.

Most of the registers mentioned below, as far as the MS. portions of them are concerned, are not indexed until the early 19th century, but where portions of them have been published they are well indexed and can consequently be quickly searched.

Registers of Hornings, Inhibitions and Adjudications
These can sometimes be of great value. The name 'horning' derives from a quaint and curious origin. A creditor was able to obtain legal redress against a debtor who had refused to obey an order of the court, namely to pay his just debts, by having him denounced as a rebel against the King with a messenger of arms blowing three blasts on a horn. Following this picturesque and noticeable action the debtor's goods were held to be escheat to the Crown against the creditor's claim, and the debtor rendered liable to imprisonment. The use of this process still survives, though creditors seldom resort to it today. The register consists of 1,289 volumes, which cover the period 1610–1902. None of this register has been published and as there is no index its consultation requires time and patience. It is best searched through the minute books, which exist from 1660 onwards.

The process of horning also took place in the sheriff courts and their registers give information similar to that in the general registers. Searches in these can also be best made through the minute books, where they survive. These sheriff court records may be held locally, or may have been handed in to the Record Office.

Information in early hornings is sometimes more valuable than in the later ones. The 17th century hornings may reveal family feuds which in turn uncover family relationships. In the 18th century the information may be disappointing, though sometimes a horning is against several members of a family, which can discover collaterals.

Letters of Inhibition

These had the result of preventing a debtor alienating or burdening his heritable property to the disadvantage of his creditors. Thus hornings deal with personal property and letters of inhibition with real property. These letters are found also in the sheriff courts. In some cases they are in the same registers as the hornings and in others in separate registers. Once again they are best searched in the minute books.

Bonds of Interdiction

These were a voluntary method of obtaining the same result as the letters of inhibition. There are two series of these registers, and a minute book covering the period 1652 to 1868 is again the easiest method of consulting them.

Court of Council and Session

The early province of the Lords of Session was both administrative and judicial but when later the Privy Council was established the administrative function of the Lords of Session was partially taken over by that body. The Privy Council was established in 1489 but the separate registers of that body begin only in 1545 and even after that date acts relating to state affairs still continue to appear among the Acts of the Lords of Council and Session.

The Acts of the Lords of Council in Civil Causes have been published in two volumes, covering the years 1478 to 1501, and selections of the Acts of the Lords of Council in Public Affairs, which are those relating to their administrative rather than their judicial actions, have been published from 1501 to 1554. These serve as a link between the previously mentioned volumes and the registers of the Privy Council.

Until 1532 the session records were called the Acts of the Lords of Council and after the establishment of the court of session the name was changed to the Acts of the Lords of Council and Session and a few years later changed again to 'Acts and Decreets'.

This vast series of MS. volumes from 1664 onwards are in three parallel series corresponding to the three clerks of session. This means that it is necessary to search through three records instead of one, because unfortunately the manuscript records of session are unindexed until 1810, after which there is an annual index. One of the great long-term tasks facing the Scottish Record Office is the indexing of the Acts and Decreets. From the point of view of the genealogist this lack of index is regrettable. Maitland Thomson states that 'the records of the Decreets of the Court of Session are a veritable museum of legal antiquities and the happiest of happy hunting grounds for the genealogist and the local historian'.[1] The process may indeed reveal a great deal of genealogical information and among the papers there may be a chart pedigree to show more clearly the relationship of the persons concerned in the action.

This was so in a process concerning the disputed succession to the lands of Archibald Buchanan of Balfunning and Croy, which took place at the beginning of the 19th century. A pedigree exists among the process papers of the court of session, and very necessarily so as the case had the complication of two persons called George Leny, as far as is known unrelated, who had married respectively the grandmother and mother of one of the parties in the proceedings.

The case was involved. It concerned the question as to whether the succession to an estate should be in the terms of a marriage contract of a great-grandfather with regard to the succession of subsequent heirs or whether it should follow the procedure of ancient investiture.

Another unusual feature of this case was that the pursuer, Andrew Leny Buchanan (who had taken the surname of Buchanan in accordance with the terms of a marriage contract) was a sergeant in the 43rd Regiment of Foot and the defender, Lieutenant (afterwards Captain) William Morison, was an officer in the same regiment. This might have been embarrassing to both parties, but by the time of Andrew Leny Buchanan's petition in June 1811 he was described as 'late sergeant' and it also appears that at any rate for a part of the proceedings William Morison was a prisoner of war in France.

The accompanying pedigree from the process papers will show more clearly the relationship. It will be seen that Andrew Leny Buchanan was the son of the elder daughter, Helen, while William Morison was the son of the younger daughter, Henrietta. Leny Buchanan claimed that he was entitled to the undivided lands of Balfunning under the marriage contract destination, but Morison claimed they should succeed jointly as heirs portioner under the ordinary laws of investiture.

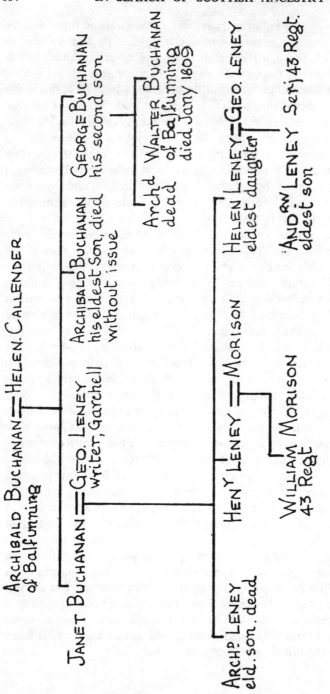

A PEDIGREE FROM A COURT OF SESSION PROCESS

Among the papers in this case is the contract of marriage dated 1 September 1713 and recorded in the books of council and session, 12 October 1809, between Archibald Buchanan of Balfunning and Helen, daughter of John Callender of Westertown; the petition of Andrew Leny Buchanan of 26 June 1811, and that of William Morison 'Captain in the 43d Regiment of Foot, at present a Prisoner of War in France and of George Morrison, [sic], writer in Glasgow, his younger brother, and Factor and Commissioner', dated 10 September 1812.

This case, like many others, dragged on for some years. The Lord Ordinary had found, 14 May 1811, that the succession of Balfunning devolved upon Andrew Leny Buchanan as eldest heir female (i.e. heir through the female line) descended of the marriage, but that the lands of Croy, which had descended in a different manner, belonged to the pursuer (Leny Buchanan) and to the defender (Morison) equally as heirs-portioners of line to their last predecessor. This decision was appealed against but was upheld by the High Court on 4 March 1813. The case had sufficient legal interest to be reported in one of the law reports, the *Scots Revised Reports*, Faculty Collection, vol. 1,[2] and those interested in the legal points can follow the lengthy arguments of the Lords of Session, but the biographer and family historian will be mainly interested in the genealogical content of such cases which, as in this instance, may be considerable.

Registers of the Privy Council
These often contain information about ordinary people of no particular prominence. Their scope, as mentioned, was both judicial and administrative. The registers have been published from 1545 to 1690 in three series, comprising altogether thirty-seven volumes, and this publication is still in progress. The registers include such matters as appeals and seditious offences against the peace.

The Exchequer Rolls and Lord High Treasurer's Accounts
These are valuable for information on all those who had financial dealings with the Crown. The exchequer rolls contain the accounts of the officials responsible for the collection of the royal revenue; for example, the sheriffs, 'custumars' (customs officers) and bailies of burghs, and they also contain the accounts of the Chamberlain, the official responsible for the receipt and expenditure of the royal revenue. His responsibilities were later divided between the Controller and the Treasurer. The Lord High Treasurer was responsible for the expenditure and receipt of that part of the revenue known as 'casualty', which was a more variable revenue.

The *Exchequer Rolls of Scotland* have been published from 1264 to 1600 in twenty-three volumes and the *Accounts of the Lord High Treasurer* have been published from 1473 to 1574 in twelve volumes.

The Register of the Great Seal

This register includes all grants of land by the Crown to its subjects, the confirmation of charters by these subjects to their vassals, patents of nobility, commissions to the great officers of state, letters of pardon and remission, of denization, charters of incorporation and a few birth briefs or certificates of descent. This register has been published from 1306 to 1668 in eleven volumes. The charters are in condensed form and in Latin until 1652 and afterwards in English. There is probably hardly a family of any note in Scotland which does not appear somewhere in this register.

The Register of the Privy Seal of Scotland

This is a well-kept register and the portion from 1488 to 1580 has been published in seven volumes. Precepts under the privy seal authorized the issue of charters and so forth under the great seal, and covered such matters as gifts of escheats and feudal casualties, letters of respite, of pensions, commissions to minor offices and presentations to churches and lesser benefices.

Cessio Bonorum

This is a process in the Court of Session which may throw considerable light on a family. It was instituted to mitigate the harshness of the laws against debtors. Under it a person who could satisfy the court that his debts were not occasioned by any fraud but due to misfortune and losses could obtain release from imprisonment, provided he made over all his assets to his creditors.

The case of Daniel Morison illustrates the kind of information which such a process can uncover. The main source for family intelligence is the 'condescendence'. This is the submission by the debtor of all the circumstances which he wishes taken into consideration in seeking the cessio. This will frequently give some account of the petitioner's life and circumstances. Daniel Morison's condescendence of 1822 reads as follows:

In the year 1795 the Pursuer entered the 3d or West Lowland Regiment of Fencibles as Ensign. He was afterwards appointed Lieut. and Adjutant and continued in the Corps in these capacities until its Reduction in the beginning of the year 1799 – The Dumfries shire Militia was then embodied and was forming under the Command of His Grace the last Duke of Buccleugh, and his Grace having occasion to notice the Pursuer's services as Adjutant in the West Lowland Fencibles desired it to be intimated to the

Pursuer that he might obtain a Commission in the Dumfries shire Regiment – accordingly the Pursuer entered that Corps as an Ensign early in the year 1799. He was afterwards appointed Lieutenant and acted occasionally as Adjutant, and continued in the Regiment until the Peace in 1802. He was married before he entered the Army, and during the period of his service, he became the father of four children. In May 1802, on the recommendation of his Grace the last Duke of Buccleugh, he was appointed Comptroller of the Customs at Glasgow, where he had gone to reside with his family. From June 1803 until the Peace of 1814, the Pursuer was Adjutant of the 1st Regiment of Glasgow Volunteers which transferred its Services, as the 5th Regiment of Lanarkshire Local Militia, and he has continued to enjoy the appointment of Comptroller of the Customs at a fixed salary, since 1812, of £400 per annum. Prior to 1812, the Salary of the office arose chiefly from certain fees.

During the period of his Military service the Pursuer's family occasioned an expenditure exceeding his pay, and he thus incurred debts to a considerable amount from which he was afterwards unable to extricate himself. Indeed his family increasing to nine children his debts were increased, in place of being diminished – The Pursuer had enjoyed the good will of all his regimental Companions, some of whom stepping forward with offers of assistance, in the way of cash advances the Pursuer was induced some years ago to feu a piece of ground in the neighbourhood of Glasgow on which he built a dwelling house and offices, which with outlays on improveing the ground cost about £1,400 Sterling. Shortly afterwards the Pursuer's health became seriously impaired, he having been attacked with a complicated nervous disorder [*in margin* vide Dr Cleghornes certificate produced in process] of a distressing and an alarming aspect, and during a depression of spirits, he was constrained to sell the property which brought only £600. He entered into an agreement for a lease of the Property, but having got into arrears of rent the Landlord relinquished the agreement on payment of £20 and the Pursuer's household furniture and whole effects were sold to pay the arrears of rent and other pressing demands. A meeting of his Creditors was then assembled and an arrangement proposed, to which some of the Creditors acceded and others would not, and indeed the Pursuer would have been unable to have fulfilled the arrangement. The maintenance and education of the Pursuer's large family was expensive. His expenditure was much increased in consequence of his own state of health, and a delicate state of health of several members of his family. He was subject to the payment of considerable sums for expenses of Diligence and his income being abridged the Pursuer got into further difficulties, from which he has been unable to extricate himself and his Creditors pressing personal diligence he has been under the necessity of bringing the present Process.

By the State produced it appears that his debts amount to £1,067.12. His only property consists of some household furniture which has been hypothecated for Landlords rent and where the loss on the Heritable property and the other circumstances of the Case are considered, it is humbly hoped the Court will grant the Pursuer the benefit of the Cessio[3].

The Lords of Council and Session on 4 July 1822 found the pursuer entitled to the benefit of this precept of Cessio upon lodging a Disposition omnium bonorum with a special Assignation to the sum of one hundred and twenty pounds per annum out of his salary as Comptroller of the Customs at Glasgow and also on his making oath in terms of the Act of Sederunt and grant cum nupia to any of the usual Magistrates of Glasgow.

It is interesting to note that, just as the celebrated vicar of Bray retained his living, Daniel Morison still remained comptroller of customs in Glasgow, but probably this was by intention, and no doubt his creditors hoped that he would do so as they realised that this was his only asset and their only hope of obtaining any repayment of his debts to them.

On 10 July following, the Lords of Council and Session, now having before them the pursuer's oath and the disposition lodged, decreed the cessio in the terms of their previous decision, 'and Dispense with his wearing the dyverne habit'. The dyverne habit was a tall pointed hat and a yellow coat which debtors were compelled to wear. This particular form of humiliation had by this date not been enforced for some considerable time.

A condition of the cessio bonorum was that the pursuer should have spent at least one month in prison before making application for it, but Daniel Morison had managed to avoid this. After spending three nights in the Canongate Tolbooth from 22–25 March, he was 'removed from Prison pursuant to Act of Sederunt 14 June 1671 on Bail to return to Prison on recovery of his health, his life being attested in the Oath of Mr Alexander Black Surgeon in Edinburgh to be then in extreme danger'.

The certificates from the doctors reveal the diagnostic methods and treatment of ailments of a century and a half ago. A certificate from a Dr W. Gavin, dated 5 May 1822, stated that he appeared to be 'afflicted with a chronic inflamation of the Stomach and of the Kidney in consequence of which it will be proper he should not at present be engaged in any sedentary employment'. An opinion was added by Dr Cleghorn. This is a long account, taking a rather pessimistic view of Daniel's health. Among other things he states that 'during the winters months a warm bath from 92 to 4 should be used once a week from 5 to 10 minutes & from the first mild weather in June the cold bath may be used every good morning till Septr.' and that 'Mr Morison should regularly shave his head once a week, wash it every evening and morning with water cold or tepid . . . dry it carefully & rub it every night with a little spirits. The wig should compress no part so much as to leave a mark & the linen should be changed every 3d day. He should not stoop or look back & he should sleep with the head as high as he can bear with the room well aired & not too hot but quite comfortable'.

Another certificate from a Dr John Thatcher, M.D., a member of the Royal College of Physicians, stated that 'Mr Daniel Morison has been, for some time, in extreme bad health, his constitution is much materially affected, & I still consider that much care & management are essentially required to prevent a serious return of those complaints which have put his life in great danger'. This certificate was dated 3 June 1822 and sent from 17 Leith Street, Edinburgh.

In spite of these somewhat gloomy medical prognostications Daniel Morison survived until 3 December 1844, attaining the age of seventy.

The *cessio bonorum* process includes a full list of creditors. These can be revealing of the pursuer's way of life and may contain names of people which provide clues as to family relationships. In the case of Daniel Morison, as well as the many creditors in ordinary walks of life, grocers, shoemakers, bakers and tailors, are distillers, spirit dealers, victuallers, innkeepers, wine merchants and brewers. This suggests a way of life and high living prevalent among the military and upper middle classes at the beginning of the last century. He was possibly fortunate in obtaining his cessio and in avoiding incarceration in the Canongate tolbooth for more than three days.

Apart from producing varied and frequently surprising personal details, the condescendence can reflect vividly on the social background of the times. A decreet of cessio bonorum by John McGillierire against his creditors dated 6 August 1765 lists:

To goods taken out of my packs when Travelling and at Markets by Thieves Thirty five pounds & sixteen shillings: To Loss sustained by my horses falling once in the Water of Tay, twice in the Water of Lyon, once in the Water of Gary and once Jumping out of the Boat under Cloud of Night at Loch rannoch mouth by which my goods were quite damnifyed Twenty seven pounds.[4]

Burgh Records

Mention has been made in Chapter IX of the independent registers of deeds in the royal burghs, commissary courts and courts of regality. In addition to the royal burghs, the records of other burghs can be valuable. The dean of guild books frequently give references to owners of tenements, and services of heirs are found in both sheriff and burgh courts. The valuable 'List of Inhabitants' in 1685 under a contemporary Act of Parliament should, where it survives, be found in the burgh records as well as in the baron court books. The burgess rolls are more fully mentioned in Chapter XIII. Extracts of a number of burgh records have been published by various societies such as the Scottish Burgh Record Society, the Scottish Record Society and the Scottish History Society. The records of the capital, as might be expected, go back a long way and are generally full and well-kept. *Extracts from the Records of the Burgh of Edinburgh, 1681–1689*, ed. M. Wood and H. Armet (1927) will give an idea of the kind of material which may be found in burgh records.

Barony Records

A barony consisted of lands usually held from the Crown and designated a free barony. The baron had jurisdiction in both civil and criminal affairs within the boundary of the barony. The baron court books, where they survive, will record the legal proceedings of the court and provide information on persons brought before it. The *Court Book of the Barony of Urie, 1604–1747*, published by the Scottish History Society[5] will indicate the kind of material which may be found in such records. A burgh of barony was a town situated within a barony in which the barony courts were held.

Regality Records

A regality was a territorial jurisdiction granted by the Crown, its lands being constituted a free regality. Persons on whom these regalities were conferred held the title of lords of regality. A grant of a regality handed over by the sovereign as much of his powers as he was able to give. The grantee thus virtually possessed the sovereignty of the territory (vide Cosmo Innes *Lectures on Scotch Legal Antiquities*, 1872). The burgh of regality was the principal town in it.

Until the abolition of the hereditable jurisdictions in 1747 the regality courts were competent to hold and record the services of heirs and registration of deeds. Where these survive they may provide valuable information on persons living within the regality, particularly in the case of services, as these were not required to be registered centrally.

A messenger of arms blowing three
      blasts on a horn

XI

CESS, CENSUS AND TAXATION LISTS

T HE TAX KNOWN as the cess tax was a means of raising funds for the support of troops in the 17th and 18th centuries. In the offices of town clerks there may be found old cess rolls, and county clerks often have old valued rent rolls as far back as the time of Oliver Cromwell. A number of these cess rolls are finding their way into the Record Office, for instance those of Peebles parish for 1738 and of Wilton parish for 1720, which came in before 1947.

Valuation rolls since 1855 have been compiled annually for each county and royal burgh. These show the landlord, tenant and occupier of every piece of property in Scotland. They may be seen locally or at the Register House. There are also to be found surviving valuation rolls of earlier periods. These may be of dates in the 17th century. A number of them, as previously mentioned, are now in the record office. Others may be held locally.

The thirteen volumes of the window tax lists 1747–1768 have been mentioned, as have the lists of inhabitants 1685. Dean of guild books will frequently give references to owners of tenements.

The Teind Office records include the valuations by the sub-commissioners in 1629, which give the names of proprietors and sometimes of the tacksmen of the lands and teinds.

Census Returns

The records of the census returns for Scotland since 1841 are preserved in the New Register House. They were held every ten years and those from 1841 to 1891 are available for searching.

A particular search may be made in respect of one person or one household at a specified address at one census for a small fee and this may be made by post provided the minimum details required, namely the exact name of the person, his address in full and the date of the census, can be supplied. For a further fee an extract of any entry which may be found is obtainable.

A general search cannot be undertaken by the staff, but must be carried out personally by the applicant or a searcher on his behalf. Full details of fees for searching the census returns and also of the special inclusive fees for a general search of the census, of the old parish registers and of the indexes to the civil registration, can be obtained from the Registrar General, New Register House, Edinburgh EH1 3YT.

The 1841 census lists the persons in each house by name, though usually only an initial is given for a second Christian name. Their relationship to the head of the household is not shown and the age of persons of fifteen or over is given only to the lowest of the term of five years, thus persons from fifteen to nineteen are shown as fifteen and someone aged twenty-nine would be shown as twenty-five. The age of children under fifteen is given to the exact year. This census shows whether a person was born in the same county or not; it does not give his exact place of birth. There is an indication or description of occupation, e.g. publican, agricultural labourer, ostler or F.S. (for female servant).

The 1851 and subsequent censuses give more exact information. They show the head of the household, and indicate the status of the other persons living in it to the head, such as wife, son, aunt, lodger, apprentice. The age is stated exactly. The occupation and the place of birth are given. The last-mentioned detail is of course particularly valuable, as it allows the searcher to go at once to the register of the parish of the person's birth.

Applicants for particular or general searches have to state their reason for wishing to search, which may be described as 'genealogical' or 'family history'. Applicants have also to undertake to consult the Registrar General before publishing anything based upon any search or extract which has been obtained from the census.

Other Taxes

After the Union there were a number of taxes which applied to the whole of Great Britain. At the end of the 18th century Pitt, anxious to pay for the wars with France, introduced a variety of taxes. Not all of these are of great genealogical value. The male servants tax of 1780 can be a useful source for information about persons of the upper or middle classes. The Society of Genealogists, London, has a list of persons who paid this tax, arranged alphabetically by counties, and covers some 24,750, indicating the number of male servants employed, but without giving their names. The original tax accounts are in the Public Record Offices.

XII

THE CLANS AND SCOTTISH TITLES

WHEN GEORGE IV visited Scotland in 1822 Sir Walter Scott wrote of him:

He is our kinsman. It is not too much to say that there is scarcely a gentleman of any of the old Scottish families who cannot 'count kin' with the Royal House from which our Sovereign is descended.

And Sir Thomas Innes of Learney in quoting the above continues:

Hardly is there a Scot today who cannot in some line of ancestry connect himself with the Royal line of Fergus Mor McEarc, and claim as a kinsman Our Sovereign Lady Queen Elizabeth II. This sense of kinship, the bond between the *Ard Righ Albann* and the great peers and chiefs, between these and the *duine-uasail*, and between the latter and the clan, has had the most far-reaching effect upon our Scottish civilization; for between the Peerage, the Houses of Chiefs and Chieftains, the Baronage, the Gudemen or lesser Lairds, and Tacksmen, it has been calculated that at the time of the Union there were (in a population of about a million) over ten thousand titled houses, each as proud and as nobly descended as any of the great continental *noblesse*.[1]

The existence of the clans was a binding force in the Highlands. While owing their chief complete loyalty the clansmen, reared in crofts and cottages, also possessed an independence which was born of a pride of race and of reflection on a glorious past. Feudalism was never imposed upon the Highlands, but feudalism appealed to the highlanders because of its principle of inheritance, fixity of tenure and traditions. In this sense the clan system was feudal, for it recognized the family basis of organization, and rural communities found happiness in this instinct of tribality and in the maintenance of subinfeudation, which the Plantagenets had abolished in England. The clansmen believed that this conferment of the lands on feudal tenure would give them a greater security and a recognition of the holding of the chief until time immemorial, or, as the charter granted by

123

McDonald to one of the vassals of the Isles stated 'to endure so long as the waves should beat upon the rock'.[2]

This subinfeudation meant that the younger sons succeeded to their shares of the family lands and they in turn proudly styled themselves by the name of that estate.

A laird was usually a tenant-in-chief of the Crown, as were the minor barons who served in the Scottish Parliament. The name derives from the word 'lord' and a laird is even today addressed by the name of his estate rather than by his surname. Thus James Stewart-Robertson of Edradynate would be addressed as 'Edradynate' without 'Mr' in front of his name. In writing he would be referred to as 'Edradynate' but addressed on the envelope as 'James Stewart-Robertson of Edradynate' without 'esquire' being added, this being implied in his style as a laird. It is usually considered that an estate should have been held in the family for at least three generations before a lairdship is established.

Until 1672 lairds would sign by the name of their estate only, but that year an act was passed which disallowed their doing so, only permitting peers to sign with their titles alone and bishops with their Christian names followed by the name of their diocese, as they still do in England today. Nevertheless lairds were allowed by law to append the name of their estate to their names and this was and still is regarded legally as part of their surname. This is a valuable means of identification in church registers and elsewhere and even tenant farmers were often known by the names of their farms and entered as such in the registers.

The traditional style of a laird is 'The Much Honoured' and this is come across in registers from time to time.

The eldest son of a laird is known as 'Younger of'. Thus John Hamilton of Bardannoch's eldest son William was known as 'William Hamilton, Younger of Bardannoch'. The wife of a laird in the past was styled 'Lady' or perhaps 'Ledy'. Thus Marie Mercer, wife of James Blair of Spoutwells, is described in a deed of 1693 as 'Marie Mercer, Lady Spoutwells'.[3] Today this custom has largely died out and the wife of Edradynate would now be known as 'Mrs Stewart-Robertson of Edradynate'.

The chiefs of clans and chieftains, who are lesser chiefs, were earlier mostly known by their estates, such as 'Macdonald of Keppoch', 'Maclain of Lochbuie', 'MacNeil of Barra' and 'Munro of Foulis', but in the 19th century the custom developed of repeating the surname, as 'Grant of Grant', 'Mackintosh of Mackintosh', or of using the style 'of that Ilk', meaning 'of the same place'. Examples of this are 'Guthrie of that Ilk' and 'Arbuthnot of that Ilk'.

Adam says that 'only the actual head of the house, his wife, and heir normally use the style "of that Ilk".' A daughter would repeat the surname, for example, a daughter of Mactavish of that Ilk would be styled 'Miss Mactavish of Mactavish'.[4]

An unusual title is that in use in the Macdougall family in which the eldest daughter of the chief while she remains unmarried is known as 'The Maid of Lorn'.

The term 'of' in documents is regarded as standing for 'heritable proprietor of'. 'In' signifies someone living in a place and 'at' refers to a sojourner or temporary resident.

The Peerage

The Scottish peerage merged into the clan system. Some peers were also chiefs of clans. All Scottish peerages belong to the period before the Union in 1707 since when, in contradistinction to Irish peerages after the Union of England and Ireland in 1801, no Scottish peerages have been created. Scotsmen made peers have been created peers of Great Britain after the Union, or of the United Kingdom after the Union of England and Ireland.

In proportion to the population of the two countries, the number of Scottish dukes is high compared with the number in England. There are six in Scotland, namely the dukes of Argyll, Atholl, Buccleuch, Hamilton, Montrose and Roxburghe. On the other hand apart from the subsidiary titles of dukes there are only four Scottish marquisates, those of Huntly, Lothian, Queensberry and Tweeddale, but this is a title which is not particularly prolific in England either. In fact when Queen Victoria, at the time of her coronation, was discussing with Lord Melbourne the peerage titles, he remarked a little impishly that marquisates were titles only given to those whom one did not wish to create dukes.[5]

Without including subsidiary titles there are at present thirty-eight earldoms, only two viscounties, those of Arbuthnott and Falkland, and twenty baronies.

A number of Scottish peerages descend in the female line in the event of there being no male heir. These go to the eldest daughter, unlike the practice in England of the descent of baronies by writ, which also descend in the female line in the absence of male heirs. In English law daughters are considered equal and therefore the eldest daughter has no precedence over the younger ones. Thus, if there are two or more daughters or descendants of these, the peerage goes into abeyance and only comes out of that abeyance on the issue of other daughters dying out or on the abeyance being terminated in favour of one of the daughters or her issue by the sovereign.

In Scotland, however, primogeniture among females is recognized and the eldest daughter will succeed. Thus the earldom of Dysart in 1821 on the death of the 6th earl devolved upon Louisa Tollemache, the elder of two surviving sisters. The present Lord High Constable of Scotland, a title hereditary in the family of Hay, Earls of Erroll, is a woman, since the 22nd earl died without male issue.

The destination of Scottish peerages is in fact very varied and often unusual. John Riddell in his *Inquiry into the Law and Practice in Scottish Peerages*, published in Edinburgh in 1842, writes that the Earl of Mansfield, the great Lord Chief Justice, held the 'arbitrary and untenable theory that, in the absence of the patent or constitution of a dignity, it could only descend to heirs-male of the body' and that Lord Rosslyn in his decision upon the Glencairn Peerage case in 1797 affirmed 'that where the limitation of a peerage is not to be discovered, the *presumption is* that it descends to the heirs male of the body of the original grantee'.[6] Research has however shown that descent to the heirs male of the body is by no means the usual descent of Scottish peerages and that Lords Mansfield and Rosslyn were in error in supposing this to be so.

In the petition in March 1967 of Bridget Helen, Dowager Viscountess Monckton of Brenchley, Lady Ruthven of Freeland, for matriculation of arms in the Court of the Lord Lyon, Sir Iain Moncreiffe of that Ilk, giving evidence in this case, explained that he had taken his degree of doctor of philosophy as a result of a research thesis into the law of succession in peerages and in other matters in Scotland and stated that his sources had been the peerages of Scotland in the *Complete Peerage* and in *The Scots Peerage* which he had gone through to compare their destinations (when they were available) with the destinations in the Great Seal Register. He stated, reading from his notes, that the number of Scottish peerages which he had examined was 366. In a considerable number of cases he admitted that no certain destination could be ascertained and stated that the most numerous category of destinations which he found were what he called 'special destinations, that is to say where the peerage was not destined to the heir female or the heir male, but to some other category of heir'. He stated later, 'There are a number, an enormous variety of special destinations, but none of them falling into any general rule of heir general or heir male.'

Of the 366 peerages examined he found that 110 had special destinations and ninety-three of these were capable of passing through or being held by a female, and fifty-eight of them actually had so passed. Peerages to the number of eighty-five were found with destinations to heirs male whatsoever. This means that such a peerage could descend to a male descendant of an ancestor in the male line of the original grantee, however remote that ancestor might be. Such heirs are frequently unable to be ascertained as their line stretches back into days before the existence of records.

Sir Iain Moncreiffe, being asked what was the position with regard to destinations to heirs male of the body had replied that 'seventy-three peerages were destined to heirs male of the body'. This is the destination that Lords Mansfield and Rosslyn had regarded as normal and usual. In fact, only about one in five of Scottish peerages were destined to heirs male of the body and this was therefore by no means the usual destination.[7]

The Dignity of Master

A title which only exists in Scotland is that of 'Master'. This is a dignity rightfully borne by heirs apparent and heirs presumptive of Scottish peerages. It is particularly to be noticed in the case of the eldest sons of viscounts and barons because with peers of higher degree the dignity is often hidden by the courtesy titles of their heirs. The eldest sons of all peers of Scotland bear by right that dignity and it is significant that the eldest son of the present Earl of Lauderdale is described in *Debrett's Peerage* as Viscount Maitland (the courtesy title) and Master of Lauderdale.[8]

The eldest sons are styled 'Master of' their father's peerage title and heirs presumptive bear the same title. Thus the eldest son of Viscount Falkland, one of the two Scottish viscounts, bears the dignity 'Master of Falkland', and the eldest son of Lord Napier and Ettrick, one of the Scottish barons, is known as 'The Master of Napier'. In this case 'and Ettrick' is not added, as the later barony of Ettrick is not a Scottish one and there is no other Scottish barony of Napier, the heir to which might also be a 'Master of Napier'. Lord Napier of Magdala, though a Scotsman, holds a peerage of the United Kingdom and not a Scottish peerage and therefore his eldest son is not entitled to be styled 'Master of Napier'.

The style of 'Master' is also by custom used by the eldest son of the heir to a Scottish peerage who bears the courtesy title of viscount or baron. Thus the 10th Earl of Southesk's eldest son, Charles Alexander, bore during his father's lifetime the courtesy title of Lord Carnegie, and his only son during the grandfather's lifetime bore the style 'Master of Carnegie'. This grandson later succeeded his aunt, Princess Arthur of Connaught, Duchess of Fife, as the 3rd Duke of Fife, since this dukedom had been granted to the 1st Duke of Fife, husband of the Princess Royal, daughter of King Edward VII, with special remainder to the two daughters and their male issue.

As mentioned above, in the absence of an heir apparent the title of Master may be borne by an heir presumptive. Thus, the 16th Earl of Lauderdale having no son, his brother Patrick Francis Maitland was known as the Master of Lauderdale and since the present Earl of Selkirk, has no son, his nephew and heir presumptive, Alasdair Malcolm Douglas-Hamilton, is known as the Master of Selkirk.

Sir Thomas Innes of Learney, when Lord Lyon, approved of heirs presumptive of the earldoms of Selkirk and Lauderdale bearing the titles Master of Selkirk and Master of Lauderdale respectively, and he would like to have seen this dignity, as an unique Scottish title, used by the eldest sons of Scottish earls rather than their father's second title as a courtesy title, as is the custom in Great Britain generally.

When the brother and heir presumptive of the 16th Earl of Lauderdale succeeded to that peerage there was a suggestion that his eldest son and heir should use the title Master of Lauderdale instead of his father's second title, Viscount Maitland, as a courtesy title. It was eventually decided that he would use the courtesy title. His eldest son, following the usual practice, is known as the Master of Maitland.

Intriguing minglings of titles sometimes occur when a Scottish peeress, in her own right is married to another peer. In this connection the marriage of the present Countess of Kintore to the first Viscount Stonehaven is interesting. On his death in 1941 his eldest son succeeded to the viscountcy, but as heir to his mother he was also by courtesy Lord Keith of Inverurie. His eldest son for this reason bears the title Master of Inverurie. This in itself is a variation from usual practice, which would have been to use the style Master of Keith, or, possibly, more lengthily, Master of Keith of Inverurie. The latter would have been cumbersome and Master of Inverurie seemed more appropriate.

In Scottish parish registers and legal documents the title 'Master' may be abbreviated to 'Mr'. As mentioned in Chapter III the Edinburgh register of baptisms for the 25 January 1642 shows the Master of Balmerinoch, eldest son of Lord Balmerinoch (or Balmerino), a witness to the baptism of John, son of John Hamilton of Muirhouse, as 'Johnne Mr of Balmirenoch'.

The previously-mentioned earldom of Selkirk has itself of all Scottish peerages perhaps the strangest of descents. Anne, Duchess of Hamilton in her own right, at the end of the 17th century married the first Earl of Selkirk, and he himself was created Duke of Hamilton for life, a not unknown occurrence in the past when a man married a peeress in her own right. This was sometimes called 'the courtesy of Scotland' and is analagous to the practice in Spain, which accounts for the present Duke of Alba being so titled through having married the daughter of the previous Duke of Alba, who became Duchess of Alba on her father's death.

After receiving the dukedom for life, the newly-created Duke of Hamilton surrendered his own peerage of Selkirk and subsidiary honours to the King, petitioning that they should be conferred upon his second son and the latter's heirs. This was done with the special remainder that, should the cadet line fail subsequently, this earldom and the other subsidiary titles should return to the dukedom and continue in that line until such time as a duke had a younger brother, when the earldom of Selkirk should revive in the latter's favour and the earldom continue in the younger brother's line.

This contingency has twice occurred in the 19th century and once in this century. In 1885 the line of Earls of Selkirk failed with the 6th earl and the earldom reverted to the ducal line. It later became vested in a brother of the 12th duke. This younger brother died unmarried, when the earldom of Selkirk again became vested in the dukedom. In this century the earldom was revived in favour of the present Duke of Hamilton's next eldest brother, Lord Nigel Douglas-Hamilton, who became the 10th earl.

These sliding peerages, as they are sometimes called, would be inadmissible in English law but are allowable under Scottish law, though it is unlikely such a remainder would or could again be granted.

Baronets

While the title of baronet was instituted by James I to encourage people to settle in Ulster, the baronets of Nova Scotia were founded to encourage Scotsmen to settle in that colony. They did not always go out there themselves and some of the soil from that country was brought to Edinburgh and laid on the esplanade near Edinburgh Castle so that the baronets could take sasine of their particular lands on Nova Scotia soil. These baronets have their own badge, incorporating the cross of St Andrew surmounted by the royal arms of Scotland.

A peculiarity of the Scottish baronetage is the existence of a few baronetcies which can descend through the female line. For long there was a difference of legal opinion between Scottish and English lawyers, the latter maintaining that such baronetcies could be transmitted through, but not held by a female, while the Scots lawyers held that the title could be held by a female. The recent case of Maureen Daisy Helen, Lady Dunbar of Hempriggs, is interesting. In August 1965 she was recognized by the

Lyon Court as a baronetess and as having succeeded her kinsman in 1963 as the eighth holder of the baronetcy under the special terms of its remainder, with the right to style herself Lady Dunbar of Hempriggs, or, if she prefers, Dame Helen Dunbar of Hempriggs. Her eldest son, who like herself has assumed the surname of Dunbar of Hempriggs, is the heir to the baronetcy.

Another historic baronetcy in Scotland which by special remainder descends through the female line in default of male heirs is Dalyell of the Binns. Mrs Dalyell of the Binns, the present holder, has not petitioned the Lyon Court to be recognized as a baronetess, but if she did so it would seem likely she would be so admitted. A third baronetcy which can descend in the female line, and has done so on two occasions, is that of Stirling Maxwell of Pollock. On the death of the 8th baronet on 6 June 1865 the baronetcy passed to his nephew, Sir William Stirling-Maxwell, who was the son of Elizabeth (sister of the 8th baronet) and her husband, Archibald Stirling of Keir, Perthshire. Again in 1956 on the death of Sir John Maxwell Stirling-Maxwell, the 10th baronet, the baronetcy passed in the female line to Anne, his only daughter, who married in 1930 John Morton Macdonald (who took the name Maxwell Macdonald). It would seem that Mrs Maxwell Macdonald has not petitioned the Lyon Court to be recognized as a baronetess, but under recent precedent it would seem she might be successful in such a claim.

XIII

UNIVERSITY AND PROFESSIONAL RECORDS

RECORDS OF UNDERGRADUATES at Scottish universities are sparse compared with those of Oxford and Cambridge. There is nothing to compare with the information found in Foster's *Alumni Oxonienses* or Venn's *Alumni Cantabrigenses*. In general, the existing records of students usually consist only of lists of those who matriculated and of those who graduated.

One of the reasons why the matriculation registers are scarce and when existing give so little information is that the system existed at Scottish universities by which the undergraduates paid fees direct to their professors or lecturers, as they did in fact at one time at Oxford. In Scottish universities, however, it is sometimes only the chance survival of the records of students kept by individual professors which will give us more than the barest information.

Edinburgh University, founded in 1582, the last of the four old universities of Scotland to be founded, has little published information. There is a list of graduates in medicine from 1705 to 1846, published in 1867, and a catalogue of graduates in the faculties of arts, divinity and law from its foundation, published in 1858. The manuscript records in the archive department include a slip index of students who have matriculated, built up from the matriculation volumes which exist from the mid-17th century, and there are lists of graduates from the late 16th century, but the matriculation registers themselves contain, until the 19th century, little but the signature of the student and, as there was a fee for matriculating and it was not compulsory until 1811 to matriculate at all, many students did not do so. From that date the place of origin is given, but this is sometimes only the county or, if from overseas, the country. After 1865 there was a *pro forma* for students matriculating, which gave the school from which they came.

Among the lists kept by professors, there is a useful one by Professor Charles Mackie of his history students from 1719 to 1744, which gives quite often the name of the father or other family information.

The graduate lists up to 1858 give little other than the date of graduation and faculty. There is a *List of Theologians in the College of Edinburgh* from about 1710 to 1727, which gives the date of graduation and the date of entry into Divinity Hall, and the county of origin, (or town if one of reasonable size).

The records of medical students are somewhat better. There are full manuscript records of students taking their MD examinations, which usually give the place of birth and age. From 1833 onwards they give the Edinburgh address of the student and dates of his first and second examination and the name of the examiner of his thesis. About 1840 a printed *pro forma* was introduced which gives the birthplace.

Sometimes the dedication of a student's thesis will give a clue to a relation. It may be dedicated to a parent or brother or sister, or to an uncle who has helped with the university expenses.

Aberdeen University was, for most of its lifetime, two separate universities, King's College and Marischal College. For King's College, founded 1495, there are *Officers and Graduates of University and King's College, Aberdeen, 1495–1860*,[1] and a *Roll of the Alumni in Arts of the University and King's College 1596–1860*,[2] while Marischal College has published the *Fasti Academiae Mariscallanae Aberdonensis 1593–1860*.[3] None of these lists, however, give information regarding parentage.

By far the best records of students at Scottish Universities are those of Glasgow. The matriculation albums, edited by W. I. Addison, have been published for the period 1728 to 1858.[4] In many cases the father's name is recorded and biographical notes of the student's career, possibly details of his marriage and death, have been given when discovered.

The oldest of the Scottish universities, that of St Andrews, founded in 1412, has published matriculation registers from 1747 to 1897,[5] the early parts of which give no information but the names and the 'nation' to which the student belonged, the latter being a somewhat arbitrary division of the students according to the place, county or country from which they came. This is therefore a possible indication of their home locality. There are some lists of graduates published, but these also give little information beyond the name. It is understood that some work is being done on the manuscript records of students and graduates at this university and possibly more details of the early students may one day be available.

The university's earliest records should be of great interest, since for a period this seat of learning must have held a monopoly of the Scottish students who sought university education at home, for it must be remembered that a great many Scotsmen went to French universities, such as Paris and Orleans, and later to other continental universities, particularly to Leyden, where Forbes of Culloden went in 1704 to finish his legal education and remarked on the studious hard work of his fellow Scots in contrast to the 'riot and debauchery' of the extravagant English youth on their grand tours. A number of Scotsmen also went to Oxford and Cambridge, until the Scottish wars and troubles of the 17th and early 18th centuries made this unpopular and sometimes impossible.

G. M. Trevelyan has emphasized that these 'students were of all classes, sons of nobles, lairds, ministers, farmers and mechanics. The most part were seeking to be beneficed clergymen, but there were far too many candidates'.[6]

Many of these aspirants for holy orders had, therefore, to eek out a sparse existence as tutors to the families of the lairds or as underpaid schoolmasters. But those who were fortunate enough to obtain a patron's presentation to a living were comparatively comfortably off by the modest standards of their times. Calamy, the English Nonconformist leader, visiting the Presbyterian ministers in Scotland in 1709, wrote of them that they had 'a competency, whereupon to live easily and conveniently and above contempt'.[7]

School Registers

A number of well-known Scottish public and grammar schools have published their registers. These include Aberdeen Grammar School, 1795–1919, annotated from 1863 by T. Wall, (1923); Edinburgh Academy, from its foundation in 1824, (1914); Fettes College, 1870 to 1909 (1909); Loretto School, 1825–1925 (1927); Melville College, (Edinburgh Institution), 1832–1932 (1933); Merchiston Castle School, 1833–1962 (1962); St Leonard's School, St Andrews, (for girls), i. 1877–1895, ii. 1895–1900 (1895 and 1901); Trinity College, Glenalmond, 1847–1954 (1955). Other schools may have surviving manuscript records of former pupils.[8]

Records of the Clergy

The *Fasti Ecclesiae Scoticanae*, edited by Hew Scott, with a new edition edited by W. S. Crockett and Sir Francis Grant, in eight volumes, 1915 to 1929, gives the succession of the ministers in the Church of Scotland from

1560 to 1929 with painstaking details. This is a true goldmine of information about Presbyterian ministers from early times. Not only are there details of their appointments and education but frequently of the minister's parentage, marriage and children. Much of this family information has been obtained from the Kirk Session records of pensions to the widows and children of ministers.

It is natural in a work of such magnitude that errors will occur from time to time, but on the whole it is a reliable record. People using it should check that there have been no corrections or additions in volume 8, *Addenda and Corrigenda* 1560–1949, published in 1950. A ninth volume, (1961), covers the period 1929 to 1954.

In tracing any family it is well worth examining the indexes of ministers in each of these volumes, as it is surprising how often one finds a member of a family went into the Church, and the details given of him may be of great value in building up details of the family history.

Most of the Kirk Session records are now in the Scottish Record Office, where they can be examined. In seeking a minister's marriage proclamation it is worth while looking in the Kirk Session minutes in addition to the register, as sometimes further information, such as the name of a parent, may be given there.

A useful work on the families of ministers is Adam W. Fergusson's *Sons of the Manse* (1923).

The historical introduction will have shown how large a part religion played in the history of Scotland. Records of the Roman Catholics are still in the hands of that Church, and are for that reason less easily accessible than those of the Presbyterian Church.[9] The schisms of the Presbyterian Church in the 18th and early 19th centuries often cause a break in records. It will have been seen how secession ministers refused to allow registration of baptisms in the orthodox parish registers even though they paid the fees in order to comply with the law. The published records of ministers of the Burgher Church are scanty and few manuscript records of their ministries survive. Lists of surviving pre-1855 registers of seceding Presbyterian Churches, of the Scottish Episcopal Church and information on surviving records of Roman Catholics, Nonconformists and of other religious bodies in Scotland, will be found in Donald Steel's *Sources for Scottish Genealogy and Family History* (1971).

Medical Men

Information about physicians and surgeons who took university degrees may be traced through the university records. Those who qualified as licentiates or fellows of the Royal College of Physicians of Edinburgh and of the Royal College of Surgeons of Edinburgh may be traced through the manuscript records of those bodies and there are printed medical directories going back to the early 19th century.

Parentage of surgeons may also sometimes be traced through the apprenticeship records of burghs, where these survive, as young men were often apprenticed to surgeons to learn the trade and be admitted to the profession. Edinburgh has published its apprentice records up to 1800.[10] Physicians and surgeons were also sometimes admitted as burgesses for good service to the burgh. Aberdeen, Banff, Canongate, Dumbarton, Edinburgh and Glasgow have published their burgess rolls for varying periods,[11] and a number of burghs may hold manuscript records of them, though some, like Brechin, had theirs destroyed during the 1745 rebellion and others have suffered loss through the all-too-frequent causes of fire and neglect.

The minutes of the Royal College of Surgeons of Edinburgh go back to 1581 and contain names of candidates who appeared before and satisfied the examiners when they were elected members of the Incorporation. Some further information about members and fellows may be obtained from the *List of Fellows* published in 1874.[12] The information in this list may be fairly full or brief, depending on the individual.

There were also licentiates of the college, surgeons who were not members of the Incorporation but allowed to practise surgery in the area covered by the Incorporation. During and after the Napoleonic wars, because of the shortage of surgeons diplomas were granted to students who had completed a recognized course at the university. The names of these appear in the minutes of the college and lists of licentiates were published in 1859 and in 1873. More details of these may be obtained from the archives of Edinburgh University.

The surgeons were in early times, as in England, associated with the barbers, but in 1722 the Court of Session effected a separation which left the college the right of licensing the barbers in respect of their trade alone. The final separation took place in 1845, when the surgeons received a new charter.

There was considerable jealousy between the College of Physicians of Edinburgh and the Surgeons, the latter claiming, according to their 17th century minutes, to be 'not only the sole teachers, but almost the sole Practitioners of the healing art within the City walls'. Naturally, this claim to eminence aroused the opposition of both the physicians and the apothecaries, neither of whom were at that time incorporated.

The surgeons decided to make their peace with the apothecaries and a 'Brotherhood of Apothecaries and Chirurgeons' was set up in 1694 and ratified by Parliament the following year.

The Royal College of Physicians of Edinburgh has published in its *Historical Sketch and Laws of the Royal College of Physicians in Edinburgh*[13] a list of fellows of the college in the original patent of 1681 and a list of fellows admitted since that date until 1925, arranged chronologically. This list gives the date of the qualification, the place where they received their degree, the date of the licence to practise and the date of admission as fellows. From 1861 onwards the information is somewhat briefer.

When the college was incorporated in 1681, only those having its licence could practise medicine in Edinburgh and its surrounding district. The licence was only granted to those having a university degree in medicine and fellows could only be elected from the licentiates. In 1829, the licentiateship was abolished, but a new class of licentiate was created thirty years later. The latter were not required to be university graduates but were admitted after examination. An intermediate rank of member was introduced in 1861.

There are biographical notices of the twenty-one fellows named in the original patent in *The Early Days of the Royall Colledge of Phisitians Edinburgh*, edited by R. P. Riches (1899). The manuscript records of this college include a list of licentiates, 1859–1951 and printed lists from 1868; also, more useful to the genealogist, a card index of MDs of Edinburgh University from 1705–1858, which contains brief biographical notes by J. D. Comrie, author of *A History of Scottish Medicine*.[14]

The Royal College of Physicians and Surgeons of Glasgow has a *List of Medical Practitioners in the Western District of Scotland, according to the Counties and Parishes, Alphabetically Arranged* (1822) and Alexander Duncan's *Memorials of the Faculty of Physicians and Surgeons of Glasgow, 1599–1850*[15] is a valuable source book. There is a catalogue of the library of the College in two volumes, published 1885 to 1901.

Many Scots medical men went into the services and William Turnbull's *The Naval Surgeon* (1806) may provide information about individuals, as may William Johnston's *Roll of Commissioned Officers in the Medical Services of the British Army 1727–1898* (1917). Those in the East India Company service may be found in D. G. Crawford's *History of the Indian Medical Service, 1600–1913*, published in two volumes in 1914.

Advocates and Attorneys
The Scottish legal system, as we have seen, differed from that existing

in England. In Scotland the equivalent of the barrister is the advocate and there are published lists of advocates with some account of their careers in *The Faculty of Advocates in Scotland, 1532–1943* (1944).

The solicitor in Scotland is known as a writer and the Writers to the Signet are a special and superior branch of the profession. They place WS after their names and their records have been published in *A History of the Society of Writers to H.M. Signet, with lists of Members . . . from 1594 to 1890* (1890). This volume contains details of parentage when known and of the master to whom they were apprenticed.

A later form of solicitor is the Solicitor in the Supreme Courts, who places SSC after his name. The records of this body have not been published but details of apprenticeship and possibly of parentage may be obtained from the Secretary of the Society of Solicitors in the Supreme Courts at 24 Hill Street, Edinburgh 2.

The Old Minute Book of the Faculty of Procurators in Glasgow, by Sir John Spencer Muirhead (1948), gives in its introduction an interesting account of the faculty and in one of the appendices there is a list of writers in Glasgow in the 17th and 18th centuries, while MS. records of members of this faculty are held in the Faculty Library, St George's Place, Glasgow.

The records of ordinary writers are only come across by chance. Some of these may be discovered in the apprenticeship records just mentioned. They were known as law apprentices.

Customs Records

The Customs and Excise were two separate departments and must be dealt with separately.

The Scottish Board of Customs was established after the Act of Union in 1707, but in 1722 a single Board of Customs for the whole of Great Britain was established. Certain commissioners of this board were appointed to reside in Edinburgh for the transaction of the Scottish business.

The history of the customs authority in Scotland is one of frequent change. In 1742 a separate and independent Scottish Board of Customs was again set up and this continued until 1823, when a unified board for the whole kingdom was once again established. Certain powers were delegated to the subordinate board in Scotland, which ceased to operate in 1829 and was finally abolished in 1833.

The records of the Scottish Boards of Customs and Excise were deposited in the Scottish Record Office in 1937. There are minute books of the Customs Board beginning in 1723, which are indexed continuously from 1781 to 1828.

The most useful records for personal details of employees in the customs are the establishment books. These volumes contain quarterly lists of officers who were employed at headquarters and show their salaries. They begin in 1715 and end in 1822. From about 1753 until about 1827 there are registers of superannuation and compensation allowances. There are also a number of outport records. The arrangement for Dumfries may be taken as typical for a small outport. The registers consist of (1) Collector to Board (2) Board to Collector, subdivided for general orders and particular correspondence addressed by the board to individual ports, (3) General Letter Books (4) Miscellanea. These in the case of Dumfries cover the dates from 1708 to 1883 and are indexed from 1825. Other ports covered are Montrose, Thurso, Kirkwall, Dunbar, Leith, Bo'ness and Glasgow.

Although the letter books are indexed for certain periods, these indexes appear to be mainly of subjects; goods, licences, etc. They did not usually index personal names. This was tested in one or two cases. For instance, in the case of a letter from Glasgow of 14 April 1826 enclosing a medical certificate regarding 'the present state of health of William Fraser, Tidesman', there was no reference found under 'F' to any Fraser in the index.[16] Only under 'O' is found the reference '1826 April 14 Officers. Wm Frazer Tidesman Medical Certe as to state of health transmitted'.

Excise Records

Minute books of the Scottish Excise Board exist from 7 November 1799 to 27 January 1830 and are all indexed. There are letter books from the Board to the Collectors 1775 to 1829, all indexed, letter books from the Board and General Commissioners in London, out-letters addressed by the Scottish Board to the principal Board in London and some letters from the London Board to the Scottish Board.

A series called Scottish Excise Board, Miscellanea, contains a register of commissions 1776 to 1808. There are also accounts of contributors to pension funds, which are not indexed, and general account books from 1707 to 1714. In 1794 there is a useful return of ages and capacities in the Scottish Excise service, and from about 1753 to 1828 there are registers of superannuation and compensation allowances, and another series covering from 1812 to 1827. There are minutes of meetings from 1818 to 1835.

Salary books exist from 1707 to about 1828 with various gaps; for Edinburgh from 1707 to 1771, Argyll 1707 to 1714 and Fife for various years from 1766 to 1783. Establishment books give names and salaries for all commissioners and officers at headquarters in Edinburgh from 1707 to about 1790. Excise duties and licences may be valuable for names of officers where salary books are missing.

Very valuable work has been done on the genealogical content of records in the Excise Department by Mr J. F. Mitchell. His article in *The Scottish Genealogist* of October 1966 entitled 'Englishmen in the Scottish Excise Department 1707–1823' gives some account of his work and is most helpful. Mr Mitchell has also compiled a card index of members of the Scottish Excise Department from 1707 to 1828, consisting of about 4,500 cards, arranged in alphabetical order, and there is a microfilm in the Scottish Record Office of these cards. This information is, of course, invaluable, and Mr Mitchell's great work in this field will be blessed by all people searching for information about excisemen.

The Exchequer records contain payments of salaries and wages to customs and excise officers and the careers of officers in early times may to a certain extent be traced through these records.

Members of Parliament
Joseph Foster's *Members of Parliament, Scotland* (2nd edn., 1882) includes the minor barons and commissioners for the shires and for the burghs, 1357 to 1882, and is based on the Parliamentary return of 1880, to which the author has added genealogical and biographical notes. The three volumes of Sir Lewis Namier and John Brooke's *The House of Commons 1754–1790*,[17] apart from the individual biographies in volumes 2 and 3, contains, in volume 1, a survey of Scottish representation during the period (pp. 38–46), some account of Scotsmen in Parliament (pp. 166–175) and details of the Scottish constituencies (pp. 469–512). The survey points out that the forty-five seats allotted to Scotland at the Union were insufficient to accommodate the Scotsmen wanting to enter Parliament during this period, and that Scotland's allotted representation was only about a twelfth of the total members, which meant that in proportion to her population she was under-represented. Romney Sedgwick's *House of Commons, 1715–1754* (1971) 2 vols., is valuable in giving biographies of Scottish members shortly after the Union and during the period of the two Jacobite rebellions.

XIV

THE NAVY, ARMY AND EAST INDIA COMPANY

SCOTLAND NEVER HAD a navy in the national sense of the word, but many Scotsmen served in the English Navy and in the British Navy after the Union. Manuscript records of officers and seamen must therefore be sought in the Public Record Office in London. The Admiralty records there are vast. Among the most useful sources of information about naval officers are the Navy Board's lieutenants' 'passing certificates', which included baptismal certificates to show that the candidates were over twenty years of age. These exist from 1789 onwards, with a few earlier ones from 1777, and there are two manuscript indexes of them in the Public Record Office, one by Miss E. H. B. Fairbrother covering the years 1777 to 1832 and the other by Miss P. Shroeder, covering the years 1789 to 1818.

For a rating, the best source for parentage is the muster roll of any ship in which he served, as this will give his place of birth. This also applies to midshipmen, but not to commissioned officers.

There are also a number of printed sources for officers. In particular may be mentioned Marshall's *Royal Naval Biography* in 12 volumes (1830) and O'Byrne's *Naval Biographical Dictionary* (1849).

Fuller details of naval records will be found in the chapter on 'Naval Ancestors' in *In Search of Ancestry*.

The Army

There was no regular and continuous Scottish army before the Union. Forces were mustered from time to time as situations required them. Troops were raised in the first and second Bishop's Wars in 1639 and 1640, after which they were disbanded. The three regiments kept in existence from 1641 formed the nucleus of the Scots force employed in putting down the rebellion in Ireland. During the Civil War various Scots forces were raised, sometimes to fight for Parliament and sometimes for the King.

Many Scottish officers had served in continental armies and a rare contemporary printed list of 1644 shows that in thirty-one regiments, five of the colonels, twenty-seven of the lieutenant colonels and twenty-five of the majors had served on the continent. Officers normally came from the aristocracy and the men by levies under acts of Parliament directing all able-bodied men between sixteen and sixty to serve. Heritors, that is landowners, were compelled to provide forces according to their financial means.

Early printed material on the Scots army of this time is scanty, but two volumes published by the Scottish History Society in 1917, *Papers relating to the Army of the Covenant 1643–47*, give information on this army and its personnel, based on the accounts of Sir Alan Hepburn Commissary-General and Treasurer of the Army. These volumes mention a great many officers and a certain number of other ranks.

Some information may be gathered from chance records, often local ones. The burgh records of Dunfermline, for instance, have the names of officers nominated to attend the 'Duns Law Expedition' from that town in 1639. The Scottish United Service Museum has a copy of detailed information gathered by the Scottish army historian, Andrew Ross, the original of which is in the possession of the Scots Guards.

The Scottish Record Office has a number of Exchequer records which include inventories of army muster rolls of the 17th century. An interesting example of these is the roll of the King's Regiment of Horse commanded by John Graham of Claverhouse, 1682–88. This lists the seventy-nine troops under their various commanders and the dates when they were formed. The troops were mainly commanded by Scottish peers and the names of these commanders include such well-known ones as the Earl of Airlie, Lord Ross, the Laird of Meldrum and the Earl of Balcarres.

Charles Dalton's published work, *The Scots Army 1661–1688* (1909), gives the names of the officers and soldiers in each company or troop and usually states the place and date of the muster.

Regiments, as in England, were almost invariably known by the names of their colonels, though it has been possible to identify some modern regiments.

The principal sources of information about officers, and to a limited extent soldiers, in the period from 1660 until the Union are the Privy Council records and the Exchequer and Treasury records. The Scottish Treasury paid the forces on the Scots establishment, but this meant normally regiments stationed in Scotland only. If they were sent abroad, they were usually placed on the payrolls of England or of the country which was paying for them. Towards the end of the 17th century there was a tendency for some of the newly-raised regiments to become more permanent, and after James II's flight in 1688 the Scots Estates impressed the forces and raised ten new troops of horse, a regiment of dragoons and six regiments of foot. Nevertheless, the regular army even after the Union was very small and far outnumbered, on paper at any rate, by the militia, which had first been raised in 1669. Lists of some of these militia officers have been preserved in the registers of the Privy Council and they are also usually found in the Treasury pay warrants.

The fencibles were an old and historic Scottish force. The heritors were under a feudal obligation to raise these fencibles and they were extensively used during the Civil Wars of 1639 to 1651 and also in suppressing the rebellions from 1666 to 1688. Sometimes larger cities, like Glasgow, raised fencibles for their own protection or use.

The registers of the Privy Council are almost complete from 1661 to 1708 and the acts and decrees of the council, with various papers and reports of committees, are printed down to 1690. There are a great number of persons mentioned in them and as the printed volumes are well indexed these can be easily traced.

A comprehensive range of the Scottish Treasury records has survived and is now in the Scottish Record Office. The two principal records are the Treasury sederunt and the Treasury registers, which sometimes overlap but between them cover the years from 1667 to 1708. There is also an interesting MS volume, anterior to this period, entitled 'Pay of Forces from Fines and Cess 1665–72.' Forces in this period were paid from three sources, from fines (imposed for not attending church), from the assessment or land taxes, known as the cess, voted by the Estates in 1667, and from taxation voted by them in 1665. This volume contains considerably more complete lists of officers than those in Dalton's *Scots Army* and in some cases names of sergeants, corporals and drummers are included.

The Treasury archives, like those of the Privy Council, contain also a number of names of militia officers. In particular the register for 1689 contains considerable information on officers of regiments recently levied.

Genealogically, the most abundant sources of information among the Treasury records are the muster rolls. Some 4,800 of them survive, mainly dating from about 1680. They cover Scots regiments when they were on the Scots establishment and not when they went abroad. These muster rolls mostly give merely the names of the officers, NCO's and men and regimental staff, and the date and place of the muster. Many are drawn

up in alphabetical order, though some, curiously enough, are in alphabetical order of Christian names. Usually the signatures of officers are on
these rolls.

Unfortunately, the standard of the majority of these rolls does not
reach that of two of them, which are of great value to the genealogist. One
of these is the troop of Life Guards of June 1678, which lists all ranks,
their parentage, their place of birth and length of service with the troop,
and interestingly reveals that a large number of them were sons of the
landed gentry of Scotland. The roll of the Earl of Argyll's Regiment for
January 1690 lists the names of the privates together with the parishes
and the counties from which they came and their occupations. Not
unnaturally, most of the men came from Argyllshire, but some came from
Perthshire, Aberdeenshire and Angus. Many were recruited from the
area of their captain's estates and Argyll's own company came mainly,
as might be expected, from around Inverary. The commonest occupations
were those of weaver, tailor, smith and mason, though six men in the
grenadier company had been fishermen.

An unbroken series of the warrant books for Scotland exist from 1670
to the date of the Union in 1707. The regular commissions were used in
Dalton's *Scots Army* up to 1688, after which they are included in that
author's *English Army Lists and Commission Registers.*

After the Union the records of the Scottish regiments become part of
the records of the British army and are to be found in the Public Record
Office, London. These include the various regiments of fencibles, militia
and volunteers raised during the French wars at the end of the 18th and
beginning of the 19th centuries. Sometimes all the officers of these regiments
would be made honorary freemen or burgesses of some town in which they
were stationed, and records of them may be found in these sources.

A certain number of works have been published on various Scottish
regiments. Sir Herbert Maxwell's *Lowland Scots Regiments* (1918) includes
in chapter VII, 'Scottish Regiments Disbanded by Andrew Ross'. The
Marchioness of Tullibardine produced *A Military History of Perthshire
1660–1902* (1908), a most valuable work and well indexed. Andrew Ross's
Old Scottish Regimental Colours (1885) is a useful volume. Arthur S.
White's *Bibliography of Regimental Histories of the British Army* (1965)
will indicate more fully the existing histories of Scottish regiments. There is
also a manuscript by Alfred Edgar Truckell on 'Dumfriesshire Militia
Records' in the Dumfries County Library.

Much of the information in this chapter has been based on 'Scottish
Military and Militia Records before 1707', a paper read by Ronald G.

Ball, MA at the World Conference on Records and Genealogical Seminar at Salt Lake City in 1969. It is hoped that this valuable contribution to Scottish military history will be published in some Scottish journal or as a booklet so that it may be more accessible to researchers.

The East India Company

A great number of Scotsmen went into the East India Company hoping, like others in that company, to make their fortune. Some of them did so, but many others perished from shipwreck and disease.

The East India Company, founded in 1601 as a trading company, expanded into one of the largest administrative units the world has known. The records of this company are housed in Orbit House, 197 Blackfriars Road, London, SE1. Their records, on the whole, have been well preserved. There is a vast amount of information in them, historical, social and genealogical.

In 1771 an official was appointed by the company to take charge of the records, and from that time onwards they are remarkably good. Prior to that date there is a great deal of material available, but this has to be searched out and is less easily accessible. The careers of early civilians can only be traced through the court minutes, original correspondence, factory records, consultations and in the public despatches from England which start in the 18th century. The last-mentioned record goods etc taken out to India by licence of the company and will even inform you of the personal baggage of the individual passengers, telling you how many hampers of beer, chests of wine, trunks of apparel and cases of cheese they took with them for their own use on the voyage. These despatches also include lists of passengers and of persons not in the company's service who had permission to proceed to or remain in the East Indies.

This civil service, as in effect it was, was divided into grades such as merchants, factors, writers and cadets. From the mid-18 century information can be discovered from the Writers Petitions, which begin in 1749 and continue until 1805. Frequently, they give you information regarding the parentage and date and place of birth of the applicant. There are also seventy volumes called Committee of College Reference from 1805 to 1856, which give similar information for those who had passed through the old East India Company College, now Haileybury College. There is a two-volume index covering the whole of the period from the date of the first writers' petitions in 1749 until 1857. There are also useful printed volumes, Dodwell and Miles, *Bengal Civil Servants, 1780–1838* (1839), and the *Record of Services of Madras Civilians, 1741–1858*, (1885) by

C. C. Prinsep. The 147 volumes of cadet papers for those entering the East India Company Army contain among other documents certificates of baptism. These are well indexed, so that the parentage of a military officer should not be difficult to ascertain in the period from 1790 to 1860, during which period some 20,000 young gentlemen entered the company's army service. From 1809 the papers should record the school at which the applicant was educated and also the profession, situation and residence of next-of-kin.

V. C. P. Hodson's *List of the Officers of the Bengal Army 1758–1834*, 4 parts (1927–47) is a most valuable work by an expert on East India Company personnel.

Prior to about 1790, when the cadet papers begin, the appointment of military officers can only be traced through the Court Minutes, Despatches, Proceedings, or Letters to or from the Court. It is fortunate that the Republic of India is continuing to publish these early records.

The embarkation lists from 1753 to 1860 give details of all ranks embarking for India and also of civilians, including free merchants and their wives.

D. G. Crawford's *History of the Indian Medical Service, 1600–1913*, 2 vols, (1914) has been mentioned earlier. There is also his later work *Roll of the Indian Medical Service, 1615-1930* (1930).

It is important to remember that the company had both a navy and a merchant navy. Details of sea-officers in these services are less easy to trace. There are three volumes of baptismal certificates of some officers, covering the period 1780 to 1830. The *List of Marine Records of the Late East India Company* (1896) gives fuller details of these records.

Ships' logs from about 1702 are fairly complete and these logs often contain lists of officers, crew and passengers on board. The registers compiled by Charles Hardy and his son, Horatio C. Hardy, of *Ships Employed in the East India Company Service* cover the period from 1707 to 1810, from which date the East India Register gives similar information. C. R. Low's *History of the Indian Navy, 1613–1863*, is also well worth consulting.

The archives department at Orbit House is working on wide-ranging indexes which will be of great value when completed. There is also an extensive card index of information about people in India compiled by Lt-Col H. K. Percy-Smith at the Society of Genealogists, London. This covers military, naval, merchant marine and civilian people.

Wills and inventories of early company servants are often recorded in the 'consultations' or 'factory miscellaneous' series. Among the archives in the Ecclesiastical Records Department there are manuscript alphabetical lists of wills and administrations covered by the Mayor's Court for the following years: Bengal, 1704–1779; Madras, 1753–1779; Bombay 1728–1753, and there is also a register of all wills proved in the three presidencies; Bengal from 1728, Madras from 1736 and Bombay from 1723 onwards.

A great deal of interest and research has been spent on East India Company records and there are a number of printed works, such works, for instance, as S. C. Hill's *Bengal in 1756*, and his *List of Europeans and Others in the English Factories in Bengal at the time of the Siege of Calcutta* in that same year. The *East India Register and Army List*, which was issued twice yearly from 1803 to 1860, covers births, marriages and deaths, lists of Europeans not in the company's service and shareholders of East India stock with their place of residence.

In Source List 1–15 in the Scottish Record Office No 5 is a 'List of MSS. relating to Indian affairs and the East India Company in H. M. Register House, Edinburgh'.

Some fuller details of East India Company records will be found in Chapter 15 of *In Search of Ancestry*.

will even inform you of the personal baggage of the individual passengers

XV

MIGRATION AND
THE SCOTSMAN ABROAD

I N THE INTRODUCTION the point has been made that Scots were driven to
migrate as much for economic as for any other reasons, but long
before permanent emigration from Scotland began Scots were going
abroad, sometimes in search of education, sometimes as traders and often
as soldiers.

Scottish students before the foundation of their own universities, had
gone to England or the continent for university education, and after the
wars with England they had gone for a time exclusively to the continent.[1]

The foundation of their own universities – St Andrews, Glasgow and
Aberdeen in the 15th century and Edinburgh in 1582 – did not completely
stop the flow to the continent. After the Reformation there was some
tendency for Scots to go to the Protestant universities in Germany and the
Low Countries, but they still continued also to go to the Catholic universities, and the University of Paris shows some 400 Scottish names in its
records for the period between 1519 and 1615.

The Scots were well-known on the continent as traders. Apart from
Scottish trading ships, the Scottish pedlar penetrated far into Europe.
Many traders lived abroad for many years and there were Scottish communities in a number of continental towns, particularly in the Low Countries. In Bruges they had a chapel dedicated to St Ninian, and the Scottish
community in Rotterdam was calculated in 1700 to number about 1,000
people. Scots tradesmen in Denmark and Sweden brought to those countries their crafts of glove-making, cloth manufacture and linen weaving,
and in Poland in the 17th century it was even estimated that there were
30,000 Scotsmen. There were colonies, too, in Hamburg and Bremen,
and in 1576 eleven Scotsmen described themselves as citizens of Regens-
burgh (Ratisbon).

Those who went abroad as soldiers in the 15th century went mainly to
serve in the French armies. In 1418, the Duke of Albany, the Regent, sent

a force there commanded by his second son, the Earl of Buchan, who later became Constable of France, and in 1424 the Earl of Douglas was created Duke of Touraine and appointed Lieutenant-General of the French Armies.

Many Scots fought against the English under the banner of Joan of Arc and many afterwards remained in France in the personal bodyguard of the king; generations later the name *Garde Ecossais* was maintained even when the personnel of that body were mainly French.

Some of these Scotsmen remained in France and were given honours and titles by the French kings, like Robert Patillo, who became Lord of Sauveterre, William Monypenny, Lord of Concressault, and best known of all, Stewart of Darnley, who was created Lord of Aubigny and Evreux. Many of their names became unrecognizably corrupted. Thus Gowrie became Gohory; Drummond, Dromont; and Williamson, D'Oillençon.

After the Reformation in England, many Protestant Scots went to England for part of their education, including two sons of John Knox, and a number of Scottish divines obtained livings in England. This tendency continued to such an extent that, in the late 19th and early 20th centuries three out of five successive Archbishops of Canterbury were Scotsmen.

Orkney and Shetland, whilst still dependencies of the united kingdom of Norway and Denmark, received migrants from Scotland, and even by the 15th century the Lowland Scottish tongue was replacing the Norse language in Orkney. In Shetland, where the penetration was slower, by 1600 a quarter of the population had surnames which suggested Scottish origins.

An attempt to colonize the Western Isles was made by James VI as a deliberate policy when a number of 'the Lowland Adventurers' from Fife endeavoured to settle in Lewis, but in 1607 they had to give up their efforts because of the determined nature of the resistance.

The settlement of Scotsmen in Ulster began in the early 17th century. When the O'Neill chieftain in County Down was forced by financial difficulties to sell his lands, these were bought by Hugh Montgomery of Braidstane and James Hamilton. Montgomery was ennobled as Viscount of Airds and Hamilton became Viscount Claneboye.

The English scheme for the plantation of the remaining counties of Ulster resulted from the flights to the continent of the Earls of Tyrone and Tyrconnel in 1607, when the English Government invited 'undertakers' to seek allocations of land on which to settle. This of course accounts for the great number of Scottish surnames in Ulster. Although this colonization came mainly from Lowland Scotland many from the Highlands also found their way to Ireland as mercenary troops and afterwards settled there.

The New World

In the 17th century when almost every major nation in western Europe was forming settlements in the New World it was natural that Scotland should do the same. James I had given his name to Jamestown, capital of Virginia; the Scots however first settled in Newfoundland, mainly through Sir William Alexander, later Earl of Stirling, who had met the English governor, Captain John Mason, in 1621. Alexander obtained a grant from the king of certain territories which were designated Nova Scotia in America and thus 'New Scotland' rose alongside New England, New France, and the New Netherlands. However the Scottish settlements there were unfortunate, the French establishing their sovereignty again in 1632, which lasted until 1713. Thus the Nova Scotia venture left no Scottish colonists at all on that side of the Atlantic and only a surviving memory of this venture remained in the baronets of Nova Scotia whose descendants are still styled as such.

The Earl of Stirling did not lose interest in the New World and in 1635 produced a further scheme for settlement in Maine. The settlements here were English and thus the idea was one of integration of Scotsmen with the English in their newly-founded colonies. This took place to a certain extent in East New Jersey but more particularly in South Carolina. When East New Jersey came under the control of twenty-four proprietors, sixteen of these were English and two Irish, but five were Scots, namely Robert Barclay of Urie, his brother David, the Earl of Perth, his brother John Drummond, and Robert Gordon, a merchant.

Emigrants came to this colony in 1683 and the next year was a peak year. The names of many of these Scottish emigrants suggests that they came from the Lowlands.

Early on, Scotsmen had turned their attention towards the south, to Florida and South Carolina, because it was from these areas that luxury goods which were much in demand in England could be produced by coloured labour. About 1682 the English proprietors of South Carolina granted 12,000 acres to Sir John Cochran of Ochiltree and Sir George Campbell of Cessnock.

Migration there was not popular with Scotsmen and more went there by compulsion than freewill, for criminals and political offenders were transported there. In 1648, a number of Scottish prisoners of the Parliamentary Army had been taken to the plantations and two years later, when the Scots were defeated by Cromwell at the Battle of Dunbar. 900 Scottish prisoners were shipped to Virginia and 150 to New England. After the Battle of Worcester in 1651 more Scottish prisoners were despatched overseas, including a shipload of about 270 to Boston in 1652. Even after the Restoration in 1665, permission was given for the transportation overseas of 'strong and idle beggars, gipsies, and criminals', mainly to Jamaica and Barbados.

Then there were the Covenanters, many of whom from 1666 onwards were shipped to these colonies and elsewhere. After the covenant rising had been defeated at Bothwell Brig in 1679 a ship carrying 200 Covenanter prisoners to the American plantations was wrecked off the Orkneys and nearly all the prisoners were drowned. Many persons also were shipped overseas after the abortive rising of the Earl of Argyll in 1681.

A number of these prisoners eventually gained their freedom and remained in America, where they in some cases prospered greatly. Many of the Scots prisoners had shown themselves such good workers that there resulted a great demand for Scotsmen and many first went out there as Scottish servants. The indexes to the testaments in the various commissariots and the services of heirs reveal a number of Scotsmen in South Carolina during the 17th and 18th centuries.

The disastrous Darien venture at the end of the 17th century came through the desire to establish an independent Scottish colony in the New World. In 1698 and 1699 over 2,500 persons left Scotland for 'New Caledonia'. This ill-conceived plan suffered initially through the bad climate in the isthmus of Darien, near Panama, but eventually failed by the Scots being driven out by the Spaniards.

After the Union in 1707 migration from Scotland was mainly to colonies already established by the English. In spite of all the difficulties and failures, the end of the 17th century had seen a number of Scottish establishments overseas in the New World. Though some settled in New England like David Melville and Duncan Campbell, who was a bookseller in Boston in 1686, most Scots were to be found in and around Virginia, either as indentured servants or as workers in the tobacco factories. Scottish settlers were to be found also in the countries around the Potomac River and in the area of the town of Dumfries. There were also a number in the West Indian islands and in 1762 it was calculated that one third of the Europeans in Jamaica were Scots. Not all of them were of the working classes. One of the Camerons of Lochiel made a fortune in

Jamaica, and it was to this island that Robert Burns the poet had contemplated emigrating in 1786 before his first volume of verses had gained sufficient fame to entice him to remain in his native country.

A number of Scottish ministers went out with these emigrants to supply their spiritual needs. One of the best known of these was James Blair, a graduate of Edinburgh and minister of Cranston before migrating to Virginia in 1685. Four years later the Bishop of London appointed Blair as his commissary in Virginia. Like so many of his countrymen, Blair was interested in education and thus in 1693 became the founder of the College of William and Mary. Mungo Inglis, another Scot, was master of the grammar school there which prepared pupils for this college. James Blair later became Governor of Virginia. He died there in 1743.

John Buchan's novel, *Salute to Adventurers*,[2] paints a vivid picture of this 17th century America, and he mentions among others 'a heap of Scottish redemptioners' or time-expired indentured servants; we meet an emigrant who had reached America from Ulster but whose forbears had come from Scotland; and we also meet 'Dr James Blair, the lately commissary of the diocese of London, who represented all that Virginia had in the way of a bishop', who 'was full of his scheme for a Virginian college to be established in the Middle Plantation'.[3]

Emigration from the Highlands
It is not true, as is often thought, that the great exodus from the Highlands was caused through the persecution of the Scotsmen after the risings of the Fifteen and the Forty-five, particularly the latter. This process of migration from Highland areas to America had been going on for a long time, mainly because of the existing economic conditions. Only about 800 Jacobite prisoners were recorded as transported after the Forty-five, their sentence being compulsory service for life which, in practice, meant that after serving seven years they received their liberty, though still remaining banished for the rest of their days. This was a very small number compared with the total and the migration to those parts was far more due to the economic and social changes in the Highlands. The change-over from cattle to sheep farming, which the landowners found themselves compelled to make, reduced the numbers of men employed on the land. Even the tacksmen found themselves without a place in the changing structure and often felt their only hope lay in migration. Frequently, these tacksmen persuaded a number of their workers to migrate with them.

Carolina continued to attract a great number of Highland immigrants and the evidence shows that between 1768 and 1772 something like 2,000 of them emigrated to that colony. A number of the Scots of the Clan Mackintosh migrated to the new colony of Georgia and Sir William Johnson, a Scottish baronet, brought many Highlanders from his estates to the Mohawk Valley, New York, in the latter half of the 18th century. In 1768 the *Scots Magazine* reported considerable emigration to Carolina and Georgia from the Western Isles.

Important causes of increasing emigration were the reports which Scotsmen already there sent back to their homes. Many of these letters gave favourable and encouraging accounts of the land to which they had gone and many brothers, cousins and even parents followed them there as a result. Scottish soldiers also, when they returned home after taking part in the campaigns of the Seven Years War in Canada, gave glowing accounts of the land in which they had served. Some Highland soldiers discharged at the end of the war had been granted land in America, mainly around New York and Prince Edward Island, and there formed a settlement which attracted other emigrants.

The work of the 5th Earl of Selkirk (1771–1820) considerably influenced migration to Canada. He was deeply concerned at the destitution of the Highlanders but at the same time possessed a desire to develop British North America rather than the United States, and it was the tract of land which he owned on Lake Ontario which became the settling ground for the numbers of migrants he brought over at his own expense. Selkirk's character and personality gave the kind of leadership which the Scots emigrants needed and on the whole this colony prospered, although other Selkirk schemes proved less successful.

Norman MacLeod (1780–1866) also was responsible for a number of emigrants, first of all to Canada and later to Australia and New Zealand. He sailed in 1817 from Loch Broom for Pictou in Nova Scotia, taking with him a number of immigrants from his home country around Assynt, and the following year a further 150 sailed from there for the new colony. Norman MacLeod combined the positions of spiritual leader and temporal magistrate of his community and acted also as schoolmaster. His severe Sabbatarianism was carried to such lengths that even the peeling of potatoes had to be done on Saturday for use on Sunday and the dishes used on the Sabbath were not to be washed up until the Monday. Perhaps it is not surprising that his flock were described as 'the most sober and orderly settlement on the island'.[4] In 1849, encouraged by a report from

MacLeod's son in Australia the community moved there, eventually settling in Melbourne.

However, they were disappointed with the opportunities in that colony and moved again to New Zealand, where they settled on the Waipu River. They found the agriculture here much easier than they had found it on Cape Breton. Many of them later became shipbuilders and mariners.

The foundation of the Highlands and Islands Emigration Society influenced emigrants in the 19th century. It invited subscriptions from the well-to-do and assisted Scotsmen in migrating by paying their fares.

Migration to the United States continued throughout the 19th century. The lack of employment in the Clyde area in the late 18th century caused many weavers from there to migrate, and among the weavers of Renfrewshire and the farmers of Stirlingshire societies or companies were founded to purchase lands co-operatively in Jamaica. The Vermont county of Caledonia resulted from the organizations of these emigrants, but the most important Scots settlements during the late 18th century were at Cape Fear valley in North Carolina, the Mohawk and Upper Hudson valleys in New York and the Attamaha valley in Georgia.

For generations the United States was the most important receiving area for emigrants from Great Britain. Ten million people are said to have migrated there between 1815 and 1910. Up to the middle of the 19th century more Scotsmen tended to go to Canada than to the United States, but between 1870 and 1920 the percentage to the United States increased to 50 per cent. of all Scottish emigrants. Nevertheless, by 1907 more Scots were migrating to Canada than to the United States. It would seem that the total number of Scots who entered the United States between 1820 and 1950 was not less than 800,000 and a great number of migrants to Canada later re-migrated from there to the United States. It has been suggested that some 60 per cent of them did so.

The great number of Scottish surnames in Canada is an indication of the importance of Scots as a migrant people. They brought to the maritime provinces not only the Scottish tongue but Scottish culture and traditions, and clan rivalries such as those between the Campbells and the MacDonalds continued in the New World. The number of Highland societies and clan societies in Canada today indicate how strongly the Scottish ties persist.

Australia

Convicts were shipped to Australia from Scotland as from England, being taken from Leith to the prison hulks preparatory to being sent to

Botany Bay. Even so, right from the earliest times, there were a number of free settlers and these grew numerically as the 19th century progressed. Australia as a largely agricultural country was a particularly suitable place for Scotsmen who wished to migrate. It was a Scot, John Hunter, who introduced sheep into Australia, although the best-known name in this connection is that of John MacArthur, born in England of a Scottish father. He went out to Australia as an army officer in 1790. Five years later he had acquired land and was breeding sheep, and the following year obtained some of the merino sheep which brought such prosperity to that colony.

Scottish names in Australia also indicate the extent to which Scotsmen explored the country. Among the mountain ranges are such names as Lindsay, Cunningham, Fraser, Aberdeen, Greenock, Dunsinane, Crawford, Murchison, MacDowall and Birnam. And it was John Macdowall Stuart who gave his name to Mount Stuart in Central Australia. In 1822 the Australian Company of Edinburgh was formed to manage shipping between Leith and New South Wales and Tasmania.

Many Scots who migrated to this dominion brought no capital, like John Robertson, who landed in Hobart with only a half-crown and a sixpence in his pocket, but many brought useful skills to a new country in need of them, and a number of the early medical men in Australia were Scotsmen. Melbourne was even described in 1839 as 'a Scotch colony. Two-thirds of the inhabitants are Scotch'.[5] To a certain extent the strength of Scotsmen in the various provinces or states can be seen by the distribution of the Scottish societies which are far more prevalent in Victoria and New South Wales than elsewhere.

Scotsmen, always keen educationalists, were prominent in the founding of such institutions. Sir Charles Nicholson, for instance, who had been trained as a physician in Edinburgh, played an important part in the foundation of the University of Sydney in 1851, but it was possibly in the field of politics that the Scotsman played the biggest part in the dominion. Their number is great and only a few can be mentioned, like Sir Thomas M'Ilwraith, Premier of Queensland; Sir Stuart Donaldson; Sir James McCulloch, four times Premier of Victoria; Sir James Milne Watson, son of a shipowner from Banff, Premier of Tasmania; Sir Robert Gordon Menzies, Prime Minister of Australia from 1939 to 1941 and from 1949 to 1967.

New Zealand
The failings of the first New Zealand Association and later the first

colonization of the lands purchased from the Maori chiefs have been mentioned in the Introduction. A number of ships sailed for New Zealand between 1839 and 1844, when sixty-three ships left Great Britain, only three however sailing from Scotland. Even so no doubt many Scots left from English ports. Some 150 Scots went out in 1839, among them being Archibald Anderson, a Stirlingshire man, who took his ploughman out with him and bought up 100 acres of land at Port Nicholas. Like many groups of Scottish emigrants they took their Presbyterian pastor with them.

Some Scots migrated first to Australia and later moved to New Zealand when the possibilities of farming and stock breeding appeared better there. A number of Scots settled in Otago in South Island, where the Association of the Free Church of Scotland purchased from the New Zealand Company 2,400 lots of sixty acres each, which they sold to emigrants at the cost of £2 per acre. The leaders of this group of settlers were the Reverend Thomas Burns, a nephew of the poet, and Captain William Cargill, a veteran of the Peninsular War. Burns arrived with 247 people from the Clyde in April 1848 and Cargill with ninety-seven in March that year.

Apart from one short outbreak of violence in the northern part of South Island the Otago settlers had peaceful relations with the Maoris, and when the thickly wooded surroundings of Dunedin were cleared they found a rich soil which gave them very profitable returns.

The Otago settlement was well publicized in Scotland and James Adam, a shipwright from Aberdeen, one of the original emigrants was sent back to Scotland by the Otago Provincial Council as an agent for further emigrants. Through his efforts some 2,000 people sailed there in eight ships in 1857.

This area continued throughout the 19th century to attract Scotsmen. The attraction increased through the discovery of gold there in 1861.

Though the particular appeal of the area around Dunedin drew many Scottish immigrants there were other Scottish settlements, such as that at Invercargill, founded in 1857, and Waipu, north of Auckland, where 1,000 Scots settled in 1860.

These settlers, engaging in farming and outdoor activities, enjoyed an expansion in the second half of the 19th century which was outstanding. Scots at home learnt that employees' hours were shorter and wages higher in New Zealand than in their native land.

South Africa

Mention has been made in the Introduction of the Scots as missionaries and explorers in Central Africa. Glasgow merchants were not unaware of the commercial possibilities in this area and Livingstone's own belief was that Christianity might go hand in hand with commerce in bringing civilization to the peoples of Africa. The African Lakes Company, founded in 1878, was a result of this thinking and somewhat similar was the founding by Sir William Mackinnon and some of his fellow Scots of the British East Africa Company.

South Africa attracted a lesser flow of Scotsmen than did Canada, Australia and New Zealand and at a later period. It is true that a small party of just over twenty people landed at Simon's Bay in 1820 and settled in the district north of Albany, known today as Bedford. Among them was Robert Pringle, whose *Narrative of a Residence in South Africa* gives some idea of the life there at that period.

The Wakefield system brought a certain number of labourers to South Africa and in 1855 the *Gipsy Bride* brought 515 people, mainly from Dumfriesshire, to Cape Town. However in general South Africa attracted fewer Scotsmen, partly because there were comparatively few openings for unskilled labourers and the demand was for people with some capital able to buy their own farms and employ native labour. Later in the century there were, however, Scotsmen of middle class and perhaps merchant families who were attracted by the commercial opportunities in this new colony. Such a man was Archibald Parker, who came from a merchant family living near Glasgow and went out originally to South Africa because of ill health. He saw there the great difficulties under which the Boer and British farmers suffered through having no organized means for the export of their goods and produce and in consequence founded the great South African export company of Wood and Parker.

By 1904 the population of Scottish birth in the colony was 41,227. In 1921 it was slightly lower, namely 35,867, but this showed that Scotsmen were still migrating to South Africa in the early part of the 20th century and their migration totals were more than twice those of Ireland and almost a third of those from England. Even so the number of Scottish settlers in a community containing many Dutch as well as English and Irish settlers was too small to make any great impression on the whole country. In consequence there are few Scottish place-names and nowhere near the number of Scottish societies in South Africa as in Canada and Australia.

Dominions Registration
The civil registration of births, marriages and deaths in the dominions overseas is fortunately based rather more on the fuller details given in the Scottish registration than on that of England and Wales.

Registration details naturally vary in the different dominions but on the whole they tend to be fairly full. The registration in New Zealand, for instance, is very good. The death certificate, for example, gives the name of the father and of the mother, with her maiden surname, the rank or profession of the father, the place of birth of the deceased and the number of years he or she had been in New Zealand; and if the deceased was married, the place of marriage, the age at time of marriage, and the name of the husband or wife and age of the widow or widower if living at the time of the death, and also the ages and sex of living issue.

The registration in Australia varies in the different states and also at the different periods of registration. A death certificate in Tasmania of 1904, for instance, will give the birthplace of the deceased, his age, rank or profession, his usual residence and how long he had resided in the dominion; if married, his age at marriage and number of issue, living and deceased, male and female.

Details in the former dominion of South Africa are also fairly full, and this is so too in Canada. Details of registration of British subjects born, married or buried in British India are now held in the India Archives, Orbit House, 197 Blackfriars Road, London, SE1.

Fuller details of the information given in these overseas registrations will be found in the Government publication, *Abstract of arrangements respecting registration of births, marriages and deaths in the United Kingdom and other countries of the British Commonwealth. . . . and in the Irish Republic* (1952). This abstract includes the lists of registers and records then kept at Somerset House and elsewhere in England and Wales.

A number of the dominions or former dominions have, of course, genealogical societies. The Australian Genealogical Society[6] has done much good work in indexing earlier registrations and census returns. An article by Dr Anthony P. Joseph, 'On tracing Australian Jewish Genealogy', in *The Genealogists' Magazine* for December 1964, although dealing with Jewish ancestry, has also much information on Australian genealogy in general. There is a genealogical society in Canada and one has recently been established in New Zealand.

A Canadian Public Archives publication, *Tracing Your Ancestors in Canada* (1966), was reprinted in *The Genealogists' Magazine* for December of that year.

The Scottish Genealogy Society has for some years been compiling a *Dictionary of Scottish Emigrants*. That portion containing emigrants to the U.S.A., compiled and edited by Donald Whyte and containing

6,479 entries, was published in 1972 by the Magna Carta Book Co. of Baltimore, U.S.A.

Work is also in progress on a Canadian section and, to a lesser extent, on emigrants to other countries.

took his plowman out with him

XVI

THE SCOTTISH RECORD OFFICE

THIS OFFICE is situated in the General Register House, Princes Street, Edinburgh EH1 3YT. The Historical Search Room, with which the genealogist is most concerned, is at the rear or north side of the building. This room was re-furnished in 1967 with comfortable chairs and individual lights, the strength of which can be increased or decreased as needed for a particular document. Apart from the additional comfort ten more seats were provided for readers and this was fortunate, because the production of documents in the Historical Search Room had in 1967 increased by one half of the 1966 figure and for the first time it exceeded the number of record volumes and documents which were produced in the Legal Search Room below, where the current work is done.

The increase in use of documents was mainly due to the stimulus of university-based research, but it was also noticed that as repertories or guides were made available for different sections of documents, these were more in demand as a consequence.

An additional search room is shortly to become available, as part of what is to be known as the West Register House. This will be located in the church building which was formerly St George's, Charlotte Square. Work on adapting this building as a record depository and reading room was started in 1967 and should be available for use in 1971.

The West Reading Room will mainly be used for housing and examining local authority and sheriff court records as they are brought into the Scottish Record Office. The process of sorting out these records and making repertories or lists of them will also take place here. A survey of them by the Record Office has been in progress in recent years and if the recommendations of the Wheatley Report on local government in Scotland, published in 1969, are adopted, under which Scotland will be divided into seven districts, these districts may possibly become the areas in which

district record offices will be established. Under that arrangement the
local and sheriff court records may later be transferred to these district
record offices, although remaining under the control of the Keeper of the
Records.

The Scottish Record Office itself has not sufficient staff to be able to
index local records but district record offices will be encouraged to do this
work.

For permission to use the Historical Search Room it is necessary to
obtain a reader's ticket (which has to be renewed annually) stating the
reasons for your research on your application: this may be designated
'genealogical research' or 'family history'. It is interesting to note that in
1968 'family history' as a subject of research was third in the list of
subjects most in demand, being preceded only by 'geographical studies
and local history' and 'social and economic history'.

The main records of genealogical value housed here have been described
in previous chapters. Matthew Livingstone's *Guide to the Public Records of
Scotland* (1905) is now much out of date, although still useful in indicating
records existing at the time of its publication. The Scottish Record Office
is looking forward to the publication of a new guide to the records but
feel that it is necessary to make fairly detailed repertories of the new records and a revision of old repertories in each class before a worth-while
guide can be produced. Additional staff would be necessary for this work.

However, the publication of sectional lists from time to time is helping
to fill the gap. In addition, volume 26 of the *Scottish Historical Review*
(1947) pp. 26–46, contains a list of 'Accessions of Public Records to the
Register House since 1905' by William Angus, then Keeper of the Records, who acknowledges his indebtedness for the preparation of the list
to Dr Gordon Donaldson, then on the staff of the Historical Search
Room, now Professor of Scottish History and Palaeography at Edinburgh
University.

This is an extensive list. Items in it of particular interest to genealogists
are briefly indicated below.

Duties levied in Scotland on houses and windows, or lights, 1747–1768 13 volumes.
Valuation rolls for the following counties:
  Argyllshire 1751; Berwickshire 1640; Dumfriesshire 1740, 1787; Forfarshire 1682;
  Kincardineshire 1657, 1669, 1744; Lanarkshire 1722, 1747; Orkney 1653; Wigtownshire
  1667.
Cess rolls of Peebles parish 1738 and of Milton Parish 1720.
Hearth money accounts 1690–1693.
A number of Excise accounts 1707–1807 and of Custom records, imports and exports
  1758–1807 and lists of officers of the Customs and Salt Duties 1752.
Army records, including muster rolls of the 17th century.
Minute Books of the Commissioners of the Forfeited Estates, 1716–1717.

A number of sheriff court records and registers of sasines from 54 burghs.
A great number of notaries' protocol books.
The heritors records of 775 parishes, but these do not usually extend back more than
a century.

For some years the *Scottish Historical Review* has included an annual
report of accessions to the Register House and notes on the year's
developments. This gives the principal accessions. A detailed account of
all accessions during the year is contained in the annual reports of the
Keeper of the Records of Scotland.

Sheriff court records continue to come in to the Record Office. Those
held there in 1970 are given below. In most cases they include registers
of deeds, sometimes with minute books.

Argyll, Ayrshire (Kilmarnock); Cromarty (deeds from 1819 only); Fife (Cupar deeds
from 1658, minute books from 1720); Dunbarton (deeds 1682); Lanarkshire (Hamilton); Midlothian (Courtyard, deeds from 1695); Orkney and Shetland (deeds 1611–
1675); Perthshire (deeds from 1507, minute books from 1652); Renfrewshire (Paisley);
Ross and Cromarty (Tain. Dingwall, Stornoway, Cromarty); Stirlingshire (Stirling,
Falkirk); West Lothian (Linlithgow, deeds from 1701, minute books from 1770;
Bathgate, deeds 1749–1751; Bo'ness, deeds 1669–1694 and 1713–1722).

There are a number of records of trades incorporations in the Record
Office, such as the Incorporation of Shoemakers, Haddington, 1747–1861
and the Incorporation of Tailors, Edinburgh, 1446–1947, which were both
received in 1964.

The Forfeited Estates papers cover the period 1745 to 1824. After the
Disannexing Act of 1784 under which the unsold estates were restored,
the management of them ended, but various letters and documents continued to come in and go out until 1824.

The Keeper's Report for 1967 (1968) includes a summary catalogue of
all burgh records (seventy-three in all) deposited in the Record Office up
to 1967.

As previously mentioned, under the Public Records (Scotland) Act,
1937 the Customs and Excise records were transferred from England to
Scotland, and under the Master of the Rolls' direction of 1948 regarding
the copying of State Papers, Home Office, Customs and Excise and
Treasury series relating to Scotland, a number of these records have been
copied and these are now in the Record Office.

Prisoners at Edinburgh and Penninghame prisons have been employed in
listing and indexing 19th century Crown Office Precognitions. This has
proved a successful venture, partly through the enthusiasm of the
responsible prison officers and partly through a particular prisoner 'who
prepared an excellent memorandum incorporating the department's

requirements for the use of prisoners employed on the project'. This work is continuing and developing.

Recent sectional lists have been the *Descriptive List of Plans in the Scottish Record Office* by I. H. Adams, volume 1 of which was published in 1966, and of particular value to genealogists, the *List of Gifts and Deposits to Date* which mainly consist of family or estate papers. This list includes all such deposits up to the end of December 1966. The list is alphabetical under the name of the family concerned. Small collections and individual items are placed in the Miscellaneous Accessions (G.D.1.). The larger collections are given individual numbers in the G.D. class and as soon as possible a brief summary list is made, a more detailed inventory being added later.

Subject indexes for some of the material are made from time to time, covering such subjects as: plans, places, correspondence, countries, art, architecture, communications, education, emigration, medicine and naval and mercantile affairs. The entries usually give the following information: the name of the family or families, the G.D. number, the countries (or counties if in Scotland), the dates covered, an indication of the size of the collection, a note sign to show if an inventory or list exists and a note of other manuscripts and printed sources. Some miscellaneous accessions are grouped under location or subject headings.

Another recent deposition of interest to genealogists is the collection of Kirk Session records of the Church of Scotland. These often throw light on a parish in which a family resided. Members of it may be mentioned if they strayed from the path of morality and had to do penance for children born out of wedlock, or for other misconduct in the eyes of the kirk elders.

The Reading Room contains a useful library of reference books, such as the publications of the Scottish Record Society, the *Fasti Ecclesiae Scoticanae*, Balfour Paul's *Scots Peerage* and other peerages, various biographical dictionaries, philological guides and dictionaries and maps of the kingdom for various periods.

Printed, manuscript or typescript indexes of the records are in the small room east of the Reading Room and there are card indexes of special collections. The method of obtaining the correct reference number of a document may seem at first a little complicated, but there are assistants available to help. Similarly, the Superintendent in the Reading Room is always available to help with the deciphering of difficult passages, although it will be appreciated that he cannot give too much of his time to one particular reader. For a document which a searcher finds too difficult to decipher himself, there are a limited number of expert professional searchers whose names can be obtained from the office. Xerox copies of documents can be obtained at low cost, but for those which are applied for by post there is an additional handling charge. Documents too large for the Xerox machine may have to be reproduced by photostat process.

Though mainly the home of the national records of Scotland, the number of local records and private muniments being deposited there is increasing all the time.

Duties levied... on... windows

XVII

SCOTS HERALDRY AND THE LYON OFFICE

SCOTTISH HERALDRY, while basically international, like all heraldry, differs considerably from that of England and Wales. The main difference is the requirement for the younger members of each generation to matriculate their arms, that is to say, to register them in the Lyon Court.

In doing this the authorities difference the coats of the cadets of the family and this continued registration of arms, in so far as it has been carried out, has resulted in a more systematic heraldry.

The control of armorial matters is in the hands of the Lord Lyon King of Arms. His office is one of great antiquity and the Lord Lyon, like the Lord Provost of Edinburgh, was from early times a privy councillor and therefore styled 'The Right Honourable'.

The Lyon Court is of great interest as a continuing and subsisting court of honour still in daily session which, since family arms are feudal heritage, still adjudicates on such 'noble fiefs' and other nobiliary causes. The Lyon King is a judge ordinary in genealogy and in questions or matters of 'family representation', namely of the chiefship of clans, in which cases his judgment is competent.

The titles and numbers of heralds in the Lyon Court have varied throughout history. At present there are three, namely Rothesay, Marchmont and Albany. Other heralds have been Islay, Ross and Snowdoun and titles used for extraordinary heralds have been Angus, Ireland, Lindsay and Orkney. The present pursuivants are Kintyre, Carrick and Unicorn, with a Falkland Pursuivant Extraordinary. Titles of previous pursuivants are Bute, Dingwall, Ormonde and March, and of extraordinary pursuivants Alishay, Darnaway, Diligence, Dragance, Ettrick, Garrioch, Hailes, Linlithgow and Montrose.

Slains and Endure are not royal pursuivants but ones appointed by peers and are interesting examples of the survival of such appointments. Slains is the pursuivant of the Earls of Erroll, Hereditary High Constables of Scotland, and Endure of the Earl of Crawford, premier earl of Scotland.

The Lyon Clerk and Keeper of Records is usually a herald or pursuivant. He holds a full-time appointment and maintains the day-to-day work of the Lyon Office, work which has been increasing annually for some time. Usually the Lyon Clerk is an advocate or a Writer to the Signet and the Procurator Fiscal may be an advocate. There is also an official Herald Painter to the Lyon Court and a Macer.

Visitations, such as were made in England and Wales in the 16th and 17th centuries, were not customary in Scotland, though the Lord Lyon's right to make them is acknowledged in the Act of 1672.

During the 17th century an attempt was made to establish the office of Lyon as an hereditary one. Sir Charles Erskine of Cambo had been succeeded as Lyon in 1672 by his son, Sir Alexander Erskine, and he in 1701 obtained a patent under the Great Seal making the office of Lyon King of Arms hereditary in his family. His son, Alexander, however, who was for a time joint Lyon with his father, predeceased him, and the father was induced by his kinsman, the Earl of Mar, to take part in the rebellion of 1715. As a result he fell into disfavour and his hopes of making his office hereditary vanished. This was no doubt a fortunate event.

There has been at least one Lyon King who was unluckier than Sir Charles Erskine. Sir William Stewart of Luthrie, who became Lyon in 1567, was within six months of entering office deprived of it and burnt at St Andrews on 16 August 1569 'for conspyring to take the Regent's lyffe by sorcery and necromancy, for which he was put to death'.[1]

One of the Lord Lyon's principal duties is the keeping of the Register of All Arms and Bearings in Scotland. This register began with the passing of the Act in 1672, which required persons to register their arms, and it contains all grants and matriculations of arms since that date; by 1970 it had reached fifty-five volumes. These constitute a fine heraldic record of Scottish armorial bearings, although it is only since the beginning of the 19th century that arms were painted in the register. The Lyon King was required to make grants of new arms to 'all virtuous and well-deserving persons' who should apply for the same, to matriculate the arms of cadets and to confirm arms to those who had neglected to register them in accordance with the requirements of the Act of 1672. It is still possible to register arms under this Act if the petitioner can show that the arms were in use by his ancestor at that date.

The Lyon King is also required to agree to additions or alterations of arms and to record family pedigrees in the Register of Genealogies, another of the records of the Lyon Office, to prepare funeral escutcheons and to be responsible for drawing up and making royal proclamations. He is also usually and traditionally King of Arms of the Most Ancient and Most Noble Order of the Thistle.

The Lyon King, heralds and pursuivants are members of the Royal Household of Scotland and wear the household uniform and over it their appropriate tabard of arms, which in all cases are the arms as borne in Scotland with the Scottish arms in the first and fourth quarters.

There have been periods when the Lyon King of Arms took his duties lightly and even irresponsibly, granting arms and supporters contrary to recognized practices and generally neglecting his responsibilities. During the last and this century, however, there have been a succession of excellent and conscientious kings of arms who have done a great deal of good work, both genealogically and heraldically. Sir James Balfour Paul, Lyon from 1890 to 1927, made great contributions in his editing, particularly of the *Scots Peerage* (1904–14) and in his *Ordinary of Arms* (1893) which contains all the Scottish arms registered in the Public Register down to the year of this work's publication. Sir Francis Grant, who was appointed Lyon Clerk in 1898 and Lyon King of Arms in 1929, in which office he remained until 1945, did a phenomenal amount of work in the genealogical and heraldic fields. Among his work was the editing of the commissariot records up to 1800, which were published by the Scottish Record Society, and his editing of the new edition of the *Fasti Ecclesiae Scoticanae* with W.S. Crockett, 8 volumes, 1915–1959. To read the list of his publications in the British Museum Printed Catalogue is to cause one to wonder how any man could have done so much in a lifetime.

His successor, Sir Thomas Innes of Learney, who was appointed in 1945 and retired in 1969, is a great authority on all heraldic, peerage and genealogical matters in Scotland, and his *Scots Heraldry* is recommended as a fascinating, informative and attractively illustrated book. J. R. H. Stevenson's *Heraldry in Scotland*[2] is one of the most authoritative works and Green's *Encyclopaedia of the Laws of Scotland* contains much interesting information under the headings: 'Heraldry', 'Lyon King of Arms', 'Name and Change of Name' and 'Precedence.' Sir Francis Grant's *Manual of Heraldry* (rev. edn. 1924) is a useful and concise account of the subject, though the illustrations are poor. Sir Iain Moncreiffe of that Ilk and Don Pottinger's *Simple Heraldry* is an example of a book full of accurate information and, at the same time, living up to its sub-title, 'Cheerfully Illustrated'.

In obtaining a new grant of arms or in matriculating arms petitioners are encouraged to give as full details of their family, in male and female lines, as they are able to substantiate. This makes the matriculation a genealogically valuable document as well as today being a fine example of heraldic painting and calligraphy. The standard of painting in the Lyon Office has in recent times been very fine. Particularly notable is the work of Graham Johnston, A. G. Law Samson, and H. L. Gordon, all Herald Painters to the Lyon Court.

The Lyon Office Records

The Lyon Court is now established in the New Register House, to which it moved in recent years. It contains a small but valuable library, which naturally possesses many of the principal printed works on heraldry and genealogy and also unique manuscript material.

One of the finest early manuscript armorials, that of Sir David Lindsay of the Mount, dated 1542, formally recognized by the Privy Council in 1630, is unfortunately not in the Lyon Office, but in the National Library of Scotland. An early manuscript in the Lyon Office is that known as the 'King's and Nobilities Arms,' and others are Sir James Balfour's and James Pont's rolls of arms.

The *Register of Genealogies* began in 1727, but there is, unfortunately, a gap from 1796 to 1827. The *Public Register of All Arms and Bearings in Scotland*, which, as previously mentioned, began in 1672, has been kept since then with complete regularity. There is a MS. ordinary of arms, which forms an index to the register itself. There are also nine volumes of *Birth Briefs, Funeral Entries and Funeral Escutcheons*. These have been indexed and published by the Scottish Record Society, once again under the editorship of Sir Francis Grant.

The *Register of Admissions of Heralds and Pursuivants* only begins in 1660, which is regrettable as these officers were the oldest known in the King's service. This admission register is also blank from 1726 to 1759.

There is here a card index to the notices of births, marriages and deaths in the *Scots Magazine* during its lifetime (1739–1826) which is an invaluable source of information about the middle and upper classes.

Those seeking information about their family should write or call on the Lyon Clerk. He and other members of the Lyon Office who happen to be there will be found to be very helpful. The department does not undertake to make researches, though the public registers and other collections of the Lyon Office will be made available at certain search fees. For either a particular or a general search enquirers will normally be required to employ

FIG. 7

Arms of a Scottish Chief: The Macnab of Macnab. *Arms:* Sa. on a chevron arg. three crescents vert in base an open boat with oars in action on a sea in base undy, arg. and az. *Crest:* The head of a savage affrontee ppr. *Supporters:* Two dragons sa. armed and langued or, having wings elevated arg. semee of crescents vert. *Motto:* Timor omnis abesto. The supporters are borne as chief of the clan. [Designed and executed by Joan Harris] a searcher. The department also does not undertake to give individual replies on such matters as name, septs or tartans, for information on which the appropriate reference books should be consulted. The Court of the Lord Lyon, in fact, only deals with tartans and septs when these matters are brought up on petition or in steps incidental to petitions or in judicial and official announcements.

Armorial bearings, designed for distinguishing persons of or within a family, cannot descend to or be used by persons who are not members of that family and armorial bearings, including the crest, are a form of individual inheritable property, devolving upon one person at a time by succession from the grantee or confirmee, and thus descend like a peerage. In Scotland a right to bear a subsidiary version of the arms and crest containing a mark of difference indicating a person's position in the family or clan may be obtained by matriculating arms in the public register.

With regard to the arms of a chief of a clan, it is not only illegal but a social crime and error to assume and purport to use your chief's arms without a due and congruent difference. There is no such thing as a 'clan coat of arms'. The arms are those of the chief and the clansmen have only the privilege of wearing the strap and buckle badge to show they are such chief's clansmen. You cannot have a crest without a shield of arms, because a crest was a later addition. Misuse of crests arises from misunderstanding of the badge rule, under which junior members of the family or clan may wear, in the specified manner, the crest of the head of the family or their chief as a badge.

People who wish to have arms granted to them personally must petition for a grant of arms or, if they can trace their ancestry back to an armigerous person, for a matriculation of those arms in their name. A person obtaining a grant or being allowed to matriculate arms receives an illuminated parchment narrating the pedigree as proved, a duplicate of which is recorded in the public register.

Commonwealth citizens, except those of English, Welsh or Irish ancestry, can apply to the Lord Lyon for a grant or matriculation of arms, but armorial bearings are not granted to foreigners, though such persons of Scottish ancestry may apply to the Lord Lyon for a cadet matriculation if their ancestors were armigerous. A foreigner of Scottish descent may sometimes be able to arrange for a collateral relative in Scotland of British citizenship to obtain a grant of arms and then they themselves may be able to obtain a cadet matriculation of these arms.

M

XVIII

SOCIETIES AND LIBRARIES

THE SCOTTISH GENEALOGY SOCIETY exists 'to promote research into Scottish family history' and 'to undertake the collection, exchange and publication of information and material relating to Scottish genealogy by means of meetings, lectures etc'. It was decided at its foundation that the society would remain an academic and consultative body and not engage itself professionally in record searching. Many of the leading genealogists in Scotland belong to this society. Information can be obtained from the honorary secretary, 21 Howard Place, Edinburgh.

The society has monthly meetings at which a talk is usually given on some genealogical subject, followed by a discussion. Membership is by election and the present annual subscription (1971) is £1·50 which includes the society's quarterly periodical *The Scottish Genealogist*. The subscription for the journal alone is £1 per annum.

The Scots Ancestry Research Society is a non-profit-making trust organization established in 1945 by the late Rt Hon Thomas Johnston, when he was Secretary of State for Scotland, to assist people of Scottish blood in tracing their Scottish ancestors. Since that date the society has investigated more than 26,000 enquiries from people of Scottish descent both at home and overseas.

The assistance of the society is obtained through filling up and returning a form to the Secretary, at 20 York Place, Edinburgh EH1 3EP. This form simply asks you to state the Christian and surnames of the person whose ancestry you wish to trace and a number of details about him as far as you can give them, such as his place of birth, whether he ever owned any land or house property there and whether he was living in Scotland in or after the 1841 census and if so where and when. There is an initial registration fee and a further fee for research work and a report.

These are the two principal national institutes dealing with research into Scottish ancestry. There are a number of other Scottish societies of interest and use to genealogists, most of which publish journals which often contain material of value.

Foremost among these must be mentioned the *Scottish Record Society*, which published the indexes to the commissariots up to 1800 and a great number of other records of genealogical value. Information can be obtained from the honorary secretary c/o the Scottish Record Office.

The *Scottish History Society* (Hon. Sec. c/o the National Library of Scotland, George IV Bridge, Edinburgh 1) has published an immense amount of valuable material, its volumes always being well indexed. Their publications include such works as MacFarlane's *Genealogical Collections concerning Families in Scotland*, edited by J. T. Clarke, 2 volumes (1887) and the *List of Persons concerned in the Rebellion* (1745–6) edited by Walter MacLeod (1890).

The *Society of Antiquaries of Scotland*, National Museum of Antiquities of Scotland, Queen Street, Edinburgh, is a body to which among others a number of well-known genealogists have been elected and the transactions of this body, including *Archaeologia Scotica* have been of great value, genealogically and otherwise. The publications of the *Spalding Club*, the *New Spalding Club* and the *Third Spalding Club* have also all been genealogically advantageous.

Other bodies which may be mentioned are the *Royal Celtic Society*, the *Scottish Burgh Record Society*, the *Saltire Society*, the *Scottish Catholic Historical Committee*, the *Scottish Church History Society*, the *Scottish Ecclesiological Society*, the *Scottish Gaelic Text Society* and the *Spottiswoode Society*.

The *Scottish Railway Preservation Society* is at 37 Montgomery Street, Edinburgh 7. In this connection it should be noted that the *Annual Report for 1969* of the Keeper of the Records of Scotland (1970) contains an appendix listing all Scottish railway archives now in the Record Office.

The *Stair Society* (Sec. 2 St Giles Street, Edinburgh 1) specializes in the history of Scots law, and a number of their publications may be of value to genealogists. The *Stewart Society* (40 Castle Street, Edinburgh), as its name implies, concentrates on information about that widespread family.

In addition to these national societies specializing in some particular field, there are a great number of local archaeological, antiquarian and historical societies, the publications of which may be of great value to searchers in those particular areas. A list of many of them will be found under 'Scotland' in *The Historical, Archaeological and Kindred Societies in the British Isles,* compiled by Sara E. Harcup, published by the University of London Institute of Historical Research, (rev. edn. 1968).

Among them may be mentioned the *Aberdeen Ecclesiological Society, Ayrshire and Galloway Archaeological Society, Bannatyne Club, Buteshire Natural History Society, Dumfriesshire and Galloway Natural History and Antiquarian Society, Edinburgh University Archaeological Society, Falkirk Archaeological and Natural History Society, Gaelic Society of Inverness, Glasgow Archaeological Society, Grampian Club, Old Glasgow Club, Maitland Club, Old Edinburgh Club, Orkney Antiquarian Society, Perthshire Society of Natural Science, Regality Club, St Andrews Society, Glasgow, St Andrews University Archaeological Society, Stirling Field and Archaeological Society, West Lothian County History Society* and the *Wigtownshire Antiquarian and Natural History Society.*

Many of these, besides publishing a periodical, have from time to time published topographical books or periodicals about their areas or parts of them, some of which have accounts of local families. Details of the publications of many of these Societies will be found in the two volumes entitled *A Catalogue of the Publications of Scottish Historical and Kindred Clubs and Societies* compiled by Charles S. Terry, 1780–1908 (1909) and Cyril Matheson, 1908–1927 (1928), and in the British Records Association pamphlet No 4, *Handlist of Scottish and Welsh Record Publications,* (the Scottish section by Peter Gouldesbrough and A. P. Kup), (1954).

Libraries

The *National Library of Scotland,* George IV Bridge, Edinburgh 1, contains, as might be expected, a number of MSS. of genealogical value. Among these are the MSS. of the Advocates Library, which were acquired in 1925 when that library became part of the National Library. The catalogue of this collection is in nine volumes of subjects (one on genealogy and heraldry with separate sections dealing with these two subjects). This is, unfortunately a catalogue of subjects rather than of contents; it mainly contains MSS. of well-known Scottish families and is not likely to be helpful to persons searching for lesser-known people.

Since 1925 three volumes have been published of catalogues of MSS. acquired after that date. These are excellent, well indexed for names and places, which may well point to genealogical sources. There are a number of catalogues of special collections, such as that of the Oliphants of Gask inventory of letters and papers, the catalogue of the annotated books and manuscripts of the late John Riddell, an advocate of Edinburgh who specialized in peerage cases (1863), and the MSS. of Sir William Fraser, all except one of which were published in *The Papers from the Collection of Sir William Fraser* by the Scottish History Society in 1924.

A great number of collections of letters have found their way into the National Library and the published indexes to these may, if one is fortunate, refer to letters of ancestors or collateral relatives which may throw light on the family. Examples are the letters of John Blair of Glasclune of the period 1710 to 1725 and the Jacobite collection of John Blair, the spy, of various dates; the account of the family of Rattray of Rannagulzion, and the papers associated with James Rattray of Rannagulzion, the Jacobite prisoner; and the large collection of letters to the Mackenzies of Delvin, advocates in Edinburgh, which contain, for instance, a number of letters from the Freer family of Lethendy over several generations.

The collection includes 'Genealogical and Heraldic collections on Scottish surnames with genealogies in alphabetical order, written about the time of James II [of Scotland]'s reign', 'The Genealogies of Several Lairds in Scotland', and a 'List of the haill knight baronets of Scotland preceding the Union'.

A great many of the MSS. are mainly heraldic. There are, for instance, the 'Orkney Genealogies and Anecdotes collected by Robert Nicholson, who served as Sheriff Substitute of Orkney from 1795 to 1814', which is a collection of a few genealogies of Orkney families, the earlier generations of which may not be reliable; the volume of 'Genealogies of the Nobility of Scotland in the hand of Sir James Balfour', which has a Latin dedication to Charles I; the 'Genealogical Account of Families of the name of Stewart with Inventar of Papers and Charters of Stewarts of Halling'; a folio volume of fifty-six pages which was purchased at Phillipp's sale in 1897 and the 'Very extensive Biographies of the Families of Sinclair, Hamilton, Abercromby, Cooper, Thring, Crawfurd, Hay, Pilkington, Cockburn, Gibson, Campbell, Cunningham, Musgrave, Murray, Riddell, Slingsby, Hannay, Balfour, Maxwell, Gordon, and several others, by Sir Egerton Bridges', a folio volume purchased at Phillipp's sale in 1896. There are a number of pedigrees of various families which are listed in the handwriting of Francis Townsend, Windsor Herald.

There are also a number of Scottish armorials, such as the 'Arms of Scottish Nobility' by Sir James Lindsay, and the famous armorial of Sir Robert Forman. There is here also the genealogical collection of Sir James Balfour of Denmilne, mainly concerned with families of Fife; that of Robert Milne relating to the Gordon, Drummond and Fraser families; and that of George Crawford relating to the Crawford family. There are 115 volumes of John Riddell's MS. collections and 156 note-books relating to a number of Scottish families. There are also pedigrees of, among other families, those of Campbell, Cunningham, Douglas, Drummond, Fraser, Leslie, Mackenzie, Mure, Rose and Sinclair.

While the library staff will indicate the principal collections they cannot undertake to give detailed replies to postal enquiries. The *University of Edinburgh Library* (George Square, Edinburgh 1) is not open to the public, but permission may be obtained to use it for approved purposes. Application should be made to the librarian. There is an index of about 30,000 cards referring to MS. material in the library which may be published shortly. Reference has already been made in Chapter XIII to MS. and printed sources of information about students at the university.

The *Edinburgh Central Public Library* (George IV Bridge, Edinburgh 1) has in its Edinburgh Room an almost complete run of the Edinburgh Post Office Directories from 1773 onwards and of the *Edinburgh Almanack* from 1742, but the latter does not contain names of ordinary inhabitants. There are also good sets of Edinburgh newspapers, a complete set of the *Scots Magazine* and John Smith's MS. 'Epitaphs and Monumental Inscriptions in the Old Carlton Burial Ground, Edinburgh, compiled with biographical and obituary notices', which contains, among other matters, details of the memorial (unveiled on 21 August 1893) to Scottish soldiers who served in the American Civil War and who presumably died in Edinburgh or elsewhere in Scotland.

In the same building is the *Scottish Library*, which contains a great deal of material of value to genealogists. It is convenient to find here, easily accessible on open shelves, such comparatively rare printed material as the decennial indexes to the services of heirs since 1700 and the indexes of the registers of deeds and those of the various sasines published by the Scottish Record Office. There are also here complete sets of the three statistical accounts of Scotland and the publications of the Stair Society, of the Scottish History Society and of other such bodies.

The *Edinburgh City Archives*, City Chambers, Edinburgh 1, has a great deal of very valuable MS. material on the capital going back to early times, including considerable information about householders and other inhabitants. Their apprenticeship registers have been published for the years 1583 to 1800 and their burgess rolls from 1406 to 1841.

The *Mitchell Library, Glasgow* (North Street, Glasgow C. 3) has MS. pedigrees of a number of families, which are listed in Marion J. Kaminkow's *Genealogical MSS. in British Libraries* (1967), and microfilms of births and marriages for the Glasgow parishes of the City and Barony, the Scottish Episcopalian churches of St Andrews-by-the-Green, Christ Church and

St Paul's, and a number of microfilms of deaths and burials from various cemeteries in Glasgow, mainly 19th century. The vast printed material of this fine library includes runs of Glasgow directories from the end of the 18th century onwards.

The *Glasgow City Archives Office*[1] houses the archives of the city, including burgess rolls,[2] and many business and family collections.

The *Aberdeen Public Library* (Rosemount Viaduct, Aberdeen) has MS. accounts of the following families: Barclays of Tollie, Barclays of Towie-Barclay, Brooker, Burness or Burns (Kincardineshire), Chalmers of Balnacraig, Collie, Cook, Craig (Brechin etc), Cruikshanks of Stracathro (1847), Dyas or Dyce, Forbes of Pitsligo, Gordon (German branch), Gordon Henderson, Hutchison of Peterhead, Keith, Lendrum, Trails of Blebe, Fergusson of Dunfallandy, Macgregor of Glenorchy, Macgregor of Dunan, Mackintosh, Maitland Mackie of Towes, Morice, Morrice (extracts from the Aberdeen parish registers), Tod (descendants of John Todd and Jessie Nimmo), Reith, Stewart of Drumin, White. There are also a number of cuttings relating to Scottish surnames, which are filed alphabetically.

The *Burgh Museum, Dumfries* (Corberry Hill, Dumfries) possesses a number of short accounts compiled by the curator of records of Dumfries and Galloway (1961) and there is in process of compilation a MS. calendar of records of Dumfries and microfilms of records of Annan, Kirkcudbright and Stranraer.

The *Ewart Public Library*, Dumfries, has a number of MSS. on Dumfriesshire families, including those of Gordon and Grierson, and records of Gretna Green marriages. These were calendared in 1958 by Dr Athol Murray of the Scottish Record Office. There is also here a useful MS. collection of Dr R. C. Reid.

The *Dundee Central Public Library* has a number of valuable genealogical and local records. They include the 'Book of the Howff' (the old burial ground) in three volumes and gravestone inscriptions made by Mr Sidney Cramer from the churchyards of Inverarity, St Rule's, Monifieth, Lundie, Dargie, Invergowrie, Easter Necropolis, Dundee (Jewish Section), Broughty Ferry, Dundee Roodyards Burial Ground and a list of tombstones in the Constitution Road Cemetery. There is also a useful MS. index of Dundee persons mentioned in a number of documents and publications including many of the Scottish Record Office, such as the Exchequer Rolls, the registers of the Great Seal and Privy Council, the Historical MSS. Commission Reports and the Registrum Episcopatus Brechinensis. There are also MS. notes on a number of families.

The *Dunfermline Public Library* possesses one of the three typescript copies of the 'Tulliallan Genealogy' compiled by John Fowler Mitchell, the tombstone inscriptions being by him and his wife, Mrs Sheila Mitchell. It is described as a reference book for any one interested in the family history of residents of Tulliallan parish, including Kincardine-on-Forth (1964).

This is an account of the parish begun through the recording of the inscriptions in the old churchyard. To this has been added information about the inhabitants gathered from various sources, resulting in a collection of material concerning the inhabitants of the parish for nearly three centuries.

The *Paisley Public Library* (High Street, Paisley) possesses 45 volumes, with an index, of a MS. known as the 'Cairn of Lochwinnoch', which is a collection of miscellaneous information about some Lochwinnoch families, with details of their birth, marriage and deaths. There are also two small volumes of monumental inscriptions from tombstones in Paisley.

The *Norman Stewart Institute, Rothesay* (Bute County Library, Rothesay, Isle of Bute) has a copy of the *Session Book of Rothesay* 1658–1758 for Rothesay Parish, which is a rare printed book.

Letters of ancestors ... which may throw light on the family

XIX

VARIOUS OTHER SOURCES

THIS CHAPTER IS rather a mixed bag, a kind of olla podrida of sources not covered elsewhere, but by no means inclusive of all such sources, for it has already been emphasized that almost any record may give information about an ancestor and the more you find out about forbears the nearer you come to discovering their line further back.

Apprentices

In Scotland perhaps even more than in England apprenticeship was the recognized path to learning not only artisan trades but also professional skills. Thus the articled clerk to a solicitor in England was known in Scotland as a law apprentice to a writer. Reference has already been made to the apprenticeship records which survive in many burghs in Scotland, but a valuable 18th century source is the typescript 'Apprentices of Great Britain' – in two alphabetical series, from 1710 to 1762 and from 1763 to 1774 – in the possession of the Society of Genealogists in London (37 Harrington Gardens, SW7). Parliament in 1710 enacted that a small tax should be paid on apprenticeship indentures and this tax, irritating no doubt to the parents and masters of the time, is of value to the genealogists of today.

Some years ago the Society of Genealogists had extracts of genealogical interest made from the registers of the receipts of this tax in the Public Record Office, London. These registers give as a rule the name of the apprentice, his parent or guardian, sometimes the place of the latter's residence, the master's name and trade and, if outside London, the town or village in which he lived, and the amount paid.

Unfortunately after about 1750 the registers do not give the name of the parent. There is an index to the masters for the first series but not for the second series. There are, however, indexes at the Public Record Office for the period 1759 to 1783 and incomplete ones from 1793 to 1803. The tax continued to 1810, but the period from 1774 to that date has not been extracted by the society.

There were, unfortunately, from a genealogical point of view, certain exceptions to this tax. It did not apply to parish apprentices nor to public charities and if the fee for the apprenticeship was only a nominal amount, this was not registered. As relatives frequently accepted apprentices for a nominal fee it is a regrettable exception.

Records of apprenticeship for all periods are also to be found in borough archives in England as well as in Scotland and particularly in the records of the city livery companies of London. The freedom records of the Corporation of the City of London are also valuable because in earlier times a person could not practise a trade without being a freeman. Freedom could be obtained by patrimony, apprenticeship or redemption and in all these cases the parentage of the freeman is usually given. Freeman registers are held by the Corporation of London Record Office, Guildhall, EC2 and information from them can be obtained for a small fee.

Trinity House Petitions
Scotsmen being a seafaring race these petitions may throw light on their family circumstances. A collection of them was presented to the Society of Genealogists by the Corporation of Trinity House in 1934. This consists of several thousands of petitions from seafaring men, most in the mercantile marine, and from their dependants, for assistance during the years from 1780 and 1854. They are bound in alphabetical order and there are 102 volumes. A detailed description of them will be found in *The Genealogists' Magazine*, vol. 6, (September 1934), p. 490. Every man or dependant who applied for assistance from the Corporation was required to give the full particulars of his or her circumstances, frequently enclosing supporting documents, possibly original certificates.

The Macleod Papers
These are the papers of the Rev. Walter Macleod of Edinburgh and his son, John Macleod, who were both professional record searchers. These are also at the Society of Genealogists and cover the father's and son's searches from 1880 to 1940.

The papers are in the process of being bound up and when this is completed they will form nearly 300 volumes. Their content is varied but of great genealogical value.

Life Assurance

In earlier days, before medical examinations for life insurance had become customary, companies relied on information about the longevity or otherwise of the applicant's family. Consequently proposal forms of the 18th and early 19th centuries frequently give details of the applicant's family, the names of his parents, brothers and sisters and possibly grandparents and their ages or, if deceased, the age at which they died.

Reference to a life policy is sometimes found in a testament and this should be followed up by writing to the head office of the assurance company. Unfortunately, a number of companies handed over these proposal forms for pulping in a drive for paper during the 1939–1945 war, but even the ledgers of these companies, which have usually been preserved, may contain information such as the addresses at the time applicants took out their policies.

Bank Records

The confidential nature of bank records entails restriction on the examination of or information from customers' accounts, but where these are of a date earlier than about 100 years these records may often be inspected or information given from them. As sons and daughters tend to go to the same bank as their parents these records may prove genealogically interesting. On a client's opening an account there may be a note that his father or uncle banked at the same bank. The 18th and early 19th centuries were of course the era of small private banks and the existence, if any, of their records may be difficult to trace. A number of these small banks were absorbed into the larger banks existing today and the latter have usually been careful of the records of banks they have taken over. It should be possible to trace the present-day bank which took over an earlier private bank. The Bank of England, Barclays, Coutts, Glyn Mills, Hoare's and the Midland Banks have, at their London offices, facilities for examining their earlier records for approved purposes.

The Hudson's Bay Company, though not a bank, may be mentioned here. Many Scotsmen served in this great company. An archivist is maintained at their London headquarters at Beaver House, Great Trinity Lane, E.C.4 and will indicate the scope of their records and assist researchers.

Tontines and Annuities

A life annuity is an annuity which ceases on the death of the nominee, who may or may not be the same person as the proprietor of the annuity.

A tontine is a scheme in which a certain number of people participate by purchasing shares and nominating some person (the nominee) who may be themselves but is more often some young child. As the nominees die the shares paid to the subscribers (or their heirs and assigns) whose nominees survive increase, until the proprietor of the share on the life of the last surviving nominee receives the total interest from the capital. In government tontines the capital sum became the property of the Government on the death of the last surviving nominee. The scheme was named after Lorenzo Tonti, a Neapolitan banker who had started the system in France in about 1653. Readers of Robert Louis Stevenson and Lloyd Osbourne's *The Wrong Box* will remember that the plot of the story hinges on a tontine.

The British Government instituted six tontines, those of 1693, 1766, 1773, 1775, 1777 and 1789, and five life annuities, those of 1745, 1746, 1757, 1778 and 1779. The earliest tontine, that of 1693, was raised to obtain funds to carry on the war against France. This tontine proved abortive, but the late Charles Bernau found a number of printed documents in the British Museum Library which included a list of all the nominees, giving their full names, age, parentage and abode for both the nominee and the parent. The tontines of 1773, 1775, and 1777 are commonly called the Irish tontines because the money for them was raised through Acts of the Irish Parliament.

Information about tontines is to be found in the tontine ledgers and papers of the National Debt Office in the Public Record Office, London, designated N.D.O.1, N.D.O.2 and N.D.O.3.

The life annuity records are not as useful as those of the tontine. The latter, among other details, give the following information: name of the subscriber, his or her address, name of the nominee (usually a young child); name of his or her parent and age of the nominee; date when the nominee died or was buried, names of the executors, administrators and assigns and the volume and folio where the will or assignment may be found; the names of attorneys, and reference to powers of attorney.

The subscribers mainly came from the middle classes and the number who subscribed is considerable. For the English tontine of 1789, for instance, there were 8,349 subscribers.

Attention was first drawn to this valuable genealogical source by the editor in *The Genealogists' Magazine*, vol. 7 (June 1935) p. 76, who mentioned the Irish tontines. More recently, Mr Francis Leeson has made a more detailed examination of these records. His booklet, *A Guide to the Records of the British State Tontines and Life Annuities of the 17th and 18th*

Centuries[1] gives a detailed description of each of the life annuities and tontines mentioned above. Details of the subscribers, nominees etc. of the 1745 life annuity have been published in *Blackmansbury*[2] and it is hoped to publish details of persons in other life annuities and in the tontines in due course. Meanwhile, the Surname Archive, Channel Sound, Sea Lane, Ferring, Sussex, holds card indexes, photo-copies and micro-films of the registers of all the listed tontines and annuities. For a small fee a search will be made among these records for a surname (including usual variants). For a common surname further fees will be charged for information additional to a complete list of all occurrences.

This comparatively recently found genealogical source is of course limited in scope, valuable mainly for upper and middle class people. Nevertheless, within that group possibilities of discovering an ancestor are by no means small. As Francis Leeson says in the introduction to his booklet, 'the records relating to the British state tontines and life annuities are practically unknown, and yet they are invaluable in that they supply, among other things, the age, parentage, residence and, in most cases, the date of death of thousands of persons living in the late 17th, the 18th, and the early 19th centuries'.

There were a number of private tontines, such as the tontine raised in 1776 to build Richmond Bridge, but the records of these, where they survive, are far less valuable genealogically. The printed list of the subscribers and their nominees to the £20,000 capital raised for building Richmond Bridge, for instance, gives only the names of the subscribers and of the nominees, with the address of the latter and his or her father's or guardian's name. As the list was published at the time the tontine was inaugurated there is of course no record of the date of death of any of the nominees, unless one comes across a copy which was obviously possessed by one of the subscribers, who has marked up the date of death of the various nominees, no doubt avidly calculating the ensuing increase in his own payment.

Civil Servants

Lists of retired civil servants were given periodically in Parliamentary papers in the 19th century. The 1836 list gives the following details: name; office, salary or retirement pay per annum; age on retirement (to the quarter-year); period of service; cause of retirement; yearly allowance (or pension). There are separate lists for those who have died or ceased to receive a pension, giving the cause of the cessation of the pension.

The 1862 list gives all officers and pensioners alive in 1860 receiving more than £150 per annum salary or pension. This is classified by different departments, the names being alphabetical in each department. It should be noted that these lists do not include the Indian Civil Service.

In the indexes under 'Superannuations' will also be found Treasury minutes of special cases of superannuation, in several cases mentioning the persons by name.

Acts of Parliament

The twelve large volumes of the Acts of Parliament of Scotland up to the time of the Union in 1707[3] are worth examining, as there are many private Acts in them referring to individuals or their property and occasionally to judicial proceedings. The indexes to them are good.

Poll Tax Rolls

The first of these was imposed in 1693, being levied the next year, to pay the debts of the army and navy, and the following year a second tax was imposed. This tax was additional to the more permanent land tax. It enacted that the sum of six shillings should be imposed on all persons of whatever age, sex or quality, exceptions being those poor subsisting on charity and children under sixteen, who lived in homes where the total poll did not exceed thirty shillings. Certain of the better-off classes were required to pay additional amounts.

Many of these polls of the last decade of the 17th century are preserved in the Scottish Record Office. A list of them will be found in D. J. Steel's *Sources for Scottish Genealogy and Family History* (1971). Although a number of these give very few names, a proportion, particularly in Berwickshire, Midlothian, West Lothian and Renfrewshire give names, occupations and the locations of houses, and quite a number also give the names of wives and children. Where these records exist their genealogical value at this comparatively early period will be appreciated.

In addition to the MS. rolls at the Scottish Record Office, some have remained in local hands and some have been published. Those for Renfrewshire for 1695, which were discovered and published by David Semple in the *Glasgow Herald* in 1864, are particularly valuable. They give as full details as any and contain the names of people in the county, their callings, residence, wives, children, servants etc. This was only published in the newspaper, but cuttings from it were made up into six complete copies in octavo volumes, with indexes. Of these six, one went to the editor, one to the British Museum Library, one to the Advocates Library (now the National Library of Scotland), one to the University of Glasgow Library, and one to the Society of Antiquaries in Scotland.

Poll Books and Directories

Poll Books were the printed books of names of those entitled to vote in the parliamentary elections and sometimes showed the candidate for whom the elector voted. They are not as prevalent in Scotland as in England, probably due to the vast areas covered by country constituencies and to the peculiar representation in towns. Examples are the *List of Freeholders . . . and of Electors in the County of Aberdeen . . . 1832* and the *Street List of Electors of the City of Edinburgh, 1854*. These poll books belong mostly to the 19th century.

Though not in itself a poll book the *View of the Political State of Scotland . . . a Confidential Report on the . . . 2662 county voters in 1788*, edited by Sir Charles Elphinstone Adam and eventually published in Edinburgh in 1887, is a useful volume.

The limited franchise of the time detracts from the value of Poll books and this is also true of the early directories, which are by no means comprehensive of the inhabitants of towns and counties, mainly listing the principal inhabitants, gentry, merchants, officials and professional men. A list of pre-1860 directories is given in Appendix E.

Police Records

The point has been made earlier that people who got into trouble with the authorities are easier to trace than those who led quiet exemplary lives and were good citizens doing their job and keeping 'the King's Peace'. The registers of the burgh councils often contain judicial proceedings and police offences and these may be preserved from very ancient days. Turning to more modern times, the 'In and Out' books of the prisons of the early 19th century sometimes give the place of birth of the prisoner.

Subscription Lists

Listed names of subscribers to books, charities and so forth should not be overlooked as these sometimes lead to information as to a person's whereabouts. It should also be remembered that when people moved from one place to another they often named their new home after their old one. This custom, which goes back to classical times, can sometimes provide a valuable clue.

XX

RECORDING RESULTS

ECTOR MCKECHNIE, that eminent Scots genealogist, in his short booklet, *The Pursuit of Pedigree* (1928), concludes, writing of the genealogist's efforts, '. . . ancestors long dead and long forgotten will have arisen to befriend him. To rescue from oblivion one's forbears, to revive their memories . . . cannot but give satisfaction. Even to catch something of the leisured spirit of bygone days and the conception of a life more lasting and more worth-while than that of an individual, is in itself no slight achievement'.[1]

But all your work, all the results of your patient, sometimes wearying and often frustrating research, will be wasted unless you leave some record of it. How often you hear people sighing, 'If only I had asked my grandfather about this . . .'! Do not yourself leave future generations to say this about you.

There are many ways of recording your work. In Chapter I the merits of a chart pedigree have been mentioned. This can be a clear and succinct way of recording your efforts. It is surprising how much information can be contained in a well-drawn-up chart pedigree. It is not necessary for this to be printed. If it is in typescript or in clear hand lettering in indian ink, this is perfectly adequate. Examples of such can be seen in the various pedigrees in this book. As previously mentioned, such pedigrees can be reproduced simply and inexpensively by one of the processes like Xerox, or by one of the photo-lithographic methods.

The next step is to try to ensure that this pedigree does not later on get lost or destroyed. The best way to do this is to get copies of it preserved at various record depositories and libraries. The British Museum Library will usually accept a reproduced pedigree of this kind and generally such pedigrees are from time to time bound up in volumes. They will be catalogued under both the name of the family to which the pedigree refers, and of the name of the compiler if this is shown on the pedigree itself.

The author of this book has had a number of pedigrees accepted and catalogued in this way. This ensures that any future family historian searching for information and consulting the British Museum catalogue will come across the pedigree. The National Library of Scotland will no doubt also be willing to accept such pedigrees, and other record depositories, such as the public library of the district to which the family belonged, should be asked to accept copies. In this way you ensure, as far as you can reasonably do so in this atomic age, that the essence of your work will be preserved for the future.

This chart pedigree should be regarded as the minimum record of your work. Many will wish to leave a fuller account in addition to, but not in substitution for, such a pedigree. Sir James Balfour Paul has written a good introduction to Margaret Stuart's *Scottish Family History* entitled 'How to Write the History of a Family'.[2] In it he mentions a number of ways in which this may be done. Some of them, as he states, are more to be warned against than recommended. One of these is that old-fashioned wheel pedigree, sometimes found among old family papers. Another is the family tree which is drawn up in the form of an actual tree, the leaves of which are inscribed with names and details of members of the family, an altogether confused and inelegant structure, more interesting as a not particularly artistic curiosity than as a pedigree. Then he mentions the anecdotal style of family history, which can be irritating in its facetiousness. It may, nevertheless, sometimes be well handled and contain valuable information, though this type of recorded history usually lacks dates and basic details.

The methods he takes more seriously are the tabulated pedigree, the historical method and the scientific method. Pedigrees in *Burke's Peerage* and *Landed Gentry* are examples of the tabulated pedigree. Each generation is given a symbol, a figure or letter, and the generations are indented so that they can be easily distinguished. This is a well-tried method which has stood the test of time and is clear and easy to follow provided the details of each generation are confined to essentials. Lengthy details about members of the family tend to prolong the layout so that the position of members in the family structure is not easily followed. A study of the above-mentioned works will soon familiarize you with this method.

Balfour Paul describes what he calls the historical method as that in which the members of the family are connected with the events of their time. His feeling was that a history of this type should be of a family which

N

has had some influence on public affairs. He mentions Sir William Fraser's histories of various Scottish families as examples of this. They are voluminous works, well documented but somewhat pedestrian in their style.

As an example of what he calls the scientific method, Balfour Paul gives *The Wedderburn Book*.[3] This has a good introduction giving an account of early notices of persons of the name in Scotland and a summary of the history itself. Then comes the main narrative, covering the various branches of the family, their armorial bearings if they were entitled to any, their tombs and so forth, and another section mentions various persons of the name in Great Britain or abroad who are not known to be connected with any particular branch of this Angus family. There are good chart pedigrees and a good key pedigree linking up the various more detailed ones. References are given in brackets throughout the work. Balfour Paul preferred footnotes, regarding, as do most people, a succession of notes in brackets in the body of the work as distracting. Another method is to have the notes at the end of the book. This has the advantage, if notes are frequent, of not disturbing with footnotes the layout of the pages of the book. Some authors use consecutive numbers for the notes throughout the book, but this leads to two- or even three-digit references, which are cumbersome. It is better to start a new sequence with each chapter. But whatever method is adopted it is important that references to authorities should be made and an index is virtually indispensable, though it is surprising and regrettable how many such books still come out without one.

Much of Balfour Paul's advice is excellent, but he was writing nearly half a century ago when family histories still tended to be of well-known families and these are the examples to which he refers. Since that time there has been a great development in the opening up of records and an increased interest in the history and genealogy of ordinary families. This has coincided with an increase in the study of demography and social history. There is no reason why the history of a family which had never played any great part in national events should not be written up interestingly by relating it to events of its period and this is probably the best way of producing the history of such a family.

There are, unfortunately, many family histories which do make rather dull reading even to members of the family. This is partly because they consist of a string of basic facts which in themselves are valuable but which are not presented in an interesting way. A narrative account of the family might remedy this, but sometimes even such an expanded account seems to lack interest.

This may be due to a number of reasons. To write a successful family history you need not only the results of basic research but also some literary ability. Genealogists do not necessarily have this and they would often do well to hand over the actual writing-up of their material to some author friend or acquaintance versed in historical work. This might involve payment, but much time and money has been spent on researches and this additional amount should not be grudged. It is a pity to spoil the ship for a ha'p'orth of tar.

However, many genealogists who want to write up their own account will be well able to do so. Certainly some knowledge of the history of the period is desirable, and it is one of the delights of genealogy that as your searches progress you learn more and more of the contemporary history.

Remembering the old proverb that 'an ounce of practice is worth a pound of precept' let us take an account of a particular family, that of Hall of Abbey St Bathans, Berwickshire.

James Hall, minister of Abbey St Bathans, was baptized at Stamfordham, Northumberland, a son of Thomas Hall in Ryall, a nearby hamlet, on 15 February 1684. He was licensed by the dissenting ministry in England in 1714 and ordained by them in 1715. He came to Abbey St Bathans on 28 July 1719. By his first wife, whose name is unknown, he had a daughter Marion, who married John Brodie, farmer of Oldhamstocks, their marriage proclamation being dated 13 August 1732 in Edinburgh.

James Hall married secondly Margaret Johnston, their proclamation being dated 27 May 1722. By her he had issue John, baptized 16 June 1723; George, baptized 11 April 1725; Janet, baptized 23 February 1727; Margaret, baptized 19 October 1729; James, baptized 18 May 1732 and Jean, baptized 1 August 1737. He died at Abbey St Bathans on 19 July 1754. His wife died 20 May 1787.

This is a factual account of some value, but it could be made more interesting by some further research and some infusion of local history and social conditions. The account might be expanded in this way:

James Hall, minister of Abbey St Bathans, baptized at Stamfordham, Northumberland 15 February 1684, son of Thomas Hall in Ryall, a nearby hamlet, was licensed by the dissenting ministry in England in 1714 and ordained by them the following year. He came to Abbey St Bathans on 28 July 1719.

He was twice married. The name of his first wife is not known, but by her he had a daughter Marion, whose marriage proclamation to John Brodie, a farmer of Oldhamstocks, was issued in Edinburgh on 13 August 1732.

James Hall's second wife was Margaret Johnston. Their marriage proclamation is dated at Abbey St Bathans 27 May 1722. By her he had three sons and the same number of daughters, whose baptisms are all recorded at Abbey St Bathans, namely: John, 16 June 1723; George, 11 April 1725; James, 18 May 1732; Janet, 23 February 1727; Margaret, 19 October 1729 and Jean, 1 August 1737.[a]

James Hall seems to have been a forthright and practical man, not averse to looking after the interests of his own family, somewhat liberal in his views and unorthodox.

Shortly before July 1731 he was in trouble with the church authorities through holding a penny wedding in his house 'which gave great scandal to the neighbourhood'.[b] A penny wedding was one at which the guests contributed a small sum of money or, occasionally food and drink for their own entertainment. Any surplus was presented to the young couple. The strait-laced church authorities of the time frowned on this custom which to us today does not appear to be deeply steeped in viciousness. So Hall was penalized by being suspended, but he was restored on 6 July 1731.

In 1738 he wrote a somewhat sycophantic letter to his patron, Alexander, 2nd Earl of Marchmont, seeking his help in the provision of a schoolmaster for the parish.c Although John Knox a century earlier had realized how religion and education went hand-in-hand and had urged the importance of establishing schools in every parish, many were frequently without such provision.

'The personal experience I have of your Lordships good inclination and ready disposition to doe good to all men and at all times, especially when its no loss to your Lordship nor hurt to any others, to give your Lordship the trouble of this for which I beg your Lordships pardon.'

Then he continues with a little factual information to put his patron in the picture:

'I having the honour and happyness to be minister at Abbey St Bathans, of whom your Lordships justly celebrated father, worthy lady and greatly honoured brother, all who now rest from their labours and I hop their works doe follow them, were the chief and only instruments, under God, of my unmerited settlement, and I having the charge of all the souls in the said parish and as I laid out myself in the instructing of the aged so for the education of the children; yet notwithstanding of all the means I could use or the pains I have taken for the space of these 19 years we had wanted a schoolmaster seven years of these nineteen . . . The occasion of this was enteirly for want of bread to a schoolmaster to live on. And now we have wanted one 2 years come July first, in which month the schoolmaster died.'

We are impressed with the worthy minister's altruism but it appears from further reading that he is not entirely disinterested.

'Now, my Lord,' he continues, 'I haveing a numerous family, eight children (and four servants) the oldest of seven of them is but 14 years old and the youngest is only 9 months old, and my stypend being only £45 sterling I am pitifull straitned in getting my children educated, which is all the patrimony I can give them, altho I should live with them 20 years, which cant be expected of one who is going in 69; yea I have been these 3 years bypast obliged to have a young man in my house to teach my children; the charges of bed and board, coal and candle and washing and his fee extended to the fourth part of my stypend besides other trouble to the familie; and for me to send my five children (which are now capable of being instructed) to Duns or to any publick town and boord them there all my stypend would not defray that charge.'

It seems that the late schoolmaster had not been a satisfactory one: 'a poor insignificant body, just naught'. However James Hall, being conscious of the advantage to his own children, was prepared to give some of his meagre stipend to assist.

'The request is this that . . . they [the heritors] would make choice of one who both can and will teach the parish children Inglish, writing, arithmetick and Latine (for my sons are begun the Latine) . . . and by their so doing it neither is nor shall be one farthing of mor charges to the heritors than the poorest, lame, criple or idiot in all the country. Plenty of such is gaping for it and seeking to be in. But I hop, as its much easier to keep out than to turn out your Lordship will be fore none of these.'

He goes on to say that, if the heritors will do this 'it will be above 100 pound Scots of advantage yearly to me in geting my children taught at home . . . I will add (for the management of a schoolmaster thus qualified) 50 marks yearly for some time, and if he be a deserveing man its possible I may give more, and by this means we both may and will get a sufficient schoolmaster.'

'I flatter myself,' the worthy minister continued, 'of a smiling return from your Lordship,' but whether he received this or not is unknown. Two, at any rate, of his sons, whether they truly acquired 'the Latine' or not, seem to have done reasonably well. John, the eldest, purchased the estate of Benacres in Ayrshired and George went into business in London. James Hall himself died at Abbey St Bathans on 19 July 1754. His wife, Margaret Johnston, survived him until 20 May 1787.

a Fasti Ecclesiae Scoticanae, new ed. 1917 ii, 2; viii, 115, Abbey St Bathans Par. Reg. and Edinburgh Marriage Reg.
b Fasti ibid.
c Historical MSS. Commission 67, Polwarth MSS, 1961, v, 149–155 (No. 218).

d Gen. Reg. Sasines vol: 497 fol. 292 (1791) and Part. Reg. Sasines Ayr vol. 45 fol. 184 (1801).

It will probably be agreed that this is a more colourful account of the minister, with his concern for the education of the parish children and in particular of his sons and their acquisition of Latin. Socially it underlines the difficulties of parish ministers in obtaining education for their often large families on their slender stipends.

It may be argued that this is an unfair example to take, because the letter among the Polwarth MSS. and published by the Historical MSS. Commission gave this family historian an unfair start in the family history stakes. These are the pearls of great price over which the genealogist rejoices when he comes across them.

Among such published and manuscript records there are few families which suffer complete oblivion. There is luck, of course, as well as skill in finding, but persistence pays and discovery brings its own feeling of satisfaction.

This example illustrates the way in which a family history can be made more attractive and diverting. Let us take another example, that of a family which might be thought to offer little prospect of interesting treatment, that of one which for generations had been farm labourers living in the same village. How can such a family story be made interesting?

This may be done by studying the agricultural history of the period and locality, in such books as T. B. Franklin's *History of Scottish Farming* (1952), James E. Handley's *Scottish Farming in the Eighteenth Century* (1953), if dealing with that period, or Isabel F. Grant's *Everyday Life on an Old Highland Farm 1769–1782* (1924). The kind of life each generation lived would have varied considerably because of the developments and inventions which have affected agricultural work. Mention has been made in the introduction of the improvements which Sir Archibald Grant of Monymusk brought about on his estate in Aberdeenshire. We know that he possessed a copy of Jethro Tull's *Horse-Hoeing Husbandry* (1731) and had adopted the turnip culture recommended in it. Tull's seed drill was also being brought into use by forward-looking Scottish farmers of the early 18th century. Then there was the foresight of men like John Cockburn and the rebuilding of the local 'farmtoun' as the English-style village.[4]

One does not want to flood a family history with contemporary accounts of such matters, but the skilfully infiltrated background of contemporary history can add greatly to the flavour of the family saga.

Whichever method we adopt in attempting to record our family researches, whether a mere brief outline or an expanded account, there will be a sense of satisfaction in completing it. José Ortega y Gasset has written 'One age cannot be completely understood if all the others are not understood. The song of history can only be sung as a whole'.[5] In a small way your account is helping towards that complete understanding. The searches of genealogists are daily unearthing minutiae of value to the historian. Goethe once wrote that 'the best thing we get from history is the enthusiasm it arouses'.[6]

The genealogist knows that enthusiasm – the pursuit of the unknown, the thrill of discovery which ties together isolated threads.

William Cowper wrote, 'When we look back upon our forefathers, we seem to look back upon the people of another nation, almost upon creatures of another species.'[7] Our careful and lengthy searches will make us feel that we know those forefathers much better.

I flatter myself ... of a smiling return from your Lordship

APPENDIX A

FAMILY QUESTIONNAIRE

The questions given below are those suggested for sending out in a *pro forma* to members of the family. The general questions will apply to most families but the more detailed ones will have to be varied as applicable to the particular family. Plenty of room should be left after each question for the reply.

THIS QUESTIONNAIRE IS sent to you in connection with the proposed production of a short account of the family. It is hoped you will fill it up and return it with as many details as possible. Even apparently trivial facts may be valuable clues in piecing together the family story. If you are uncertain of something please mark it 'possibly' or with some similarly appropriate phrase. If you have not enough room, please add a separate sheet.

General Questions

Do you know of the existence of any of the following, relating to earlier members of the family. They are mainly valuable if they belong to the period before about 1860.

Family Bible, giving details of baptism, marriage, burial etc?

Family pedigree or written account or notes about the family, baptism, marriage proclamation, burial certificates, receipts for use of mortcloth, leasehold or freehold of burial plots or lairs in graveyards?

Any piece of land, house or cottage, however small, at any time owned by the family?

Letters of introduction from kirk elders when moving to a new parish?

Deeds, sasines, service of heirs, testaments testamentar or dative, hornings, inhibitions, cessio bonorum?

Certificates of membership of clan societies?

Army, Navy, Merchant Service, East India Company certificates of service, war or other medals or miniatures, apprenticeship indentures, degree certificates, burgess or guild brethren certificates?

Letters of past members of the family, particularly from those overseas?

Any marriage contracts or settlements, the name of any family solicitors?

Receipt (or recipe) books in which the recipes are named after the people giving them (often relatives)?

Estate books or maps, bank books, life assurance policies, tontine or stock and share certificates?

Diaries, note-books, birthday books, family samplers, funeral cards, visiting cards, mourning rings, memorial cards, bookplates, paintings of arms or crests, seals, certificates of grants or matriculations of arms, silver bearing armorial emblems?

Old family portraits, miniatures, daguerreotypes or photographs?

Any family tradition regarding service in any particular regiment, ship, Civil Service, trade or occupation?

Old books containing names of owners who are possibly forbears?

Any information as to former homes, their names, parishes, indications of localities in which the family lived?

Example of a Specific Question
The earliest member of the family known to me is IAN MACTAVISH, whose marriage proclamation to MARGARET LINDSAY is recorded at Aberfoyle, Perthshire, 11 May 1820. He died in Perth 14 July 1842 aged forty-five so was born about 1796 or 1797. Have you information as to where he was born, who his father and mother were and where they lived or where they were married or any other information about them or other earlier members of the family?

APPENDIX B

LATIN WORDS AND PHRASES USED IN LEGAL DOCUMENTS IN SCOTLAND.

Abavus: a great-great-grandfather.
Amita: a father's sister; an aunt.
Atavus: a great-great-great-grandfather.
Avia: a grandmother.
Avunculus: a mother's brother.
Avunculus magnus: great-uncle on the mother's side.

Consobrinus: a cousin (strictly on the mother's side) see also *patruelis*.
Cum brevi regio incluso: with the royal brief included.

Filius: a son.
Filius fratris: a nephew (brother's son).
Filius sororis: a nephew (sister's son).
Frater: a brother.

Germana: a full sister.
Germanus: a full brother.

In curia balivatus: in the bailie's court.

Jurati dicunt magno sacramento interveniente: having been sworn under the great oath.

Lator praesentium: bearer of these presents.
Loco die mensis et anno praedictii: (with the) place, day of month and year as aforesaid.

Mater: a mother.
Matertera: a mother's sister.

Nepos: a grandson; a nephew.
Neptis: a grand-daughter.

Obiit ad fidem et pacem S.D.N. [Supremi Domini Nostri] regis: died at the faith and peace of our sovereign lord the king.

Pater: a father.
Patruelis: a cousin on the father's side.
Patruus: a father's brother.
Patruus magnus: a great-uncle on the father's side.
Praetorium: courthouse.
Proavia: a great-grandmother.
Proavus: a great-grandfather; a grandfather's or grandmother's father.
Probos et fideles homines patriae: worthy and faithful men of the district.
Pronepos: a great-grandson.

Sobrinus: see *Consobrinus*.
Soror: a sister.

Tritavus: great-great-great-great-grandfather.

Vicecomitatu: sheriffdom.

APPENDIX C

GLOSSARY OF TERMS FOUND IN EARLIER LEGAL AND OTHER DOCUMENTS

Fuller accounts of the underlisted words and phrases will be found in the works listed in the bibliography under *Legal, Ecclesiastical and Trade Terms*.

Abbreviate of adjudication: an abstract of a decree of adjudication; it contains such details as the names of debtors and creditors of the lands adjudged and the amount of the debt.

Agnates: persons related through the father.

Aiker: an acre. *Aiker daills:* land divided into acres and let or feued.

Allenarly: only. It prevents a life rent being construed as a fee.

Allodial: of land held absolutely, without acknowledgement to an overlord; not held under any feudal tenure, e.g. church property.

Annual rent: interest on money which has been lent.

Attour: (prep.) over, out of, above, besides, in addition to; (adv.) farther off or out, across, apart, besides, in addition.

Availl: worth, value. *Availl of marriage:* the sum payable to a superior by the heir of a deceased ward vassal on his becoming of marriageable age (abolished 20 Geo. II).

Averment: positive statement, affirmation; proof of.

Bailie, (baillie, etc.): the baron's deputy in a burgh of barony; a municipal magistrate or officer (corresponding to the English alderman); a person who looked after river fisheries; a man or boy in charge of the cows on a farm.

Barony: lands held of the crown and erected into a barony, with civil and criminal jurisdiction within its bounds.

Bateing: providing refreshments.

Batt: a term used in plumbing, etc.

Bear, (bere, beer, bar): a kind of barley; a festival celebrating the stooking of the bear.

Beastial: cattle, animals.

Bigging: a building.

Biggit: (adj.) built.

Birlymen: ground officers; those who assessed damages; referees.

Blair: part of flax used in manufacture.

Blanch-duty: a duty paid in kind or money in lieu of rent.

Bloodwyte: a fine imposed for drawing blood.

Boll: a dry measure of varying amount; a measure of grain equivalent to six bushels.

Bond: in Sc. law usually related to money lent on the security of land, thus more equivalent to a mortgage in England. *Bond of caution:* a bond by which someone acted as security for another; a *heritable bond* gave power to enter into possession and receive rents to recover payment. *Bond of thirlage:* in Sc. law a condition of servitude or state of obligation, in which the tenants of lands or persons living in certain areas are bound to use only a particular mill, forge, *etc.*, particularly at a later period of the obligation to have their corn ground at a particular mill (originally that of the lord or his assignee) and pay the recognized consideration (multure q.v.) or dues in lieu.

Bord: board.

Brewarie: brewery.

Brieve: a legal writ; an official document; a warrant issued from Chancery authorizing an inquest by a jury, such as for a service of an heir.

Brother-bairn: literally a brother's child, but used to signify the child of an uncle, denoting the relation of a cousin.

Browdenster: an embroiderer.

Burgage: a tenure in a royal burgh in which property was held direct of the Crown.

Burgh: a town. *Burgh of barony:* a town lying within a barony and in which the courts of barony were held. *Burgh of regality:* the head town of a regality.

Burghal aikers: acres belonging to a burgh.

Burrow: burgh, borough. *Burrow mailles:* rents due to or levied by a burgh.

Bye: (prep.) beyond.

Bygane: past.

Byre: cowhouse.

Cachepool: a tennis court.

Caddie: a boy who ran errands; a young fellow; a junior officer.

Cain (kain): a custom or rent paid in kind.

Caitchpoole: see *cachepool*.

Cattband: the name given to the strong hook on the inside of a door or gate and fixed to the wall, keeping it shut.

Cautioner: a surety, e.g. in the confirming of a testament.

Cess: a land tax.

Chamberlain: an officer-of-state concerned with royal burghs and the conduct of their magistrates.

Charter of resignation: the means by which a feu was reconveyed to another vassal.

Chassnutree: chestnut-tree.

Clare constat, precept of: the deed to the heir of a tenant granted by the superior. It was followed by a sasine.

Closs: a close, a street.

Clouer: clover.

Cnow: a hill.

Coal heuch: a coal-pit.

Coble: (n.) a rocking motion; a see-saw or titter-totter; (v.) to rock; to play see-saw; to cause to rock.

Coble (cobble, cowble): (n.) a small flat-bottomed rowing boat mainly used for river or lake fishing; a ferry boat.

Co-heir of provision: one of several heirs having a right by will or settlement.

Collateral: strictly in legal succession confined to brothers and sisters, but sometimes used to include descendants of collaterals and brothers and sisters of ascendants.

Commissariot (Commissariat): a court mainly concerned with the confirmation of testaments.

Commissary: a judge in the commissary court. His judicial powers included the confirmation of testaments and matters of nullity in actions for divorce, *etc.*

Compear: (of a defender) to appear in an action.

Compter: accountant.

Condescendence: that part of a pursuer's written pleading which contained the statement of facts on which he relied.

Confirmation: the completion of the probate of a testament by the executors.

Conquest: the comprehensive name for an inheritance acquired by purchase or gift and not by inheritance. The heir of conquest was not necessarily the heir of line.

Cousin-red: kinship.

Cruive (cruve): a box or inclosure made of spars and placed across a river generally in a dam or dike, to trap fish which enter into it.

Cruize (crusie): a lamp, lantern.

Cum (come, kum): a bend, curve of a crook; the angle made by certain tools when held in working position with the user's hand or body; a thaw; a tub, e.g. a milk-*cum* or -*kim*; a large ladle for baling out a boat.

Curator: an administrator of another person's affairs, either one nominated in a testament or appointed by the court; the curator to a minor or idiot (equivalent to the English guardian).

Customer (custumer): a custom-house officer.

Daill: deal, share.

Dative: appointed by the court instead of by the testator; the decree dative is the technical name given to the decree of the commissaries conferring on an executor (not being an executor-nominate) the office of executor (Bell's Dict. Laws Scot. (1890) p. 294). *Executor dative*: the executor appointed by the decree-dative; *tutor-dative*: a tutor, the guardian of a minor appointed by the court where there is no *tutor-nominate* or *tutor-at-law*.

Decreet: judgement, decree of a court of law.

Decreet arbitral: the final sentence of an arbitrator.

Defender: the defending party in a civil action.

Diligence: a warrant issued by a court to ensure the attendance of a witness or the production of some document; the process under which a person's lands or effects are attached on execution or (in Sc. law) in security for a debt; (v.) to sue or prosecute for debt.

Discharge: (Sc. law) forbid.

Dispone: (in Sc. law) to assign, make over or grant; to convey land, before 1869 an essential word in any valid conveyance of land; *to dispone upon:* to dispose of.

Disposition: (in Sc. law) a deed of conveyance and assignation of property.

Dominum directum: (in Sc. law) the right retained by the superior in all feudal grants; the *dominum utile* is that which the vassal acquires.

Doucat: a dove-cote.

Eikit: added.

Eschapit: to escape.

Executor dative: an executor appointed by a magistrate or court (see also Testament and Dative).

Executor nominate: an executor named by the testator.

Exerce (exerse): to carry out duties (e.g. of an office); to act; (n.) an exercise, function.

Expede: (in Sc. law) officially to issue (a document, *etc.*) to write out the principal writ and have it sealed, signed, *etc.*

Extent, old: see Old extent.

Feal: fee.

Fee: a servant's wages; a hiring-fair or market; *very fee:* full wage.

Feu: a perpetual lease.

Fennies: see *Tennies*.

Ferme: rent, duty.

Fiars: prices for grain 'struck' annually in each county on which the stipends were calculated. *Fiars Court:* originally formed to fix the value of Crown rents.

Firlot (firlat, -let, *etc.*): a measure for grain, the fourth part of a boll and equivalent to four Sc. pecks; the vessel in which a firlot was measured.

Firr: fir, fir-tree.

Flitting and removing: moving to another house or dwelling.

Forethocht: premeditated.

Foss: a pit for drowning culprits; the right of dealing with them in this way.

Free-ish and -entry: the right of way to or from a property.

Garbal teind: the tenth sheaf of the cut corn to which the rector of a parish was entitled.

Gavill: a gable.

Goofing: underpinning.

Graith: apparatus, furnishings.

Grandsher (gransher, *etc.*): a great-grandfather; an old man (see *guidsire*).

Guidsire (gudesirr, *etc.*): a grandfather; *great gudsire:* a great-grandfather (see also
   gutcher).
Gutcher (gou(t)cher, gowcher, geetcher): a grandfather; a relation, a cousin.

Habit and repute: (in Sc. law) 'held and reputed' (to be of a certain reputation); in the
   law of theft it means 'having the reputation of being a thief'; in civil law it means the
   reputation of being married, such a reputation combined with cohabitation consti-
   tuting an irregular marriage.
Haill: all, the whole of.
Heir: without qualication means the nearest heir-at-law. *Heir Male and of Provision:*
   service in these terms signifies that the lands are destined to the heir male general
   not merely to male descendants, that is, the heir may be a collateral male or an
   ascendant: *Heir Male of the Body and of Provision:* service when lands are destined
   to male descendants excluding all female descendants and the issue of all females:
   Heir of Conquest: real property acquired by purchase or otherwise than by inheritance
   (e.g. by gift) was known as 'conquest'. Where a man died childless and intestate his
   conquest went to his immediate elder brother (or to his issue) and heir of conquest.
   Heir of Entail, Taillie or Talzie: an heir who succeeds under the destination of an
   entail. *Heir of Line:* means simply *heir*, that is, the nearest heir-at-law. *Heir cum
   Beneficio Inventarii:* an heir who doubted his predecessor's solvency might submit an
   inventory of the latter's real property and by doing so obtain exemption from liability
   beyond the value of that property. *Heir of Provision:* an heir whose right lay in a
   settlement or will in the Scottish form. *Heir Portioner:* one of a number of females (or
   their issue) succeeding jointly.
Herezeld: heriot, the best horse or ox or other animal of a vassal which became the
   property of his lord on his death.
Heritor: strictly any landowner; in practice, a landowner liable to contribute to upkeep
   of the parish church.
Hutch: a measure of coals which contained two Winchester bushels.

Ilk: same (name, place or landed estate) particularly in *of that ilk* (of the same – name
   etc.) used after the surname to distinguish the senior from cadet branches of landed
   families.
Indweller: an inhabitant, resident, occupant, one who lives in a place (in Scotland 'of'
   implies 'heritable proprietor of'; a person living in a place would be described as
   'in', e.g. John Ogilvie in Kirriemuir).
Incidents: refreshments.
Infangthef: the right of judging and punishing a thief caught 'within the fang', i.e.,
   within the limit of the estate to which the right belonged.
Interdict: judicial prohibition, comparable with an injunction in England.
Intromit with: to handle or deal with, such as funds or property.
Investiture: the process by which a person is vested with a right to lands.
Ish: termination, lease: issue, means of exit. See also *free-ish and entry.*

Kain: see *Cain.*
Kest: to cast.
Knaveship: a small due in meal which by established custom was paid to the undermiller.
Knocking stock: a crude kind of mallet, sometimes called a knocking-mell, used in
   beating the hulls of barley.
Kum: see *cum.*
Ky: cows.

Labouring: tilling.
Laigh: low.
Lair: a grave, particularly a burial plot in a graveyard.
Lamb: Lammas, Candlemas.
Letter: (in Sc. law) a writ or warrant issued by the court of session under the signet,
   which contained a narrative of the facts and an order that certain things should be
   done by the addressee.
Ley (lea): untilled ground, ground left fallow.

Liferent: property held for a lifetime which cannot be disposed of further by the holder.
Litster (lister): a dyer of cloth; (v.) to dye, follow the trade of a dyer.

Mail: rent.
Mail-land: land unit containing three soums (q.v.).
Maress: marsh.
Mark (merk): an old Scottish coin worth about 1s 2d sterling (1946).
Martinmas: a term-day in Scotland, 11th November.
Meal: oatmeal.
Mercate: market.
Merchet: a marriage tax; *merchets of women:* taxes paid at marriages on behalf of the women.
Merkland: land so called because the duty paid on it to the sovereign or superior was one merk.
Miln (milln(e), myln): a mill.
Missue: a missive.
Monie: many.
Moveable estate: property not heritable, which in consequence passes to the next of kin instead of to the heir-at-law.
Muir: a moor.
Multure: the duty, in the form of a proportion of grain, taken by the proprietor or tenant of a mill on all corn ground in it: *multure court:* the court which fixed this share; *multurer:* the tacksman of a mill, a miller.

Nevoy (nevo, nefo, nevey, *etc.*): Scottish forms of nephew.

Octo: a measure of arable land, an eight part of a *Pennyland* (q.v.).
Oe (o, oi(e), oy(e), oey): a grandchild; a nephew.
Old extent: an ancient valuation of land or other property for purposes of assessment.
Orchyeard: orchard.
Oun: oven.
Outfangthef: the right of judging and punishing a thief caught outside the jurisdiction of the lord (see also *Infangthef*).
Outputter: a person who passes counterfeit coins.
Oy: see *oe*.

Passive title: denotes legal position of someone who is held liable for the debts of a deceased person because of interference in his property.
Patestones: the steps at the corner of a roof of a house to facilitate climbing to the top.
Pend: a covered entry.
Pendicle: (in Sc. law) an adjunct, accessory of privilege pertaining to heritable property or land; *all parts pendicles and pertinents:* everything forming part of or connected with the lands being conveyed (other than the regality).
Pennyland: a division of land in parts of Scotland once under Norse occupation, also arable land in Galloway and in most parts of the Highlands still reckoned in pence, farthings and octos, the average extent being about eight or nine acres.
Penny wedding: a wedding at which the guests gave a small sum of money towards the food and drink, any balance being handed over to the bride and bridegroom.
Pit and gallows: the right of punishing by hanging or drowning.
Plewed: ploughed.
Poinding: rounding up (stray animals, *etc.*).
Possess: (in Sc. law) to occupy as a tenant; seizure of movables, cattle, *etc.*, for payment of debt; to lease; *possessory judgement:* the legal rule under which a tenant of at least seven years standing cannot be turned out by another claimant other than by an action of reduction in court (see *quots*).
Pot: a dungeon; the rights of imprisoning.
Precept of sasine: a written order for the delivery of land or property as described in it.
Probative: (in Sc. law, generally in combinations) *probative document -writ -writing, etc;* a document which contains its own evidence of authenticity and validity.
Procurator Fiscal: a solicitor or lawyer practising in a lower court.

Procuratory: (in Sc. law) the authorization of one person to act for another.
Procure: (in Sc. law) to persuade or induce someone to do something criminal.
Provision: see *Heir Male and of Provision.*
Pupil: a child up to 12 (girl) and 14 (boy).
Pursuer: plaintiff, person suing in an action.

Qu-: wh-
Quha: who.
Quhytt: white.
Quot: a twentieth part of a deceased person's estate, previously paid as duty to the
  commissaries on confirmation of a testament.

Racked: strained.
Reduce: annul or set aside by legal process.
Regality: a territorial jurisdiction granted by the sovereign, with lands given *in liberam
  regalitatem,* those to whom it is granted being styled *Lords of Regality*; the territories
  over which this right existed.
Relief: (in Sc. law) a payment made by the heir of a deceased vassal to the superior in
  recognition of his legal succession to the deceased vassal.
Reset: the crime of receiving stolen property, knowing it to be such.
Resignation: see *Charter of Resignation.*
Retour: the return of extract of a decision sent to Chancery by a jury on an inquest
  declaring their decision as to heirship; the verdict of a jury.
Roup: an auction.

Sak: a plea of suit at law; the right to judge in law suits; jurisdiction in matters of
  dispute.
Sasine: a method of investiture in lands in accordance with ancient laws in which the
  presenting or delivering of earth and stone (and sometimes other symbols) was made.
Sclate: slate.
Sconcing: bevelling the scuntions of a window.
Scuncheon (scuntion, scontion, skimshion): the internal return or reveal of a window or
  door case, the inner edge of a window or doorjamb.
Seasin: see *Sasine.*
Sederunt, Acts of: the procedural rules drawn up by the court of session judges in
  accordance with their statutory powers; the acts by which lands were reseigned into
  a superior's hands.
Sequels: small amounts of corn or meal given to the servants at a mill as fees in addition
  to what was paid to the multerer (q.v.).
Sett (set): a letting or lease, synonymous with a *tack*: the pattern of cloth, especially of
  tartan.
Sickerly: surely, certainly, smartly, earnestly.
Shaw: a wood.
Sheriff: a former judicial and administrative officer, once hereditary; his duties were
  mainly carried out by the sheriff-depute.
Sheriff Depute: the principal administrative office in a county or sheriffdom, now
  obsolete.
Silver rent: rent paid in money and not in kind.
Sister-bairn: literally the child of a sister, but used to signify the child of an aunt in
  denoting cousin relationship.
Smethy (smiddy): a smithy.
Soccage: the tenure by which land was granted to a vassal on condition of his cultivating
  other lands belonging to the granter, in lieu of the performance of military service.
Sok: a jurisdiction; the district of such jurisdiction.
Sorners: gangs of vagrants.
Soum: a unit of grazing; a term expressing the proportion of cattle or sheep to a pasture.
  A *soum of sheep:* five, or in some districts, ten sheep.
Spait: flood.
Spulzie: the act of despoiling; spoliation; self-help.
Steading (stedding): a piece of ground set apart for building upon.

Stobb: a post, a stout piece of wood for driving into the ground.

Stoop: a post or support fixed in the ground or in other ways fixed in its position.

Subtack: sublet.

Sucken (or thirl): dues paid at a mill; the feudal jurisdiction having its own mill at which the tenants were bound to have their grain ground (see also *multure*).

Superior: the grantor of land to a person, who became his vassal, in return for the perpetual payment of feu-duty.

Swey: a movable instrument made of iron, rectangular in shape, fastened to one of the jambs of the chimney, from which kettles and pots were suspended over the fire.

Tack: a lease.

Tacksman: one who holds a lease.

Talzie: see *Heir of Entail, Taillie or Talzie*.

Teind: a tithe.

Tenement: a house; a building containing several separate dwellings.

Tenendry: tenants; land occupied by tenants.

Tennandry: service in harvest; labour on the roads of a barony exacted by the lord from his tenants.

Tennies: slaughter-house.

Terce: a life-rent allowed by law to a widow, being the third of the heritable subjects possessed by her husband on his death, provided the marriage has lasted for a year and a day or that there is a living child of it.

Terce land: land, the rent of which is assigned to the widow as her terce.

Testament: a will or administration; *Testament Testamentar* is one made by the testator; *Testament Dative* exists when a person dies intestate and an executor is appointed by the court.

Thame: them.

Theme: the right by which a person in whose possession stolen or looted property is found to name the person from whom he received it.

Thirl: see *sucken*.

Thole: the right of an owner to exact custom or payment for goods being taken through his land.

Threedmiln: treadmill.

Tocher: the dowry or marriage portion of a wife.

Tutor: a guardian appointed for a minor; tutors are frequently designated after the estate of a minor. *Tutor Dative:* one appointed by a court. *Tutor nominate:* one designated in a will. *Tutor-at-law:* one having a legal right of appointment.

Tyking: ticking, a linen used for making mattresses or beds, *etc.*

Uent: a vent, chimney.

Umquhile: former, late.

Unco: (adj. and adv.) extreme(ly), unusual(ly), strange(ly); (n.) a stranger.

Unlaw: any transgression of the law; an act of injustice, an injury; a fine; a law which has no real authority.

Uterine: born of the same mother but different fathers.

Vassal: a tenant holding lands under a lord.

Vitious intromission: the unwarranted dealing with the movable estate of a deceased person.

Wadset: a pledge of land with right of recovery by the debtor on payment.

Waith: a waif.

Walkmylne: a fuller's mill.

Wobster (wobstar): a weaver.

Wrak: wreck; whatever is thrown up by the sea; seaweed; trash, refuse of all kinds.

Writer: a solicitor.

Yard: a garden.

Yett: a gate.

APPENDIX D

LIST OF PRE-1855 PARISHES SHOWING COUNTY AND COMMISSARIOT

List of Parishes showing County and Commissariot

Abbreviation used	County	Commissariot
Abn	Aberdeen	Aberdeen
Ang	Angus	
Arg	Argyll	Argyll
Ayr	Ayr	
Ban	Banff	
Ber	Berwick	
Bre		Brechin
But	Bute	
Cai	Caithness	Caithness
Cla	Clackmannan	
Dbl		Dunblane
Dbn	Dunbarton	
Dfs	Dumfries	Dumfries
Dkd		Dunkeld
Edn		Edinburgh
ELn	East Lothian	
Fif	Fife	
Gla		Glasgow
Ham		Hamilton and Campsie
Inv	Inverness	Inverness
Isl		The Isles
Kdn	Kincardine	
Kin	Kinross	
Klr	Kirkcudbright	Kirkcudbright
Lan	Lanark	Lanark
Ldr		Lauder
Mid	Midlothian	
Mor	Moray	Moray
Nai	Nairn	
Ork	Orkney	Orkney and Shetland
Pbl	Peebles	Peebles
Per	Perth	
Ren	Renfrew	
Ros	Ross and Cromarty	Ross
Rox	Roxburgh	
Sel	Selkirk	
She	Shetland	
StA		St Andrews
Sti	Stirling	Stirling

O

Abbreviation used	County	Commissariot
Sut	Sutherland	
WLn	West Lothian	
Wig	Wigtown	Wigtown

NOTES

a in the commissariot column indicates parishes formed in or after 1823 from which date the boundaries of the commissariots (until abolished in 1876) co-incided with those of the sheriffdoms.

[1]Part in Lan.
[2]Part in Gla.
[3]Part in StA.
[4]Part in Sti.
[5]Part in Sti.
[6]During Commonwealth.

	County	Commis- sariot		County	Commis- sariot
Abbey	Ren	Gla	Auchterderran	Fif	StA
Abbey St Bathans	Ber	Ldr	Auchtergaven	Per	Dkd
Abbotshall	Fif	StA	Auchterhouse	Ang	Dkd
Abdie	Fif	StA	Auchterless	Abn	Abn
Abercorn	WLn	Dkd	Auchtermuchty	Fif	StA
Aberdalgie	Per	Dkd	Auchtertool	Fif	Dkd
Aberdeen	Abn	Abn	Auldearn	Nai	Mor
Aberdour (Aberdeen)	Abn	Abn	Avoch	Ros	Ros
Aberdour (Fife)	Fif	Dkd	Avondale	Lan	Gla
Aberfeldy	Per	a	Ayr	Ayr	Gla
Aberfoyle	Per	Dbl	Ayton	Ber	Edn
Aberlady	ELn	Dkd			
Aberlemno	Ang	StA	Baldernock	Sti	Gla
Aberlour	Ban	Mor	Balfron	Sti	Gla
Abernethy	Pcr	Dbl	Ballachulish and Cor-		
Abernethy and			ran of Ardgour	Arg	a
Kineardine	Kdn	StA	Ballantrae	Ayr	Gla
Abernyte	Per	Dkd	Ballingry	Fif	StA
Aboyne	Abn	Abn	Balmaclellan	Kir	Kir
Acharacle	Arg	a	Balmaghie	Kir	Kir
Airlie	Ang	StA	Balmerino	Fif	StA
Airth	StA	Sti	Balquhidder	Per	Dbl
Alford	Abn	Abn	Banchory-Devenick	Kin	Abn
Alloa	Ayr	Gla	Banchory-Ternan	Kin	Abn
Alness	Ros	Ros	Banff	Ban	Abn
Alva (Stirling)	Sti	Sti	Bargrennan	Wig	a
Alvah (Banff)	Ban	Abn	Barony	Lan	Gla
Alves	Mor	Mor	Barr	Ayr	Gla
Alvie	Inv	Inv	Barra (Inverness)	Inv	a
Alyth	Ang	Dkd	Barry (Forfar)	Ang	StA
Ancrum	Rox	Pbl	Barvas	Ros	Isl
Annan	Dfs	Dfs	Bathgate	WLa	Edn
Anstruther-Easter	Fif	StA	Beath (Fife)	Fif	Dkd
Anstruther-Wester	Fif	StA	Bedrule	Rox	Pbl
Anwoth	Kir	Kir	Beith (Ayr)	Ayr	Gla
Appin	Arg	Arg	Belhelvie	Abn	Abn
Applecross	Ros	Ros	Bellie	Mor	Mor
Applegarth (and			Bendochy	Per	StA
Sibbaldbie)	Dfs	Dfs	Benholm	Kin	StA
Arbilot	Ang	StA	Bervie	Kin	StA
Arbroath	Ang	StA	Biggar	Lan	Lan
Arbuthnott	Kin	StA	Birnie	Mor	Mor
Ardchattan	Arg	Arg	Birsay	Ork	Ork
Ardclach	Nai	Mor	Birse	Abn	Abn
Ardersier	Inv	Ros	Blackford	Per	Dbl
Ardnamurchan	Arg	a	Blair-Athol	Per	Dkd
Ardrossan	Avr	Gla	Blairgowrie	Per	StA
Arisaig	Inv	a	Blantyre	Lan	Gla
Arngask	Per	Dkd	Boharm	Ban	Mor
Arrochar	Dbn	Gla	Boleskine	Inv	Inv
Ashkirk	Sel	Pbl	Bolton	ELn	Edn
Assynt	Sut	Cai	Bonhill	Dbn	Gla
Athelstaneford	ELn	Edn	Borgue	Kir	Kir
Auchindoir and			Bo'ness	WLn	Edn
Kearn	Abn	Abn	Borthwick	Rox	Pee
Auchinleck	Ayr	Gla	Bothkennar	Sti	Sti
Auchterarder	Per	Dbl	Bothwell	Lan	Gla

	County	Commis-sariot		County	Commis-sariot
Botriphnie	Ban	Mor	Clatt	Abn	Abn
Bourtie	Abn	Pbl	Cleish	Kin	StA
Bowden	Rox	Pbl	Closeburn	Dfs	Gla
Bower	Cai	Cai	Clunie (Perth)	Per	Dkd
Bowmore (or			Cluny (Aberdeen)	Abn	Abn
Kilarrow)	Arg	Arg	Clyne	Sut	Cai
Boyndie	Ban	Abn	Cockburnspath	ELn	Edn
Bracadale	Inv	Isl	Cockpen	Edn	Edn
Brechin	Ang	Bre	Coldingham	Ber	Ldr
Bressay	She	Ork	Coldstream	Ber	Ldr
Broughton	Rox	Pbl	Colinton	Edn	Edn
Brydekirk	Dfs	a	Coll	Arg	Isl
Buchanan	Sti	Sti	Collace	Per	StA
Buittle	Kir	Kir	Collessie	Fif	StA
Bunkle and Preston	Ber	Ldr	Colmonell	Ayr	Gla
Burntisland	Fif	StA	Colonsay	Arg	Isl
Burra and Quarff	Ork	Ork	Colvend	Kir	Dfs
			Comrie	Per	Dbl
Cabrach	Ban	Abn	Contin	Ros	Ros
Cadder	Lan	Gla	Corsock-Bridge	Kir	a
Caddonfoot	Sel	a	Corstorphine	Mid	Edn
Cairney	Abn	Abn	Cortachy and Clova	Ang	Bre
Callander	Per	Dbl	Coull	Abn	Abn
Cambuslang	Lan	Gla	Coupar-Angus	Per	Dkd
Cambusnethan	Lan	Gla	Covington and		
Cameron	Fif	StA	Thankerton	Lan	Lan
Cambeltown	Ard	Ros	Coylton	Ayr	Gla
Campsie	Sti	Ham	Craig	Ang	StA
Canisbay	Cai	Cai	Craigie	Ayr	Gla
Canonbie	Rox	Dfs	Craignish	Arg	Arg
Canongate	Edn	Edn	Crail	Fif	StA
Caputh	Per	Dkd	Crailing	Rox	Pbl
Cardross	Dbn	Ham	Cramond	Edn	Dkd
Careston	Ang	Bre	Cranshaws	Ber	Ldr
Cargill	Per	Dkd	Cranston	Mid	Edn
Carlaverock	Dfs	Dfs	Crathie and Braemar	Abn	Abn
Carloway	Ros	a	Crawford	Lan	Lan
Carluke	Lan	Lan	Crawfordjohn	Lan	Lan
Carmichael	Lan	Lan	Creich (Sutherland)	Sut	Cai
Carmunnock	Lan	Gla	Crichton	Mid	Edn
Carmylie	Ang	Bre	Criech (Fife)	Fif	StA
Carnbee	Fif	StA	Crieff	Per	Dkd
Carnock	Fif	Sti	Crimond	Abn	Abn
Carnwath	Lan	Lan	Cromarty	Ros	Ros
Carriden	ELn	Edn	Cromdale, Inverallan,		
Carrington	Edn	Edn	(and Advie)	Mor	Mor
Carsphairn	Kir	Kir	Crossmichael	Kir	Kir
Carstairs	Lan	Lan	Croy and Dalcross	Nai	Inv
Castleton	Rox	Pbl	Cruden	Abn	Abn
Cathcart	Ren[1]	Ham[2]	Cullen	Ban	Abn
Cavers	Rox	Pbl	Culross	Per	Dbl
Cawdor	Nai	Mor	Culsalmond	Abn	Abn
Ceres	Fif	StA	Culter	Lan	Lan
Channelkirk	Ber	Ldr	Cults	Fif	StA
Chapel of Garioch	Abn	Abn	Cumbernauld	Dbn	Gla
Chirnside	Ber	Ldr	Cumbraes	But	Isl
Clackmannan	Cla	StA	Cumlodden	Arg	Arg

	County	Commis-sariot		County	Commis-sariot
Cummertrees	Dfs	Dfs	Dundonald	Ayr	Gla
Cupar	Fif	StA	Dunfermline	Fif	StA
Currie	Edn	Edn	Dunino	Fif	StA
			Dunipace	Sti	Sti
Dailly	Ayr	Gla	Dunkeld	Per	Dkd
Dairsie	Fif	StA	Dunlop	Ayr	Gla
Dalavich	Arg	Arg	Dunnet	Cai	Cai
Dalbeattie	Kir	a	Dunnichen	Ang	Bre
Dalgetty	Fif	Dkd	Dunning	Per	Dbl
Dalkeith	Edn	Edn	Dunnottar	Kin	StA
Dallas	Mor	Mor	Dunoon and Kilmun	Arg	Arg
Dalmellington	Ayr	Gla	Dunrossness	She	Ork
Dalmeny	WLn	Edn	Dunscore	Dfs	Lan
Dalry (Ayr)	Ayr	Gla	Dunse	Ber	Ldr
Dalry (Kirkcud-			Dunsyre	Lan	Lan
bright)	Kir	Kir	Durness	Sut	Cai
Dalrymple	Ayr	Gla	Duror	Arg	a
Dalserf	Lan	Ham	Durris	Kin	StA
Dalton	Dfs	Dfs	Durrisdeer	Dfs	Dfs
Dalziel	Lan	Gla	Duthil and		
Daviot	Abn	Abn	Rothiemurchus	Inv	Inv
Daviot and			Dyce	Abn	Abn
Dunlichty	Nai	Inv	Dyke	Mor	Mor
Deerness	Ork	Ork	Dysart	Fif	StA
Delting	She	Ork			
Denny	Sti	Sti	Eaglesham	Ren	Gla
Deskford	Ban	Abn	Earlston	Ber	Ldr
Dingwall	Ros	Ros	Eassle and Nevay	Ang	StA
Dirleton	ELn	Edn	East Kilbride	Lan	Ham
Dollar	Cla	Sti	Eastwood	Ren	Gla
Dolphington	Lan	Lan	Eccles	Ber	Ldr
Dores	Kdn	StA	Ecclesmachen	WLn	Edn
Dornoch (Suther-			Echt	Abn	Abn
land)	Sut	Cai	Eckford	Rox	Pbl
Dornock (Dumfries)	Dfs	Dfs	Eday and Pharay	Ork	Ork
Douglas	Lan	Lan	Edderton	Ros	Ros
Dowally	Per	Dkd	Eddlestone	Pbl	Pbl
Drainie	Mor	Mor	Eddrachillis	Sut	Cai
Dreghorn	Ayr	Gla	Edgerston	Rox	a
Dron	Per	Dbl	Edinburgh	Edn	Edn
Drumblade	Abn	Abn	Edinkillie	Mor	Mor
Drumelzier	Rox	Pbl	Ednam	Rox	Pbl
Drumoak	Abn	Abn	Edrom	Ber	Ldr
Dryfesdale	Dfs	Dfs	Edzell	Ang	StA
Drymen	Sti	Gla	Elgin	Mor	Mor
Duddingston	Edn	Edn	Elie	Fif	StA
Duffus	Mor	Mor	Ellon	Abn	Abn
Duirinish	Inv	Isl	Enzie	Mor	a
Dull	Per	Dkd	Errol	Per	StA
Dumbarton	Dbn	Gla	Erskine	Ren	Gla
Dumfries	Dfs	Dfs	Eskdalemuir	Dfs	Dfs
Dun	Ang	StA	Ettrick	Sel	Pbl
Dunbar	ELn	Edn	Evie and Rendall	Ork	Ork
Dunbarney	Per	StA	Ewes	Rox	Dfs
Dunblane	Per	Dbl	Eyemouth	Ber	Ldr
Dunbog	Fif	StA			
Dundee	Ang	StA	Fair Isle	Ork	Ork

	County	Commissariot		County	Commissariot
Fala and Soutra	Edn	Edn	Glass	Abn	Mor
Falkirk	Sti	Sti	Glassary	Arg	Arg
Falkland	Fif	StA	Glasserton	Wig	Wig
Farnell	Ang	Bre	Glassford	Lan	Gla
Farr	Sut	Cai	Glenbervie	Kdn	Bre
Fearn (Forfar)	Ang	Dkd	Glenbucket	Abn	Abn
Fearn (Ross)	Ros	Ros	Glencairn	Dfs	Dfs
Fenwick	Ayr	Gla	Glencoe and		
Ferry-Port-on-Craig	Fif	StA	Ballachulish	Arg	a
Fetlar	She	Ork	Glencross	Mid	Edn
Fettercairn	Kdn	StA	Glendevon	Per	Dbl
Fetteresso	Kdn	StA	Glenelg	Inv	Arg
Findo-Gask	Per	Dbl	Glenholm	Pbl	Pbl
Fintray (Aberdeen)	Abn	Abn	Glenisla	Ang	StA
Fintry (Stirling)	Sti	Gla	Glenmuick, Tullich,		
Firth and Stennes	Ork	Ork	etc.	Abn	Abn
Flisk	Fif	StA	Glenorchy & Inishail	Arg	Arg
Flotta	Ork	Ork	Glenrinnes	Ban	a
Fodderty	Ros	Ros	Glenshiel	Ros	Ros
Fogo	Ber	Ldr	Golspie	Sut	Dfs
Fordoun	Kdn	StA	Gorbals	Lan	Ham
Fordyce	Ban	Abn	Gordon	Ber	Ldr
Forfar	Ang	StA	Govan	Lan	Ham
Forgan	Fif	StA	Graitney (or Gretna)	Dfs	Dfs
Forgandenny	Per	Dkd	Grange	Ban	Mor
Forglen	Ban	Abn	Greenlaw	Kir	Kir
Forgue	Abn	Abn	Greenock	Ren	Gla
Forres	Mor	Mor	Guthrie	Ang	Bre
Fort-Augustus or					
Abertarff	Inv	Inv	Haddington	ELn	Edn
Forteviot	Per	StA	Halfmorton	Dfs	Dfs
Fortingall	Per	Dkd	Halkirk	Cai	Cai
Foss	Per	Dkd	Hamilton	Lan	Lan
Fossoway and			Harray	Ork	Ork
Tulliebole	Kin	Dbl	Harris	Inv	a
Foula	Ork	Ork	Hawick	Rox	Peb
Foulden	Ber	Ldr	Heriot	Mid	Edn
Foveran	Abn	Abn	Hobkirk	Rox	Pbl
Fowlis-Easter	Per	StA	Hoddam	Dfs	Dfs
Fowlis-Wester	Per	Dbl	Holm and Paplay	Ork	Ork
Fraserburgh	Abn	Abn	Holywood	Dfs	Dfs
Fyvie	Abn	Abn	Houston and Killel-		
			lan	Ren	Gla
Gairloch	Ros	Ros	Hownam	Rox	Pbl
Galashiels	Sel	Pbl	Hoy and Graemsay	Ork	Ork
Galston	Ayr	Gla	Humbie	ELn	Edn
Gamrie	Ban	Abn	Hume	Ber	Ldr
Gargunnock	Sti	Sti	Huntly	Abn	Abn
Gartly	Abn	Mor	Hutton (Berwick)	Ber	Ldr
Garvald	ELn	Edn	Hutton and Corrie		
Garvock	Kdn	StA	(Dumfries)	Dfs	Dfs
Gigha	Arg	Isl			
Girthon	Kir	Kir	Inch (Wigtown)	Wig	Wig
Girvan	Ayr	Kir	Inchinnan	Ren	Gla
Gladsmuir	ELn	Edn	Inchture	Per	StA
Glamis	Ang	StA	Innerleithen	Pbl	Pbl
Glasgow	Lan	Gla	Innerwick	ELn	Edn

	County	Commis-sariot		County	Commis-sariot
Insch (Aberdeen)	Abn	Abn	Killearn	Sti	Gla
Inverallan	Inv	Inv	Killearnan	Ros	Ros
Inveraray (and			Killin	Per	Dkd
Glenaray)	Arg	Arg	Kilmacolm	Ren	Gla
Inverarity and Methy	Ang	StA	Kilmadock	Per	Dbl
Inveravon	Ban	Mor	Kilmalie	Inv	Arg
Inverchaolain	Arg	Arg	Kilmany (Fife)	Fif	StA
Inveresk	Mid	Edn	Kilmarnock	Ayr	Gla
Inverkeillor	Ang	StA	Kilmaronock	Dbn	Dbn
Inverkeithing	Fif	StA	Kilmartin	Arg	Arg
Inverkeithny	Ban	Mor	Kilmaurs	Ayr	Gla
Inverkip	Ren	Gla	Kilmelford	Arg	Arg
Inverness	Inv	Inv	Kilmeny (Argyll)	Arg	Isl
Inverurie	Abn	Abn	Kilmodan	Arg	Arg
Iona	Arg	a	Kilmonivaig	Inv	Arg
Irongray	Kir	Dfs	Kilmorack	Ros	Ros
Irvine	Ayr	Gla	Kilmore and		
			Kilbride	Arg	Arg
Jedburgh	Rox	Pbl	Kilmorich	Arg	Arg
Johnstone (Dumfries)	Dfs	Gla	Kilmory	But	Isl
Jura	Arg	Isl	Kilmuir	Inv	a
			Kilmuir-Easter	Ros	Ros
Keig	Abn	Abn	Kilmun	Arg	Arg
Keir	Dfs	Dfs	Kilninian and		
Keith	Ban	Mor	Kilmore	Arg	Isl
Keith-hall and			Kilninver	Arg	Arg
Kinkell	Abn	Abn	Kilrenny	Fif	StA
Kells	Kir	Kir	Kilspindie	Per	StA
Kelso	Rox	Pbl	Kilsyth	Sti	Sti
Kelton	Kir	Kir	Kiltarlity	Inv	Inv
Kemback	Fif	StA	Kiltearn	Ros	Ros
Kemnay	Abn	Abn	Kilwinning	Ayr	Gla
Kenmore	Per	Dkd	Kincardine (Perth)	Per	Dbl
Kennoway	Fif	StA	Kincardine (Ross)	Ros	Ros
Kettins	Ang	StA	Kincardine O'Neil	Abn	Abn
Kettle	Fif	StA	Kinclaven	Per	Dkd
Kilbarchan	Ren	Gla	Kinfauns	Per	StA
Kilberry	Arg	Arg	Kingarth	But	Isl
Kilbirnie	Ayr	Gla	King-Edward	Abn	Abn
Kilbrandon and			Kinghorn	Fif	StA
Kilchattan	Arg	Arg	Kinglassie	Fif	StA
Kilbride	Arg	Arg	Kingoldrum	Ang	Bre[3]
Kilbucho, etc.	Pbl	Pbl	Kingsbarns	Fif	StA
Kilcalmonell and			Kingussie and Insh	Inv	Inv
Kilberry	Arg	Arg	Kinloch	Per	Dkd
Kilchoman	Arg	Isl	Kinloch-Rannoch	Per	Dkd
Kilchrenan and			Kinlochspelvie	Arg	a
Dalavich	Arg	Arg	Kinloss	Mor	Mor
Kilconquhar	Fif	StA	Kinnaird	Ang	Bre
Kildalton	Arg	Isl	Kinneff and		
Kildonan	Sut	Cai	Catterline	Kdn	StA
Kildrummy	Abn	Abn	Kinnell	Ang	StA
Kilfinan	Arg	Arg	Kinnellar	Abn	Abn
Kilfinichen and			Kinnethmont	Abn	Abn
Kilvickeon	Arg	Isl	Kinnettles	Ang	StA
Killean and			Kinnoull	Per	StA
Kilchenzie	Arg	Arg	Kinross	Kin	StA

	County	Commis-sariot		County	Commis-sariot
Kintail	Ros	Ros	Leochel-Cushnie	Abn	Abn
Kintore	Abn	Abn	Lerwick	She	Ork
Kippen	Per	Dbl	Leslie (Aberdeen)	Abn	Abn
Kirkbean	Kir	Dfs	Leslie (Fife)	Fif	Dkd
Kirkcaldy	Fif	StA	Lesmahagow	Lan	Lan
Kirkcolm	Wig	Wig	Leswalt	Wig	Wig
Kirkconnel	Dfs	Dfs	Lethendy and		
Kirkcowan	Wig	Wig	Kinloch	Per	Dkd
Kirkcudbright	Kir	Kir	Lethnott and Navar	Ang	Bre
Kirkden	Ang	StA	Leuchars	Fif	StA
Kirkgunzeon	Kir	Kir	Libberton (Lanark)	Lan	Lan
Kirkhill	Inv	Inv	Liberton (Edinburgh)	Mid	Edn
Kirkhope	Sel	a	Liff, Benvie, and		
Kirkinner	Wig	Wig	Invergowrie	Ang	StA
Kirkintilloch	Dbn	Gla	Lilliesleaf	Rox	Pbl
Kirkliston	WLn	Edn	Linlithgow	WLn	Edn
Kirkmabreck	Kir	Kir	Linton	Rox	Pbl
Kirkmahoe	Dfs	Dfs	Lintrathen	Ang	StA
Kirkmaiden	Wig	Wig	Lismore	Arg	Arg
Kirkmichael (Ayr)	Ayr	Gla	Little Dunkeld	Per	Dkd
Kirkmichael (Banff)	Ban	Mor	Livingston	WLn	Edn
Kirkmichael			Lochalsh	Ros	Ros
(Dumfries)	Dfs	Dfs	Lochbroom	Ros	Ros
Kirkmichael (Perth)	Per	Dkd	Lochcarron	Ros	Ros
Kirknewton and			Lochgilphead	Arg	a
East-Calder	Mid	Edn	Lochgoilhead	Arg	Arg
Kirkoswald	Ayr	Gla	Lochlee	Ang	Bre
Kirkpatrick-Durham	Kir	Dfs	Lochmaben	Dfs	Dfs
Kirkpatrick-Fleming	Dfs	Dfs	Lochranza	But	Isl
Kirkpatrick-Juxta	Dfs	Dfs	Lochrutton	Kir	Dfs
Kirktown			Lochs	Ros	a
(Roxburgh)	Rox	Pbl	Lochwinnoch	Ren	Gla
Kirkurd	Pbl	Pbl	Logie (Fife)	Fif	StA
Kirkwall and St Ola	Ork	Ork	Logie (Perth)	Per	Dbl[5]
Kirriemuir	Ang	StA	Logiealmond	Per	a
Knockando	Mor	Mor	Logie-Buchan	Abn	Abn
Knockbain	Ros	Ros	Logie-Coldstone	Abn	Abn
			Logie-Easter	Ros	Ros
Ladykirk	Ber	Ldr	Logie-Pert	Ang	StA
Laggan	Inv	Inv	Logierait	Per	Dkd
Lairg	Sut	Cai	Longforgan	Per	StA
Lamington-see			Longformacus	Ber	Ldr
Wandell			Longside	Abn	Abn
Lanark	Lan	Lan	Lonmay	Abn	Abn
Langholm	Dfs	Dfs	Loth	Sut	Cai
Langton	Ber	Ldr	Loudoun	Ayr	Gla
Larbert	Sti	Sti	Lumphanan	Abn	Abn
Largo	Fif	StA	Lunan	Ang	StA
Largs	Ayr	Gla	Lundie and Fowlis	Ang	StA
Lasswade	Mid	Edn	Luss	Dbn	Gla
Latheron	Cai	Cai	Lyne and Megget	Pbl	Pbl
Lauder	Ber	Ldr			
Laurencekirk	Kdn	StA	Madderty	Per	Dkd
Lecropt	Sti	Dbn[4]	Mains	Ang	StA
Legerwood	Ber	Ldr	Makerston	Rox	Pbl
Leith (North)	Mid	Edn	Manor	Pbl	Pbl
Leith (South)	Mid	Edn	Markinch	Fif	StA

	County	Commissariot		County	Commissariot
Marnoch	Ban	Mor	Newburgh	Fif	StA
Maryculter	Kdn	Abn	Newburn	Fif	StA
Marykirk	Kdn	StA	New Cumnock	Ayr	Gla
Maryton	Ang	Bre	New Deer	Abn	Abn
Mauchline	Ayr	Gla	New Kilpatrick	Dbn	Sti[6]
Maxton	Rox	Pbl	Newhills	Abn	Abn
Maybole	Ayr	Gla	Newlands	Pbl	Pbl
Mearns	Ren	Gla	New Luce	Wig	Wig
Megget	Pbl	Pbl	New Machar	Abn	Abn
Meigle	Per	Dkd	New Monkland	Lan	Ham
Melrose	Rox	Pbl	New Spynie	Mor	Mor
Menmuir	Ang	Dkd	Newton	Mid	Edn
Merton	Ber	Ldr	Newton-on-Ayr	Ayr	Gla
Methlick	Abn	Abn	Newtyle	Ang	StA
Methven	Per	StA	Nigg (Kincardine)	Kdn	StA
Mid-Calder	Mid	Edn	Nigg (Ross)	Ros	Ros
Middlebie	Dfs	Dfs	North Berwick	ELn	Edn
Midmar	Abn	Abn	North Bute	But	a
Mid and South Yell	She	Ork	North Knapdale	Arg	Arg
Minnigaff	Kir	Wig	North Leith	Mid	Edn
Minto	Rox	Pbl	Northmavine	She	Ork
Mochrum	Wig	Wig	North Ronaldshay	Ork	Ork
Moffat	Dfs	Dfs	North Uist	Inv	Isl
Moneydie	Per	Dkd	North Yell	She	Ork
Monifieth	Ang	StA			
Monikie	Ang	Bre	Oa	Arg	a
Monimail	Fif	StA	Oathlaw	Ang	Bre
Monkton and			Ochiltree	Ayr	Gla
Prestwick	Ayr	Gla	Old Cumnock	Ayr	Gla
Monquhitter	Abn	Abn	Old Deer	Abn	Abn
Montrose	Ang	Bre	Oldhamstocks	ELn	Edn
Monymusk	Abn	Abn	Old, or West,		
Monzie (Perth)	Per	Dbl	Kilpatrick	Dbn	Gla
Monzievaird	Per	Dbl	Old Luce	Wig	Wig
Moonjie (Fife)	Fif	StA	Old Machar	Abn	Abn
Mordington	Ber	Ldr	Old Meldrum	Abn	Abn
Morebattle	Rox	Pbl	Old Monkland	Lan	Ham
Morham	ELn	Edn	Olrig	Cai	Cai
Mortlach	Ban	Abn	Ordiquhill	Ban	Abn
Morton	Dfs	Dfs	Ormiston	Mid	Edn
Morvern	ELn	Edn	Orphir	Ork	Ork
Moulin	Per	Dkd	Orwell	Kin	StA
Mousewald	Dfs	Dfs	Oxnam	Rox	Pbl
Moy and Dalarossie	Inv	Inv	Oyne	Abn	Abn
Muckairn	Arg	Arg			
Muckart	Per	StA	Paisley	Ren	Gla
Muiravonside	Sti	Sti	Panbride	Ang	Bre
Muirkirk	Ayr	Gla	Papa-Stour	Ork	Ork
Murroes	Ang	StA	Papa-Westray	Ork	Ork
Muthill	Per	Dbl	Parton	Kir	Kir
			Peebles	Pbl	Pbl
			Pencaitland	ELn	Edn
Nairn	Nai	Mor	Penicuik	Mid	Edn
Neilston	Ren	Gla	Penninghame	Wig	Wig
Nenthorn	Ber	Ldr	Penpont	Dfs	Dfs
Nesting	She	Ork	Persie	Per	a
New Abbey	Kir	Dfs	Perth	Per	StA
Newbattle	Mid	Edn	Peterculter	Abn	Abn

	County	Commis-sariot		County	Commis-sariot
Peterhead	Abn	Abn	St Cuthberts	Mid	Edn
Pettinain	Lan	Lan	St Cyrus	Kdn	StA
Petty	Inv	Mor	St Fergus	Ban	Abn
Pitsligo	Abn	Abn	St Kilda	Inv	Isl
Pittenweem	Fif	StA	St Madoes	Per	Dbl
Polmont	Sti	Sti	St Martins	Per	Dkd
Polwarth	Ber	Ldr	St Monance (or		
Port-Glasgow	Ren	Gla	Abercrombie)	Fif	StA
Port of Menteith	Per	Dbl	St Mungo	Dfs	Dfs
Portmoak	Kin	StA	St·Ninians	Sti	Sti
Portnahaven	Arg	a	St Quivox, etc.	Ayr	Gla
Portpatrick	Wig	Wig	St Vigeans	Ang	StA
Portree	Inv	Isl	Salen (Argyll)	Arg	a
Premnay	Abn	Abn	Saline (Fife)	Fif	Sti
Prestonkirk	ELn	Edn	Salton	ELn	Edn
Prestonpans	ELn	Edn	Sanday	Ork	Ork
			Sandness	She	Ork
Queensferry	WLn	Edn	Sandsting and		
			Aithsting	She	Ork
Rafford	Mor	Mor	Sandwick	Ork	Ork
Rathen	Abn	Abn	Sandwick and		
Ratho	Mid	Edn	Cunningsburgh	She	Ork
Rathven	Ban	Abn	Sanquhar	Dfs	Dfs
Rattray	Per	Dkd	Savoch	Abn	a
Rayne	Abn	Abn	Scone	Per	StA
Reay	Cai	Cai	Scoonie	Fif	StA
Redgorton	Per	Dkd	Seafield	Ban	a
Renfrew	Ren	Ham	Selkirk	Sel	StA
Rerrick	Kir	Kir	Shapinshay	Ork	Ork
Rescobie	Ang	StA	Shotts	Lan	Ham
Resolis	Ros	Ros	Skene	Abn	Abn
Rhynd	Per	StA	Skipness	Arg	Arg
Rhynie and Essie	Abn	Mor	Skirling	Pbl	Pbl
Riccarton	Ayr	Gla	Slains	Abn	Abn
Roberton	Rox	Pbl	Slamannan	Sti	Sti
Rogart	Sut	Cai	Sleat	Inv	Isl
Rosemarkie	Ros	Ros	Smailholm	Rox	Pbl
Roseneath	Dbn	Gla	Small Isles	Inv	a
Rosskeen	Ros	Ros	Snizort	Inv	a
Rothes	Mor	Mor	Sorbie	Wig	Wig
Rothesay	But	Isl	Sorn	Ayr	Gla
Rothiemay	Ban	Mor	Southdean (and		
Rothiemurchus	Inv	Inv	Abbotrule)	Rox	Pbl
Ronsay and Egilshay	Ork	Ork	Southend	Arg	Arg
Row	Dbn	Gla	South Knapdale	Arg	Arg
Roxburgh	Rox	Pbl	South Leith	Mid	Edn
Rutherglen	Lan	Gla	South Ronaldshay		
Ruthven	Ang	Dkd	and Burray	Ork	Ork
Ruthwell	Dfs	Dfs	South Uist (Outer		
			Hebrides)	Inv	a
Saddell and Skipness	Arg	Arg	Speymouth	Mor	Mor
St Andrews (Orkney)	Ork	Ork	Spott	ELn	Edn
St Andrews-			Sprouston	Rox	Pbl
Lhanbryde	Mor	Mor	Stair	Ayr	Gla
St Andrews and St			Stenton	ELn	Edn
Leonards (Fife)	Fif	StA	Stevenston	Ayr	Gla
St Boswells	Rox	Pbl	Stewarton	Ayr	Gla

	County	Commissariot		County	Commissariot
Stirling	Sti	Sti	Trinity-Gask	Per	Dbl
Stitchel (and Hume)	Rox	Pbl	Troqueer	Kir	Dfs
Stobhill	Mid	a	Tulliallan	Fif	StA
Stobo	Pbl	Pbl	Tullynessle, Forbes,		
Stonehouse	Lan	Gla	(and Kearn)	Abn	Abn
Stoneykirk	Wig	Wig	Tundergarth	Dfs	Dfs
Stornoway	Ros	Isl	Turriff	Abn	Abn
Stow	Mid	Edn	Tweedsmuir	Pbl	Pbl
Stracathro	Ang	Bre	Twynholm	Kir	Kir
Strachan	Kdn	Bre	Tynron	Dfs	Dfs
Strachur	Arg	Arg	Tyree	Arg	Isl
Straiton	Ayr	Gla	Tyrie	Abn	Abn
Stralachlan	Arg	Arg			
Stranraer	Wig	Wig	Udny	Abn	Abn
Strath	Inv	Isl	Uig	Ros	a
Strathblane	Sti	Gla	Unst	She	Ork
Strathdon	Abn	Abn	Uphall	WLn	Edn
Strathfillan	Per	a	Urquhart (Elgin)	Mor	Mor
Strathmartine	Ang	StA	Urquhart and		
Strathmiglo	Fif	Dkd	Glenmoriston	Inv	Inv
Strichen	Abn	Abn	Urquhart and		
Stromness	Ork	Ork	Logie-Wester	Mor	Mor
Stronsay	Ork	Ork	Urr	Kir	Kir
Sunart or Strontian	Arg	Arg	Urray	Ros	Ros
Swinton (and					
Simprim)	Ber	Ldr			
Symington (Ayr)	Ayr	Gla	Walls (Shetland)	She	Ork
Symington (Lanark)	Lan	Lan	Walls (Orkney)	Ork	Ork
			Walston	Lan	Lan
Tain	Ros	Ros	Wamphray	Dfs	Dfs
Tannadice	Ang	StA	Wandell and		
Tarbat	Ros	Ros	Lamington	Lan	Lan
Tarbert	Arg	a	Wanlockhead	Dfs	a
Tarbolton	Ayr	Gla	Watten	Cai	Cai
Tarland (and Migvie)	Abn	Abn	Weem	Per	Dkd
Tarves	Abn	Abn	Wemyss	Fif	StA
Tealing	Ang	Dkd	West Calder	Mid	Edn
Temple	Mid	Edn	Westerkirk	Dfs	Dfs
Tenandry	Per	a	West Kilbride	Ayr	Gla
Terregles	Rox	Dfs	West Linton	Pbl	Pbl
Teviothead	Rox	a	Westray	Ork	Ork
Thurso	Cai	Cai	Westruther	Ber	Ldr
Tibbermore	Per	Dkd	Whalsay and Skerries	She	Ork
Tillicoultry	Cla	Dbl	Whitburn	WLn	Edn
Tingwall	She	Ork	Whitekirk and		
Tinwald	Dfs	Dfs	Tynninghame	ELn	Edn
Tobermory	Arg	a	Whiteness and		
Tongland	Kir	Kir	Weisdale	She	Ork
Tongue	Sut	Cai	Whithorn	Wig	Wig
Torosay	Arg	Isl	Whitsome (and		
Torphichen	Mid	Edn	Hilton)	Ber	Ldr
Torryburn	Fif	StA	Whittinghame	ELn	Edn
Torthorwald	Dfs	Dfs	Wick	Cai	Cai
Tough	Abn	Abn	Wigtown	Wig	Wig
Towie	Abn	Abn	Wilton	Rox	Pbl
Tranent	ELn	Edn	Wiston and		
Traquair	Pbl	Pbl	Roberton	Lan	Lan

	County	Commis-sariot
Yarrow	Sel	Pbl
Yester (or Gifford)	ELn	Edn
Yetholm	Rox	Pbl

APPENDIX E

DIRECTORIES PRIOR TO 1860

GENERAL

Findley's Directory to Gentlemen's Seats, Villages, etc. in Scotland 1843.

Pigot's Commercial Directory of Scotland, Ireland and the four most northern counties of England for 1820–21 and 1822, containing a representation of the professional and mercantile inhabitants of the principal towns. . . Embellished with . . . maps of Scotland and Ireland. (Manchester, 1820).

Pigot's New Commercial Directory of Scotland . . . containing . . . directories of Edinburgh, Glasgow, and every other town . . . and village. 1825–6, 1826–7, 1837.

Slater's (Kelly's) Royal National . . . Directory and Topography of Scotland etc. 1852, 1860, 1867 etc.

ABERDEEN

The Aberdeen Almanack and Northern Register etc. [1834 etc.].

A Directory for the city of Aberdeen, and its vicinity 1824–25 (1828–29) 2 vol. (Aberdeen, 1824–28).

DUNDEE

The Dundee Directory for 1818 . . . by A. Abbot, Dundee [1818] [continued as *The Dundee Register and Directory . . . for 1824–5,* (Dundee, 1824).].

EDINBURGH

Gray's Annual Directory 1834–35 . . . of Edinburgh and its vicinity etc. (Edinburgh, 1834).

The Post office Annual Directory (and Calendar) from Whitsunday 1813 to Whitsunday 1814 [———1845] containing an alphabetical list of the noblemen . . . gentlemen . . . traders, and others . . . in . . . Edinburgh and Leith etc. Edinburgh 1813–44 [continued as *The Post Office Edinburgh and Leith Directory.* (Edinburgh, 1846, etc.).].

Williamson's Directory for the City of Edinburgh, Canongate, Leith and suburbs, from June 1775 to June 1776 etc. (Edinburgh, [1776]).

Williamson's Directory for the City of Edinburgh, Canongate, Leith and suburbs, from June 1778 to June 1779 (Edinburgh, [1778]).

Williamson's Directory for the City of Edinburgh, Canongate, Leith, and suburbs, from June 1780 to June 1781 etc. (Edinburgh, 1780 etc.).

GLASGOW

Glasgow Directory . . . edited by Nathaniel Jones for the year 1787.

The Glasgow Directory . . . containing a list of the merchants, manufacturers, traders . . . in the city and suburbs . . . corrected till July 1801 [1813, 1817, 1818] (Glasgow, 1801 [———1818]).

Glasgow Post Office Directory for 1828–29 etc. (Glasgow 1828 [etc.]).

HADDINGTONSHIRE (now East Lothian)

Haddingtonshire Annual Register for 1850: being a directory to the nobility, gentry, tenantry, and commercial inhabitants of East Lothian. Haddington (1850).

PERTH

Morison's Perth and Perthshire Register for 1818; containing accurate lists of the institutions, public offices etc. in the city and county of Perth [1818].

Morison's Perth and Perthshire Register for 1846 [1854 etc.]; containing accurate lists of the institutions, public offices etc. in the city and county of Perth (Perth [1854–60]).

The Perth Directory for 1852–3 . . . *Compiled and arranged by J. Marshall and J. Mackie,* etc. Perth [1852, 1853].
[continued as]
The Post Office Perth Directory for 1854–55 . . . *compiled* . . . *by J. Marshall and J. Galloway* [1856–57 etc. compiled by J. Marshall etc.] Perth [1856 etc.].

NOTES AND REFERENCES

Introduction: Outline of Scottish History

[1]Gordon Donaldson, *The Scots Overseas* (1966), p. 14.
[2]Quoted in 'James V of Scotland', *Dictionary of National Biography*.
[3]*Reg. of Privy Council* 3rd ser. vol. 10 p. 28.
[4]*Ibid.* p. 208.
[5]*Ibid.* vol xi p. 318.
[6]Quoted Janet R. Glover, *The Story of Scotland* (1960), p. 219.
[7]*Sinclair's Statistical Account* (1791–9), 'Lintrathen, Angus'.
[8]*Ibid.* 'Lethendy, Perthshire'.
[9]*Ibid.* 'Coupar Angus, Perthshire'.
[10]Pub. 1952.
[11]Quoted Glover *op. cit.* p. 232.
[12]*Ibid.* p. 241.
[13]*Ibid.* p. 242.
[14]*Ibid.* p. 257.
[15]Lord Cockburn, quoted Glover *op. cit.* p. 258.
[16]*Ibid.* p. 272
[17]Quoted Glover *op. cit.* p. 341
[18]*Ibid.* p. 348.

CHAPTER I: Family Information

[1]Edin. (1904–14).
[2]2nd edn (1935).
[3]Gerald Hamilton-Edwards, *In Search of Ancestry*, 2nd edn. (Phillimore, 1971).

CHAPTER III: Parish and Non-conformist Registers

[1]Quoted J. Maitland Thomson, *The Public Records of Scotland* (1922), p. 123.
[2]Although the Society of Friends had no ordained ministers there were in Scotland in the 18th century Friends who voluntarily acted and were known as such.

CHAPTER IV: Surnames and Christian Names

[1]A similar map is on book jacket of Frank Adam, *The Clans, Septs and Regiments of the Scottish Highlands*, 8th edn (1970) [reproduced in black and white on p. 62].
[2]Vol XIII Nos 2 and 3.
[3]See Scottish Record Soc. XXI *Orkney and Zetland Testaments, 1611–1684.*
[4]*Ibid.*
[5]*The Exchequer Rolls of Scotland*, S.R.O., Vol. V
[6]Edin. City Archives.

CHAPTER VI: Testaments

[1]Testament testamentar and codicil of William Stewart of Middle Gourdie, confirmed Dunkeld 12 April 1699.
[2]Testament testamentar of Isobell Ramsay of Alyth, Angus, confirmed Dunkeld 9 June 1713.
[3]Vol. XXXIV, ed. by F. J. Grant (1909).

CHAPTER VII: The Sasine Registers

[1]Part. Reg. Sasines Ayr VI, pt 2 fol. 386.
[2]Vol. XXIX fol. 431.

CHAPTER VIII: Service of Heirs

[1]*Abbreviationis Inquisitionum* II, Perth No. 279.

CHAPTER IX: Registers of Deeds

[1]J. Maitland Thomson *op. cit.* p. 42.
[2]Durie 264 fols 16–20.
[3]Durie 238 fol. 571.
[4]Vol. II, 70–72 (1876).
[5]See *Local Authority Records* (The Boyle Committee), 1967.
[6]See *Sheriff Court Records* (The Kidd Committee), 1967.
[7]David Littlejohn, *ed. Records of the Sheriff Court of Aberdeenshire* (1904 etc.).
[8]Sheriff Court of Argyllshire Register of Deeds, new ser. I 1809–1818. It is interesting to note that this Daniel Morison's Testament Testamentar was proved 29 Mar. 1810. In it he nominated his father and his heirs universal legator and executor.

CHAPTER X: Other Court Registers

[1]J. Maitland Thomson *op. cit.* pp 37–38.
[2]Edin. (1905), p. 720 No. 66, 4 March 1813 1st Div.
[3]Process Papers, Court of Session, 22 June 1822.
[4]Decreet of Cessio Bonorum, John McGillierire, recorded Reg. of Deeds 6 August 1765 (Mack fol. 11).
[5]Edited by D. G. Barron (1892), (*Scot. Hist. Soc.* 1st ser. vol. xii).

CHAPTER XII: Clans and Scottish Titles

[1]*The Tartans of the Clans and Families of Scotland* 7th edn. (1964).
[2]*Scottish National Manuscripts* Vol. 2, p. xiv.
[3]Reg. of Deeds 1693 Mack 73 fol. 143.
[4]Frank Adam, *The Clans, Septs and Regiments of the Scottish Highlands*, 7th edn. rev. by Sir T. Innes of Learney (1965), p. 408.
[5]Reginald B. Brett, *Viscount Esher, The Girlhood of Queen Victoria: a selection from H.M.'s diaries 1832–1840*, 2 v. (1912), i, 362.
[6]Vol. 1, pp 373–6.
[7]Proceedings, Lyon Court, March 1967.
[8]1969 edn., Lauderdale p. 656.

CHAPTER XIII: University and Professional Records

[1]Ed. by P. J. Anderson (New Spalding Club), (1893).
[2]Ed. by P. J. Anderson (1900).
[3]Ed. by P. J. Anderson, 3 v. (1908), vol. ii being officers, graduates and alumni and vol. iii being an index to vol. ii compiled by J. F. K. Johnstone.
[4]*Matriculation Albums of the University of Glasgow from 1728 to 1858*, ed. by W. I. Addison (1913).

[5]*Matriculation Roll of the University of St Andrews 1747–1897*, ed. by J. M. Anderson (1905).
[6]*Illustrated English Social History III. The Eighteenth Century* (1949–52), p. 129.
[7]Quoted *ibid.* 129–30.
[8]For a fuller list of school registers in Scotland see Phyllis M. Jacobs *Registers of the Universities, Colleges and Schools of Great Britain and Ireland*, (1964).
[9]See p. 58.
[10]*Edinburgh Apprentices 1583–1800*, Scottish Record Soc. vols 28, 60, 61, 92.
[11]Aberdeen 1399–1700 (New Spalding Club 6, 34); Banff (honorary burgesses) 1549–1892 (New Spalding Club 10); Canongate (Edinburgh) 1622–1733 (S.R.S. 83); Dumbarton 1600–1925 (S.R.S. 73); Edinburgh 1406–1841 (S.R.S. 59, 62, 68); Glasgow 1573–1846 (S.R.S. 56, 66).
[12]*List of Fellows of the Royal College of Surgeons of Edinburgh from . . . 1581 to . . . 1873* (1874).
[13]Pub. 1925.
[14]2 v. 2nd edn (1932).
[15]Pub. 1896.
[16]Letter Books – Glasgow – Collector to Board [C.E. 59].
[17]3 v. (1964).

CHAPTER XV: Migration and the Scotsman Abroad

[1]See Gordon Donaldson *The Scots Overseas* (1966), p. 23. Much of this chapter is based on information in Professor Donaldson's book.
[2]Pub. 1940.
[3]Quoted Donaldson *op. cit.* p. 46.
[4]Flora McPherson, *Watchman against the World* (1962), p. 122.
[5]Margaret Kiddle, *Men of Yesterday*, Melbourne (1961), pp 517–8.
[6]Heritage House, 413 Riley St., Surrey Hills, New South Wales 2010, Australia.

CHAPTER XVII: Scots Heraldry and the Lyon Office

[1]Sir J. Balfour Paul, *Heraldry in relation to Scottish History and Art* (Rhind Lectures on Archaeology for 1898) (1900), p. 84.
[2]2 v. (1914).

CHAPTER XVIII: Societies and Libraries

[1]Address PO Box 27, City Chambers, Glasgow, but callers use 249 George Street.
[2]Pub. 1573–1846 (S.R.S. vols 56 and 66).

CHAPTER XIX: Various Other Sources

[1]1968 (Pinhorn Handbooks 3).
[2]Vol. V Nos 1 & 2 (April and June 1968).
[3]*The Acts of the Parliaments of Scotland 1124–1707*, 12 v. in 13 (v. 6 being in 2 pts), 1814–1875. (Vol. 12 is an index).

CHAPTER XX: Recording Results

[1]Hector McKechnie, *Juridical Review* XL No. 4 (Dec 1928) p. 339.
[2]*Scottish Family History*, 1930, pp 3–33.
[3]Alexander Wedderburn, *The Wedderburn Book*, 2 v. priv. pr. (1898).
[4]See T. C. Smout *A History of the Scottish People 1560–1830* (1969), p. 293 *et seq.*
[5]Quoted W. H. Auden and Louis Kronenberger *The Faber Book of Aphorisms* (1964), p. 231.
[6]Quoted Rudolf Flesch ed. *The Book of Unusual Quotations* (1959), p. 121.
[7]*Ibid.* p. 121.

BIBLIOGRAPHY

Unless otherwise stated, the place of publication is London.

HISTORY

BINGHAM, Madeleine, *Scotland under Mary Stuart: an account of everyday life* (1971).

BONSER, K. J., *The Drovers* (1970), pp. 21–37.

CAMPBELL, Roy Hutcheson, *Scotland since 1707: the rise of an industrial society* (1965).

COCKBURN, Henry, Lord Cockburn, *Journal of Henry Cockburn: being a continuation of the Memorials of his Time 1831–1854*, ed. by Thomas Cleghorn (Edinburgh 1874), 2 vols.

—— *Memorials of his Time* (Edinburgh 1856).

DICKINSON, William Croft, *Scotland: from the earliest times to 1603* (1961).

DONALDSON, Gordon, 'Foundations of Anglo-Scottish Union' in *Elizabethan Government and Society*, ed. S. T. Bindoff and others (1961).

—— *Scotland: James V to James VII* (Edinburgh 1965).

—— *Scottish Kings* (1967).

EYRE-TODD, George, *The Highland Clans of Scotland* (1923), 2 vols.

FORBES, Robert, *The Lyon in Mourning*, 3 vols. (1895–96), ed. by H. M. Paton. Material relating to the 1745–46 rebellion.

FRANKLIN, Thomas Bedford, *A History of Scottish Farming* (1952).

GLOVER, Janet Reaveley, *The Story of Scotland* (1966).

GRAHAM, Henry Grey, *The Social Life of Scotland in the Eighteenth Century* (1937).

GRANT, Sir Francis James, *Zetland Family Histories* (1907). New edn. of *The County Families of the Zetland Islands*.

GRANT, Isabel Frances, *Everyday Life in Old Scotland etc.* [1932].

GRAY, Malcolm, *The Highland Economy* (Edinburgh 1957).

GREGORY, Donald, *History of the Western Highlands and Isles of Scotland, from . . . 1493 to . . . 1625* (Edinburgh 1836, 2nd edn. London 1881).

HALDANE, Archibald Richard Burdon, *The Drove Roads of Scotland* (1952). With a map.

HAMILTON, Henry, *Selections from the Monymusk Papers, 1713–55* (Edinburgh 1945). Scot. Hist. Soc., ser. 3, vol. 39.

HANDLEY, James Edmund, *The Agricultural Revolution in Scotland* (Glasgow 1963).

—— *Scottish Farming in the Eighteenth Century* (1953). With a useful bibliography.

HUNTER, Thomas, *Woods, Forests and Estates of Perthshire, with Sketches of the Principal Families in the County* (1883).

KNOX, Henry Macdonald, *Two Hundred and Fifty Years of Scottish Education 1696–1946* (1953).

LAWSON, John Parker, *The Book of Perth* (1847). Contains extracts from the Kirk Session records.

LOCHHEAD, Marion, *The Scots Household in the Eighteenth Century* (1948).

MACKENZIE, Agnes Mure, *The Kingdom of Scotland: a short history* (Edinburgh 1957). A new edition.

MACKENZIE, Donald Alexander, *Scotland: the Ancient Kingdom* (1930).

MACKENZIE, William Mackay, *The Scottish Burghs* (Edinburgh 1949).

MACKIE, Robert Laird, *Scotland* (Edinburgh 1962), ed. by G. Donaldson.

218

MACKINNON, James, *The Social and Industrial History of Scotland* (1920–21), 2 vols.
MACLEAN, Sir Fitzroy Hew, Bart., *Concise History of Scotland* (1970).
MACLEOD, Robert Charles, *The Island Clans during Six Centuries* [1930].
MACLEOD, Walter, ed., *A List of Persons Concerned in the Rebellion* [1745–46] (1890). Scot. Hist. Soc., ser. 1, vol. 8.
MEIKLE, Henry William, ed., *Scotland: A Description of Scotland and Scottish Life* (1947).
MILLAR, Alexander Hastie, ed., *A Selection of Scottish Forfeited Estate Papers, 1715; 1745* (Edinburgh 1909). Scot. Hist. Soc., ser. 1, vol. 57.
MURRAY, Eunice Guthrie, *Scottish Women in Bygone Days* (1930).
NICHOLAISEN, W. F. H., 'Norse Settlements in the Northern and Western Isles,' *Scot. Hist. Review*, vol. 48, no. 145 (April 1969).
NICHOLLS, Sir George, *A History of the Scotch Poor Law in connection with the Condition of the People* (1856).
PATON, Henry, ed., see FORBES, Robert.
PAUL, Sir James Balfour, 'Social Life in Scotland in the 16th Century', *Scot. Hist. Review*, vol. 17, no. 68 (July 1920), pp. 296–309.
PETRIE, Sir Charles Alexander, Bart., *The Jacobite Movement* (1948).
PLANT, Marjorie *Domestic Life of Scotland in the Eighteenth Century* (Edinburgh 1952). Edin. Univ. Press.
PRYDE, George Smith, *Scotland: from 1603 to the Present Day* (1962).
—— *Social Life in Scotland since 1707* (1934). Hist. Assoc. pamphlet no. 98.
RAIT, Sir Robert Sangster, *A History of Scotland . . .*, rev. edn. (1939).
RAMSAY, Edward Bannerman (Dean of Edinburgh), *Reminiscences of Scottish Life and Character* (Edinburgh 1947). Scottish Classics no. 2.
REID, James Macarthur, *Scotland, Past and Present* (1959).
ROGERS, Charles, *Social Life in Scotland* (Edinburgh 1884–86), 3 vols.
SANDERSON, William, *Scottish Life and Character, painted by H. J. Dobson . . . described by W. Sanderson* (1904).
SCOTLAND, James, *Modern Scotland: a short history from 1707 to the present day* (1953).
Scots Year Book (1926 – date). Previously *London-Scottish Assoc. Year Book.* Contains lists of clan societies and associations throughout the world.
SMOUT, Thomas Christopher, *A History of the Scottish People, 1580–1830* (1969). A useful book for genealogists, containing comprehensive bibliographies at the end of each chapter.
TYTLER, Patrick Fraser, *The History of Scotland to 1603*, 3rd edn. (Edinburgh 1845), 8 vols. With index.
YOUNGSON, Alexander John, *The Making of Classical Edinburgh, 1750–1840* (Edinburgh 1966).

CHURCH HISTORY

ANSON, Peter Frederick, *The Catholic Church in Modern Scotland, 1560–1937* (1937).
BARNETT, Thomas Ratcliffe, *The Makers of the Kirk* (1915).
BELLESHEIM, Alphons, *History of the Catholic Church of Scotland, translated with notes and additions by D. O. H. Blair* (Edinburgh 1887–90), 4 vols.
BURNET, George Bain, *The Story of Quakerism in Scotland, 1650–1850, with an epilogue on the period 1850–1950 by William H. Marwick* (1952).
CAMPBELL, Andrew James, *Two Centuries of the Church of Scotland, 1707–1929* (Paisley 1930).
CUNNINGHAM, John, *The Church History of Scotland*, 2nd edn. (Edinburgh 1882), 2 vols.
DAICHES, Salis, 'The Jew in Scotland', *Scot. Ch. Hist. Soc. Rec.* 3 (1929).
DONALDSON, Gordon, *Scotland: Church and nation through sixteen centuries* (1960).
ESCOTT, Harry, *A History of Scottish Congregationalism* (1960).
EWING, William, *Annals of the Free Church of Scotland, 1843–1900* (Edinburgh 1914), 2 vols.
GOLDIE, Frederick, *A Short History of the Episcopal Church in Scotland from the Restoration to the Present Time* (1951) [1952].

HALLEN, Arthur Washington Cornelius, 'Huguenots in Scotland', *Proc. Huguenot Soc. London*, vol 2 (1889).

HEWISON, James King, *The Covenanters* (Glasgow 1908) 2 vols.

HUTCHISON, Matthew, *The Reformed Presbyterian Church in Scotland, 1680–1876* (Paisley 1893).

LAWSON, John Parker, *History of the Scottish Episcopal Church from the Revolution to the Present Time* (Edinburgh 1843).

—— *The Roman Catholic Church in Scotland: its establishment, subversion and present state* (Edinburgh 1835).

LEITH, William Forbes, *Memoirs of Scottish Catholics during the 17th and 18th Centuries* (1909) 2 vols.

LUMSDEN, Sir John, *The Covenants of Scotland* (Paisley 1914).

MACEWEN, Alexander Robertson, *A History of the Church in Scotland* [1913–16] 2 vols.

MACPHERSON, John, *A History of the Church in Scotland* (Paisley 1901).

MAIDMENT, James, ed., 'Extracts from the Kirk Session Register of Perth, 1577–1634', *Spottiswoode Miscellany*, vol. 2, pt. 9 (Edinburgh 1845), pp. 225–311.

SMALL, Robert, *History of the Congregations of the United Presbyterian Church from 1733 to 1900* (Edinburgh 1904), 2 vols.

STORY, Robert Herbert, ed., *The Church of Scotland Past and Present* [1890–91], 5 vols.

SWIFT, Wesley Frank, *Methodism in Scotland: the first hundred years* (1947). Wesley Hist. Soc., lecture no. 13.

TORRANCE, John, *The Quaker Movement in Scotland* [Edinburgh 1927]. Extracted from the *Records of the Scot. Ch. Hist. Soc.*

—— *The Early Quakers in North-East Scotland* [Banff 1936]. Extracted from the *Trans. of the Banffshire Field Club.*

WODROW, Robert, *The History of the Sufferings of the Church of Scotland from the Restoration to the Revolution*, ed. by Rev. R. Burns (Edinburgh 1829–30), 2 vols.

GENEALOGICAL AIDS

ANDERSON, William, *The Scottish Nation; or the surnames, families, literature, honours and biographical history of the people of Scotland* (1866–77), 3 vols.

BEATON, Donald, *Genealogical Bibliography of Caithness and Sutherland* (1909). Publications of the Viking Club (Old Lore series), vols 2–5 (1909–1912).

BELL, George Joseph, *Principles of the Law of Scotland*, 10th edn. (Edinburgh 1899).

BELL, Sydney S., *Dictionary of Decisions* [1808–1833], (Edinburgh 1841–2).

BLACK, George Fraser, *A List of Works Relating to Scotland* (New York 1916).

BLACK, William George, *Hints as to how to Compile a Pedigree in Scotland*, repr. from the *Trans. of the Glasgow Arch. Soc.* new series, vol. 8, pt. 1 (April 1927).

BURNS, Thomas, *Church Property: the Benefice Lectures, with a preface by James Macgregor* (Edinburgh 1905).

CRAIGIE, John, *Scottish Law of Conveyancing: Heritable Rights*, 3rd edn. (Edinburgh 1899); Re-written and enlarged; pp. 43–5 give form of instrument of sasine and explanation of its clauses.

DICKINSON, William Croft, DONALDSON, Gordon and MILNE, Isabel A., eds., *A Source Book of Scottish History* (1952–4), 3 vols.

DONALDSON, Gordon, 'Church Records', pts. 1 and 2, *Scot. Genealogist*, vol. 2, nos. 3 and 4 (July and Oct. 1955).

Faculty Collection, Court of Session Reports, 1752–1824.

FERGUSON, Joan Primrose Scott, comp., *Scottish Family Histories held in Scottish Libraries*, 1st edn. repr. (Edinburgh 1968). Scottish Central Library publication; includes MS and TS material.

GOULDESBROUGH, Peter, KUP, A. P., and LEWIS, Idwal, *Handlist of Scottish and Welsh Record Publications* (1954). The Scottish Section is by P. G. and A. P. K. British Record Soc. Pamphlet no. 4.

GREEN, William and Sons, *Green's Encyclopoedia of the Law of Scotland*, ed. by John Chisholm (Edinburgh 1896–1904), 14 vols.

HAMILTON-EDWARDS, Gerald Kenneth Savery, *In Search of Ancestry*, 2nd edn. (1971), pp. 122–139.

HANCOCK, Philip David comp., *A Bibliography of works relating to Scotland 1916–1950* (Edinburgh 1959–60), 2 pts. Edin. Univ. publications.

KAMINKOW, Marion J., *Genealogical Manuscripts in British Libraries: a descriptive guide* (U.S.A. Baltimore 1967).

LIVINGSTONE, Matthew, *A Guide to the Public Records of Scotland deposited in H.M. Register House, Edinburgh* (1905). See also *Scot. Hist. Rev.*, vol. 26 and 27 (1946–7).

MACFARLANE, Walter, *Genealogical Collections concerning Families in Scotland, made by W. Macfarlane, 1750–1751*, 2 vols., ed. by J. T. Clarke (1900). Scot. Hist Soc., vols. 33, 34.

MCKECHNIE, Hector, 'The Pursuit of Pedigree', *The Juridical Review*, vol. 40 (1928), pp. 205–34, 304–40.

MACKENZIE, Sir George, Lord Advocate, *Families of Scotland* [1636–91]. MS copies in Nat. Lib. of Scot., Lyon Office and B.M.   See desc. and list of included families in 'Notes on Sir George Mackenzie's Families of Scotland' in *Scot. Genealogist*, vol. 4, no. 2 (April 1957).

MATHESON, Cyril, *A Catalogue of the Publications of Scottish Historical and Kindred Clubs and Societies and of Papers Relative to Scottish History issued by H.M.S.O. 1908–27* (Aberdeen 1928). A continuation of the work by C. S. Terry (q.v.).

MITCHELL, John Fowler, 'Hearth Tax and Poll Tax', *Scot. Genealogist*, vol 11, no. 3 (Sept. 1964).

MORRISON, F. H., *Synopsis of Bell's Principles of the Law of Scotland for Students* (Edinburgh 1903).

MORRISON, William Maxwell, *Dictionary of Decisions* [1540 to 1808].

MUNRO, Robert William and MUNRO, Jean, 'Highland Genealogy in Local Publications', *Scot. Genealogist*, vol. 11, no. 1 (May 1964) pp. 1–7. A guide to genealogical material in the *Celtic Mag.*, *Celtic Monthly*, *Trans. Gaelic Soc. of Inverness* and *Trans. Inverness Scientific Soc. and Field Club.*

SANDISON, Alexander, *Tracing Ancestors in Shetland* (Lerwick 1969).

SCOTTISH RECORD SOCIETY, *List of Publications 1897–1964* (1964). Reprod. from typewriting.

STEEL, Donald John, *Sources of Scottish Genealogy and Family History* (1970).

STUART, Margaret, *Scottish Family History* (1930). A guide to printed and some MS sources, with an essay, 'How to Write the History of a Family' by Sir James Balfour Paul.

TAYLOR, Alexander Burt, 'Registration and Censuses and the Information they Supply', *Scot. Genealogist*, vol. 9, no. 4 (Dec. 1962).

TAYLOR, James, of Glasgow, *The Great Historic Families of Scotland*, (1887), 2 vols.

TERRY, Charles Sandford, *A Catalogue of the Publications of Scottish Historical and kindred Clubs and Societies etc., 1780–1908* (1909). Continued by Cyril Matheson (q.v.).

THOMSON, John Maitland, *The Public Records of Scotland* (Glasgow 1922).

TURNBULL, William Barclay David Donald, *Scottish Parochial Registers: memoranda of the state of the parochial registers of Scotland* (Edinburgh 1849).

MONUMENTAL INSCRIPTIONS

GARDNER, David E., 'Burial Grounds of Glasgow and District', *Scot. Genealogist*, vol. 3, no. 4 (Oct. 1956).

GILCHRIST, George, assisted by M. Conran, A. Shannon, M. Shannon and Robert A. Shannon, has compiled and published (reprod. from type-writing) pre-1855 inscriptions from churchyards and graveyards in the following parishes in Dumfriesshire, usually including heraldic designs, maps of locations, plans of graveyards and notes:

Applegarth	Dryfesdale
Caelaverock	Ewes
Canonbie	Graitney
Cummertrees	Hoddam
(Repentance Tower)	Half-Morton and Morton
Dalton	(Tower of Sark)
Dornock	Hutton and Corrie

Johnstone	Mouswald
Kirkmichael	Sibbaldbie
Kirkpatrick-Fleming	Torthorwald
(Kirkconnell)	Tundergath
Langholm	Unthank
Lochmaben	Wamphray
Middlebie	Wauchope

HENDERSON, John Alexander, *Aberdeenshire Epitaphs and Inscriptions: with historical, biographical, genealogical and antiquarian notes* (Aberdeen 1907-). Printed for subscribers.

JERVISE, Andrew, *Epitaphs and Inscriptions from Burial Grounds and Old Buildings in the North-East of Scotland* (Edinburgh 1875-9), 2 vols.

MCNAUGHTON, Duncan, 'Campbell Street Burying Ground, Port Glasgow', *Scott. Genealogist* vol. 6, no. 2 (April 1959).

MACPHERSON, Alan G., 'Headstones in the Graveyard at Cluny', *Scot. Genealogist*, vol. 15, no. 4 (Dec. 1968).

MITCHELL, John Fowler and MITCHELL, Sheila, have compiled and published (reprod. from typewriting) for the Scottish Genealogy Society pre-1855 monumental inscriptions from graveyards in the following counties: *Clackmannan, Dunbarton, Kinross, Renfrew and West Lothian*. J. F. Mitchell is also author of the following articles in *Scot. Genealogist*:
'Tombstones in Detached Portion of Old Carlton Cemetery, Edinburgh', vol. 3, no. 2 (April 1956).
'Tombstones in North Leith Cemetery', vol. 3, no. 3 (July 1956).
'The Quaker Burial Ground in Glasgow', vol. 4, no. 2 (April 1957).
'Lists of Books which contain Records of Burials', vol. 4, no. 1 (Jan. 1957). With additions, etc. vol. 9, no. 3 (Sept. 1962).
'Burial Ground Inscriptions', vol. 9, no. 1 (April 1963).
[A continuation of those listed in vol. 9, no. 3 (Sept. 1962) is contained in vol. 10, no. 4 (Feb. 1964), vol. 11, no. 1 (May 1964), vol. 12, no. 2 (Aug. 1965), vol. 14, no. 3 (Nov. 1967).]
'Old Burial Ground at Gourock' from *Gourock Times* 10 April 1970 with Historical Note by Colin Milne in issue of 7 Feb. 1969, in *Scot. Genealogist*, vol. 17, no. 4 (Dec. 1970).

SELKIRKSHIRE ANTIQUARIAN SOCIETY, *Gravestone Inscriptions prior to 1855, vol 1. Selkirk, Askirk and Lindean Old Churchyards* [1968].

CIVIL, PARISH AND OTHER REGISTERS

BURN, John Southerden, *The History of Parish Registers in England, also of the Registers of Scotland*, 2nd edn. (1862).

CARGILL, David C., 'The Presbyterian Meeting-Houses and their Baptismal and Marriage Registers', *Scot. Genealogist*, vol. 10, no. 2 (Oct. 1963), and vol. 15, no. 2 (June 1968).

HOGAN, E. A., 'Parish Registers in the New Register House', *Scot. Genealogist*, vol. 3, no. 2 (April 1956).

MARSHALL, James Scott, ed., *Calendar of Irregular Marriages in the South Leith Kirk Session Records, 1697-1818* (Edinburgh 1968). Scot. Record Soc., vol. 95.

MARWICK, William Hutton, 'Scottish Friends' Records', *Scot. Genealogist*, vol. 7, no. 3 (Aug. 1960).

RENNIE, Archibald L., Registrar General of Scotland, 'Recent Developments at New Register House', *Scot. Genealogist*, vol. 18, no. 2 (June 1971).

SCOTTISH OFFICE, Registrar-General of Births, Deaths and Marriages for Scotland, *Detailed List of the old Parochial Registers of Scotland, etc.* (Edinburgh 1872).

SCOTTISH RECORD OFFICE, *Records of the Church of Scotland preserved in the Scottish Record Office and General Register Office, Register House, Edinburgh* (Glasgow 1967). *Scot. Rec. Soc.*, vol. 96.

SETON, George, *Sketch of the History and Imperfect Condition of the Parochial Records of Births, Deaths and Marriages in Scotland* (Edinburgh 1854).

STEEL, Donald John, *Sources for Scottish Genealogy and Family History*, pp. 67-95.

NAMES

ANDERSON, William, *Genealogy and Surnames* (Edinburgh 1865).
BLACK, George Fraser, *The Surnames of Scotland, their Origin, Meaning and History* (New York 1946).
BLAKE, J. L., 'Distribution of Surnames in the Isle of Lewis', *Scot. Studies* 10 (1968), pp. 154–61.
EVANS, David Ellis, *Gaulish Personal Names: a study of some Continental Celtic formations* (1967).
MACBAIN, Alexander, *An Etymological Dictionary of the Gaelic Language*, 2nd edn. (Stirling 1911).
—— *Etymology of the Principal Gaelic National Names, Personal Names and Surnames* (Stirling 1911).
—— 'The Old Gaelic System of Personal Names', *Trans. Gael. Soc. of Inverness*, vol. 20 (1894–6), pp. 279–315.
—— *Personal Names and Surnames of the Town of Inverness* (Inverness 1895).

CENTRAL AND LOCAL COURT REGISTERS

ARMET, Helen, and WOOD, M., eds., *Extracts from the Records of the Burgh of Edinburgh, 1681–1701* (1927).
BARON, Douglas Gordon, ed., *The Court Book of the Barony of Urie in Kincardineshire, 1604–1747* (Edinburgh 1892). Scot. Hist. Soc., [ser. 1], vol. 12.
Census Reports of Great Britain, 1801–1931 (1951). (Guides to Official Sources, no. 2, H.M.S.O.
DELL, Richard F., 'The Glasgow City Archives Office', *Scot. Hist. Rev.*, vol. 47, no. 144 (Oct. 1968), pp. 211–6.
DICKINSON, William Croft, ed., *Court Book of the Barony of Carnwath, 1523–42* (1937). Scot. Hist. Soc., ser. 3, vol. 29.
LINDSAY, Sir John, ed., *Inventory of the Records of the City of Glasgow* (1913).
LIVINGSTONE, Matthew, *Calendar of Charters etc. relating to Lands etc.* (1907).
—— *A Guide to the Public Records of Scotland, deposited in H.M. General Register House* (Edinburgh 1905).
MACGREGOR, Malcolm Blair, *The Sources and Literature of Scottish Church History* (Glasgow 1934).
MALCOLM, Charles Alexander, 'The Sheriff Court: sixteenth century and later', *Introduction to Scottish Legal History* (1958) (Stair Society), p. 356.
METCALFE, William M., ed., *The Lordship of Paisley* (1912). Contains useful glossary.
MILL, Anna Jean, *Inventory of the Early Manuscript Records of the Older Royal Burghs of Scotland* (1923). St Andrews Univ. Pub. no. 17.
MITCHELL, John Fowler, 'Hearth Tax and Poll Tax', *Scot. Genealogist*, vol. 9, no. 3 (Sept. 1964).
—— 'Scottish-American Heirs, 1800–1819', *Scot. Genealogist*, vol. 14, no. 4 (Dec. 1967).
—— 'Scottish-Australian Heirs before 1860', *Scot. Genealogist*, vol. 15, no. 1 (Mar. 1968).
MURRAY, David, *Scottish Local Records and the Report of the Departmental Committee of 1925 on Sheriff Court Records* (Glasgow 1927). Repr. from *Scot. Hist. Rev.*
PATON, Henry, *The Scottish Records: their history and value* (Edinburgh 1933). Hist. Assoc. of Scotland.
PRYDE, George Smith, *The Burghs of Scotland: a critical list* (1965).
RODGER, William, 'The Poll Tax Rolls, 1695', *Scot. Genealogist*, vol. 10, no. 4 (Feb. 1964).
ROMANES, Charles S., *Selections from the Records of the Regality of Melrose, I 1605–1661, II 1662–1676, III 1547–1706* (Edinburgh 1914–17). Scot. Hist. Soc. ser 2, vols. 6, 8, 13.
SCOTTISH BURGH RECORD SOCIETY publications, 1898–.
SCOTTISH RECORD SOCIETY, *Records of the Church of Scotland preserved in the Scottish Record Office and General Register Office, Register House, Edinburgh* (Glasgow 1967).
SHAW, Samuel, *An Accurate Alphabetical Index of the Registered Entails in Scotland, 1685 to 1784* (Edinburgh 1784).
SKINNER, B. C., 'Local History of Scotland', *Scot. Hist. Rev.*, vol. 47, no. 2 (Oct. 1968), pp. 160–67.

STAIR SOCIETY, *Sources and Literature of Scots Law* (1936). Printed Law Reports listed on pp. 47–58; Burgh Records pp. 104–10; Sheriff etc. Court Records, pp. 117–132.

STEEL, Donald John, *Sources for Scottish Genealogy and Family History* (1970), pp. 132–168, 171–4, 176–184.

TAYLER, Alistair Norwich and TAYLER, Henrietta, eds., *Jacobite Cess Roll of the Co. of Aberdeen in 1715* (Aberdeen 1932). Spalding Club pub.

—— *The Valuation Roll of the County of Aberdeen for the year 1667* (1933).

WATSON, Charles Brodie Boog, 'List of Owners of Property in Edinburgh 1635', extracted from the 13th volume of the *Book of the Old Edinburgh Club* [Edinburgh 1924].

PROFESSIONAL RECORDS

Army

DALTON, Charles, *The Scots Army 1661–1668: with memoirs of the commanders-in-chief* (1909), 2 pts.

FERGUSON, James, ed., *Papers illustrating the History of the Scots Brigade in the Service of the United Netherlands, 1572–1782* (Edinburgh 1899–1901), 3 vols. Scot. Hist. Soc., vol. 38.

MCLACHLAN, T., 'McLachlans who served as Officers in the British Army', *Scot. Genealogist*, vol. 18, no. 2 (June 1971).

STEWART-MURRAY, Katharine Marjory, Marchioness of Tullibardine, afterw. Duchess of Atholl, ed., *A Military History of Perthshire, 1660–1902* (Perth 1908), 2 vols.

Church

COUPER, William James, *The Reformed Presbyterian Church in Scotland, its Congregations, Ministers and Students* (Edinburgh 1925). A fasti of this church from 1743 to 1876, with useful data of congregations, ministers and students.

DOWDEN, John, *The Bishops of Scotland* (Glasgow 1912).

FERGUSSON, Adam Wightman, *Sons of the Manse* (1923).

KEITH, Robert, *Bishop of the Scottish Episcopal Church in Fife: an historical catalogue of the Scottish bishops*, new edn. (Edinburgh 1824).

KINNIBURGH, Robert, *Fathers of Independence, or Biographical Sketches of Early Scottish Congregational Ministers A.D. 1798–1851* (Edinburgh 1851).

MACGREGOR, William Malcolm and BLAKE, Buchanan, *A Historical Sketch of the United Free Church College, Glasgow: with a complete alumnus roll from 1856 to 1929* (Glasgow 1930).

ROBERTSON, David, comp., *South Leith Records 1588–1700* (Edinburgh 1911). Many full extracts.

SCOTT, Hew, *Fasti Ecclesiae Scoticanae: the succession of ministers in the parish churches of Scotland from 1560*, new edn. rev. by W. S. Crockett and Sir Francis J. Grant, (1915–1961), 9 vols. Vol. 9 (1961) *Ministers 1929–1954*, ed. by John Alexander Lamb, D.D. Vol. 8 (1950) contains *Ministers 1914–1928* and *addenda and corrigenda 1560–1949*.

SMALL, Robert, *History of the Congregations of the United Presbyterian Church from 1733 to 1900* (Edinburgh 1904). Gives summaries of the various congregations of this church.

East India Company

Asiatic Journal and Monthly Register for British India, vol. 1–25 (1816–28), 26–28 (1828); continued under various titles to 1845 [45 vols.].

BULLOCK, Humphrey, 'Anglo-Indian Family History', *The Amateur Historian*, vol. 1 (Feb.–Mar. 1953), pp. 117 *et seq.*

CAMPBELL of Barcaldie, Sir Duncan, Bart., *Records of Clan Campbell in the Military Service of the Honourable East India Company, 1600–1858* (1925).

DANVERS, F. C., ed., *List of Marine Records in the late East India Company, preserved in the Record Department of the India Office* (1895).

DODWELL, Edward and MILES, James Samuel, *East India Company's Bengal Civil Servants, 1780–1838* (1839).

—— *East India Company's Bombay Civil Servants, 1798–1839* (1839).
—— *East India Company's Madras Civil Servants, 1780–1839* (1839).
DODWELL, Henry Herbert, *Calendar of the Madras Despatches, 1744–1765* (Madras 1920–30), 2 vols.
—— *A Calendar of the Madras Records, 1740–1744* (Madras 1917).
East India Register and Directory, continued under various titles (1803–1895).
FOSTER, Sir William. *Guide to the India Office Records, 1600–1858* (1919 repr. 1966).
GOVERNMENT OF INDIA, Indian Records Series, *Fort William – India House Correspondence*. (Delhi 1958–1963). Nat. Archives of India.
HARDY, Charles, *A Register of Ships employed in the Service of the . . . East India Company from 1760 to 1810 . . . rev. with considerable additions by H. C. Hardy* (1811). [The India Office Records have a copy of the very scarce edn. covering the period 1707–1760].
HILL, Samuel Charles, *Bengal in 1756–1757* (1905), 3 vols.
—— *Catalogue of the Home Miscellaneous Series of the India Office Records* (1927).
—— *List of Europeans and others in the English Factories in Bengal at the time of the Siege of Calcutta in the year 1756, with an appendix containing lists of European Sufferers* (Calcutta 1902).
HODSON, Vernon Charles Paget, *List of the Officers of the Bengal Army, 1758–1834* (1927–47), 4 pts.
—— 'Some Families with a Long East India Connection'. *The Genealogists' Magazine*, vol. 6 (Mar. 1932–Dec. 1933).
HYDE, Henry Barry, *The Parish of Bengal, 1678 to 1788* (Calcutta 1899).
INDIA OFFICE publications:
    List of Factory Records of the late East India Company (1897).
    Lists of Consultations, Proceedings, etc. for Bengal, Madras, Bombay, North-Western Provinces and other minor administrations for various periods between 1702 and 1900 (1899–1900).
    List of Marine Records of the late East India Company (1896).
LANCASTER, Joan C., 'The India Office Records: a brief description'. *Archives*, vol. 9, no. 43 (April 1970).
—— *The India Office Records: a guide to lists and catalogues* (1966).
LOVE, Henry Davison, *Vestiges of Old Madras, 1640–1800*, 4 vols. From original records, well documented and indexed.
LOW, Charles Rathbone, *History of the Indian Navy, 1613–1863* (1877), 2 vols.
PRINSEP, Charles Campbell, *Records of Services of the Honourable East India Company's Civil Servants in the Madras Presidency, from 1741 to 1858 etc.* (1885).
SAINSBURY, Ethel Bruce, ed., *A Calendar of the Court Minutes etc. of the East India Company, 1635–39* [etc.] (1907 – in progress).
WILSON, William John, *History of the Madras Army* (Madras 1882–3), 3 vols.

Law

GRANT, Sir Francis James, ed., *The Faculty of Advocates in Scotland, 1532–1943: with genealogical notes* (Edinburgh 1944). Scottish Record Office pub., pt. 15.
HENDERSON, John Alexander, ed., *History of the Society of Advocates in Aberdeen* (1912). New Spalding Club, vol. 40.
History of the Society of Writers to H.M. Signet . . . with List of Members . . . from 1594 to 1890 (1890).
MCKECHNIE, Hector, ed., *The Society of Writers to H.M. Signet* (1936).
OMOND, George William Thomson, *The Lord Advocates of Scotland* (1883–1914), 3 vols.

Medicine

Catalogue of the Library of the College of Physicians and Surgeons of Glasgow (1885–1901), 2 vols. Contains list of medical practitioners in the Western district of Scotland, alphabetically arranged according to the counties and parishes.
COMRIE, John Dixon, *History of Scottish Medicine to 1860*, 2nd edn. (1932), 2 vols.
CRAWFORD, Dirom Grey, *A History of the Indian Medical Service, 1600–1913* (1914), 2 vols.

—— comp., *Roll of the Indian Medical Service, 1615–1930* (1930).
DODWELL, Edward and MILES, James Samuel, *Medical Officers of the Indian Army, 1764–1838* (1839).
DRUMMOND, C. G., 'Pharmacy and Medicine in Old and New Edinburgh', *Scot. Genealogist*, vol. 12, no 1 (May 1965).
DUNCAN, Alexander, *Memorials of the Faculty of Physicians and Surgeons of Glasgow, 1599–1850* (Glasgow 1896).
GUTHRIE, Douglas, 'Dynasties of Doctors', *Scot. Genealogist*, vol. 5, no. 2 (April 1958).

Navy

CHARNOCK, John, *Biographia Navalis* (1794–8), 6 vols. Memoirs of officers of the Royal Navy from 1660 to 1797.
CLOWES, Sir William Laird, *The Royal Navy: a history from the earliest times to the present* (1897–1903), 7 vols.
JAMES, G. F., 'Collected Naval Biography', *The Bulletin of the Inst. of Hist. Research*, vol. 15 (1937–8).
LEWIS, Michael Arthur, *England's Sea Officers* (1939).
—— *A Social History of the Navy, 1793–1815* (1960).
LLOYD, Christopher and COULTER, Jack Leonard Sagar, *The Royal Naval Medical Service* (1954). History of the second world war [Series title], U.K. Medical Series.
Lloyd's Captains' Register (1869). British mercantile marine officers, giving their place of birth.
MAINWARING, George Ernest. *A Bibliography of British Naval History* (1930).
MARSHALL, John, *Royal Naval Biography*, 12 vols. There is a TS index of this at the Soc. of Genealogists, London.
NATIONAL MARITIME MUSEUM, *Commissioned Sea Officers of the Royal Navy* [1954], 3 vols.
O'BYRNE, William Richard, *A Naval Biographical Dictionary* (1849). Covering all officers from lieutenant upwards living in 1845.
—— *Naval Biographical Dictionary*, new and enlarged edn. (1861). Includes Royal Marines, pursers and chaplains, but only vol. 1 and 4 pts of vol. 2 (up to name 'H. S. G. Giles') published. Copies are very scarce.
RALFE, James, *The Naval Biography of Great Britain* (1828), 4 vols. A rare book.

Parliament

FOSTER, Joseph, *Members of Parliament, Scotland*, 2nd edn. (1882).
NAMIER, Sir Lewis and BROOKE, John, *History of Parliament, The House of Commons, 1754–1790* (1964), 3 vols.
RAIT, Sir Robert Sangster, *The Parliaments of Scotland* (Glasgow 1924).
SEDGWICK, Romney, *History of Parliament, The House of Commons, 1715–1754* (1971), 2 vols.
TAYLER, Alistair Norwich and TAYLER, Henrietta, *Banffshire M.P.s since the Act of Union* (Elgin 1930).
—— *Morayshire M.P.s since the Act of Union* (Elgin 1930).

Other Professions

GUNNIS, Rupert, *Dictionary of British Sculptors, 1660–1851* (1953).
HARVEY-JAMIESON, H. M., 'The Company of Merchants of the City of Edinburgh', *Scot. Genealogist*, vol. 8, no 3. (July 1961).
KENNEDY, Ian M., 'Some Scottish Banking Families', *Scot. Genealogist*, vol. 6, no. 1 (Jan. 1959), and vol. 7, no. 2 (April 1960).
MITCHELL, John Fowler, 'Burns' Excise Associates', *Scot. Genealogist*, vol. 6, nos. 1 and 2 (Jan. and April 1959) and vol. 7, no. 2 (April 1960).
—— 'Englishmen in the Scottish Excise Department, 1707–1823', *Scot. Genealogist*, vol. 13, no. 2 (Oct. 1966).
WHYTE, Donald, 'Schoolmasters of Abercorn Parish, 1646–1872', *Scot. Genealogist*, vol. 15, no. 1 (Mar. 1968).

UNIVERSITY AND SCHOOL RECORDS

Universities

Aberdeen

ANDERSON, Peter John and JOHNSTONE, James Fowler Kellas, eds., *Fasti Academiae Mariscallanae Aberdonensis, 1593–1860* (Aberdeen, 1889–98), 3 vols. New Spalding Club. Vols. 4, 18, 19.

ANDERSON, Peter John, ed., *Officers and Graduates of University and King's College, Aberdeen, 1495–1860* (Aberdeen 1893). New Spalding Club. Vol. 11.

—— *Roll of Alumni in Arts of the University and King's College of Aberdeen, 1596–1860* (Aberdeen 1900).

JOHNSTON, William, *Roll of the Graduates of the University of Aberdeen, 1860–1900* (Aberdeen 1906). With Roll of Graduates 1901–1925; with Supplement 1860–1900 compiled by Theodore Watt (Aberdeen 1935).

RAIT, Sir Robert Sangster, *The Universities of Aberdeen* (Aberdeen 1895).

Edinburgh

GRANT, Alexander, *The Story of the University of Edinburgh, during its First Three Hundred Years* (1884).

Glasgow

ADDISON, William Innes, ed., *The Matriculation Albums of the University of Glasgow from 1728 to 1858* (Glasgow 1913).

—— comp., *A Roll of the Graduates of the University of Glasgow from 1727 to 1897* (Glasgow 1898).

—— *The Snell Exhibitions from the University of Glasgow to Balliol College, Oxford* (Glasgow 1901). Lists holders 1679–1900.

COUTTS, James, *History of the University of Glasgow, 1451–1909* (Glasgow 1909).

MACKIE, John Duncan, *The University of Glasgow, 1451–1951: a short history* (Glasgow 1954).

St Andrews

ANDERSON, James Maitland, ed., *Early Records of the University of St Andrews: the graduate roll 1413–1579 and the matriculation roll 1473–1579* (Edinburgh 1926). Scot. Hist. Soc. 3rd ser. vol. 8.

—— *The Matriculation Roll of the University of St Andrews, 1747–1897* (Edinburgh 1905).

CANT, Ronald Gordon, *The University of St Andrews: a short history* (Edinburgh 1946).

Schools

Aberdeen Grammar School, *Roll of Pupils 1795–1919: annotated from 1863 by T. Wall* (Aberdeen 1922).

Cargilfield, Barnton, Edinburgh, *Cargilfield Register, 1873–1927* (Leith 1928).

Chanonry House School, Aberdeen, *Spirat adhuc amor: the record of the Gym (Chanonry House School), Old Aberdeen*, comp. by A. Shewan (Aberdeen 1923). App. A: Roll of Old Boys [1849–79].

Edinburgh Academy Register: a record of all those who have entered the school since its foundation in 1824, ed. by T. Henderson and P. F. Hamilton-Grierson (Edinburgh 1914).

Fettes College. *The Fettes College Register 1870 to 1909*, 4th edn., ed. by M. J. C. Meiklejohn (Edinburgh [1909]).

Loretto School, *The Lorettoin Register 1825–1925*, 2nd edn., ed. by A. H. Buchanan-Dunlop (Edinburgh 1927).

Melville College, *Edinburgh Institution 1832–1932*, ed. J. R. S. Young (Edinburgh 1933).

Merchiston Castle School, *Merchiston Castle School Register, 1833 to 1962*, 5th edn. ed. by E. O. Connell (Edinburgh [1962]).

St. Leonard's School, St. Andrews, Register, vol. 1 (1877–95), vol. 2 (1895–1900) [St. Andrews 1895 and 1901].

HERALDRY, CLANS AND TITLES

ADAM, Frank, *The Clans, Septs and Regiments of the Scottish Highlands*, rev. by Sir T. Innes, 8th edn. (1970).

ADDINGTON, Arthur Charles, *The Royal House of Stuart: the descendants of King James VI of Scotland, James I of England*, vol. 1 (1969).

CUNNINGHAM, Audrey, *The Loyal Clans* (Cambridge 1932).

DOUGLAS, Sir Robert, *The Baronage of Scotland* (1798).

FAIRBAIRN, James, *Fairbairn's Crests of the Families of Great Britain and Ireland*, rev. by *Laurence Butters* (1968). Originally published in 2 vols., Edinburgh 1860.

GAYRE, George Robert and GAYRE, Reinold, eds., *Roll of Scottish Arms*, pt. 1, vol. 1 A-G [1965]. Vol. 2, H-Z [1969].

GRANT, Sir Francis James, *The Manual of Heraldry*, new and rev. edn. with 350 illus. (1924).

INNES of Learney, Sir Thomas, 'Heraldic Law', in Stair Society's *Sources and Literature of Scots Law* (1936), ch. 32, pp. 379–95.

—— *The Scottish Tartans, with Historical Sketches of the Clans and Families of Scotland*, 4th edn. (1963).

—— *The Tartans of the Clans and Families of Scotland*, 7th edn. (Edinburgh 1964).

MONCREIFFE, of that Ilk, Sir Rupert Iain Kay, Bart., *The Highland Clans: dynastic origins, chiefs and background of the clans connected with Highland history and some other families* (1967).

PAUL, Sir James Balfour, *Heraldry in Relation to Scottish History: the Rhind Lectures* (1900).

RENNIE, James Alan, *The Scottish People: their clans, families and origins* (1960). Has a useful clan map.

RIDDELL, John, *Inquiry into the Law and Practice in Scottish Peerages before and after the Union* (Edinburgh 1842), 2 vols.

Scottish Clans and Their Tartans: history of each clan and full list of septs, 41st edn. (Johnston & Bacon, Edinburgh 1968).

STEVENSON, John Robert Horne, *Heraldry in Scotland* (Glasgow 1914), 2 vols. Including a recension of 'The Law and Practice of Heraldry in Scotland' by George Seton.

STODART, Robert Riddle, *Scottish Arms, 1370–1678: reproduced in facsimile from contemporary MSS* (Edinburgh 1881), 2 vols.

SCOTS OVERSEAS

BERRY, E. M. E., 'Seeking the Emigrant Scot', *Scot. Genealogist*, vol. 7, no. 4 (Oct. 1960).

BERTHOFF, Rowland Tappan, *British Immigrants in Industrial America, 1790–1950* (Cambridge, Mass. 1953).

BOLTON, Charles Knowles, *Scotch Irish Pioneers in Ulster and America* (1910).

BOND, John, *They Were South Africans* (1956).

BRYCE, George, *The Scotsman in Canada: Western Canada* [1912], 2 vols.

BURTON, John Hill, *The Scot Abroad*, new edn. (Edinburgh 1881).

CAMPBELL, Colin Turing, *British South Africa A.D. 1795 – A.D. 1825* (1897). Deals in detail with the 1820 settlers.

CAMPBELL, William Wilfred, *The Scotsman in Canada: Eastern Canada* [1912], 2 vols.

DONALDSON, Gordon, *The Scots Overseas* (1966). A valuable work, containing excellent bibliographies.

FISCHER, Thomas Alfred, *The Scots in Germany* (Edinburgh 1902).

—— *The Scots in Eastern and Western Prussia: a sequel to 'The Scots in Germany'* (Edinburgh 1903).

—— *The Scots in Sweden* (Edinburgh 1907).

GRANT, William Lawson, ed., *Makers of Canada*, rev. edn. (Oxford 1926), 12 vols. Vol. 12 forms the *Oxford Encyclopaedia of Canadian History*.

GREENE, J., 'Scottish and English Families in Livonia', *Scot. Genealogist*, vol. 10, no. 3 (Jan. 1964)

GUILLET, Edwin Clarence, *The Great Migration* (Toronto 1937). The Atlantic crossing by sailing ship since 1770.

HARRISON, John, *The Scot in Ulster* (Edinburgh 1888).

HATTERSLEY, Alan Frederick, *The British Settlement of Natal* (Cambridge 1950). Good on Scottish emigration to the colony.

HILL, George, *The Plantation of Ulster* (Belfast 1877).

JONES, H. R., 'Migration within Scotland', *Scot. Geog. Mag.* no. 83 (1967), pp. 151–60.

KIDDLE, Margaret, *Men of Yesterday* (Melbourne 1961). A social history of Victoria, Australia, in the 19th century.

KING, Helen L., 'Scottish Links with Kansas', *Scot. Genealogist*, vol 17, no. 1 (Mar. 1970).

LOGAN, Robert Archibald, 'Highlanders from Skye in North Carolina and Nova Scotia: 1771–1818', *Scot. Genealogist*, vol. 12, no. 4 (Feb. 1966).

McLACHLAN, T., 'Ancestors Overseas', *Scot. Genealogist*, vol. 17, no. 2 (1970).

MacLEAN, J., 'Scottish Families in Holland', *Scot. Genealogist*, vol. 12, no. 3 (Dec. 1965).

MacLEOD, Mrs Neil A., 'Early History of Glengarry and its Settlers', *Scot. Genealogist*, vol. 18, no 2 (June 1971).

MACMILLAN, David S., *Scotland and Australia, 1788–1850: emigration commerce and investment* (1967).

MARAIS, Johannes Stephanus, *The Colonization of New Zealand* (1927). Concerns only the early period.

MEYER, Duane, *The Highland Scots of North Carolina, 1732–66* (1961).

MUNRO, R. W., 'Scots in South Africa', *Scot. Genealogist*, vol. 14, no. 21 (Oct. 1967).

SCOTTISH HISTORY SOCIETY, *Papers Relating to the Scots in Poland.*

REED, Alfred Hamish, *The Story of Early Dunedin* (Wellington 1956).

SMITH, Abbot Emerson, *Colonists in Bondage* (Univ. of N. Carolina Press, 1947).

SOLTOW, J. H., 'Scottish Traders in Virginia, 1750–75', *Economic History Review*, 2nd ser., vol. 12 (1959–60).

STEUART, Archibald Francis, ed., *The Scots in Poland, 1576–1793* (Edinburgh 1915). Scot. Hist. Soc., vol. 59.

WHYTE, Donald, Ed., *Dictionary of Scottish Emigrants to the U.S.A.* (Baltimore, U.S.A. 1972).

LEGAL, ECCLESIASTICAL AND TRADE TERMS

CRAIGIE, Sir William Alexander, *A Dictionary of the Older Scottish Tongue: from the twelfth century to the end of the seventeenth* (1931–   ). In progress, pt. 18 (to word 'Law') 1959.

DU FRESNE, Charles, *Glossarium ad Scriptores Mediae et . . . Latinitatis* (1840–57), 7 vols.

GIBB, Andrew Dewer, *Students' Glossary of Scottish Legal Terms* (1946).

GRANT, William, ed., *The Scottish National Dictionary . . . containing all the Scottish words known to be in use or to have been in use since* c. *1700* (1931–   ). In progress, vol. 8 (to word 'Selkirk') 1970.

JAMIESON, John, *An Etymological Dictionary of the Scottish Language . . . a new ed. . . . rev. . . . with the entire supplement incorporated by J. Longmuir and D. Donaldson* (Paisley 1879–87), 5 vols.

LATHAM, Ronald Edward, comp., *Revised Medieval Latin Word-List: from British and Irish Sources* (1965). Pub. for the British Academy: based on the work by J. H. Baxter and C. Johnson.

TOPOGRAPHY AND SURVEYS

EMERY, F. V., 'A "Geographical Description" of Scotland prior to the Statistical Accounts', in *Scot. Studies*, 3 (1959).

GENEALOGICAL SOCIETY OF . . . LATTER-DAY SAINTS, *The Social, Economic, Religious and Historical Background of Scotland as it affects Genealogical Research* (Salt Lake City, Utah, U.S.A.). Useful chronological outline of main events in Scotland affecting genealogical research.

JOHNSTON, W. and JOHNSTON, Alexander Keith, *Johnston's Gazetteer of Scotland*, 2nd edn. (1958).

LEWIS, Samuel, *Topographical Dictionary of Scotland* (1851), 2 vols. and atlas.

MITCHELL, Sir Arthur and CASH, C. G., *A Contribution to the Bibliography of Scottish Topography* (1917), 2 vols. *Scot. Hist. Soc.*, 2nd ser., vol. 14, etc.

New Statistical Account of Scotland by the Ministers of the Respective Parishes (1845), 15 vols.

Ordnance Gazetteer of Scotland (1903), 3 vols. [With bibliography of the principal towns.]

SINCLAIR, Rt Hon. Sir John, Bart, *The Statistical Account of Scotland: drawn up from the communications of the ministers of the different parishes* (1791–99), 21 vols.

WEBSTER, Alexander, 'An Account of People in Scotland in the year 1755', in J. G. Kyd, *Scottish Population Studies*. (*Scot. Hist. Soc.*, 3rd ser., vol. 44, 1952.)

SCOTTISH NEWSPAPERS 1740 TO 1855 WHICH CONTINUED IN PUBLICATION TWO OR MORE YEARS

The earliest title of the paper is given, with cross references from later titles. The dates of publication are given up to 1855 and where the paper continued beyond that date the date is followed by a dash, e.g. *Dundee, Perth and Cupar Advertiser* 1803–1855—. *The Cambridge Bibliography of English Literature*, vol. 2, gives details of Scottish newspapers to 1800 and *The New Cambridge Bibliography of English Literature*, vol. 3, gives details of newspapers 1800–1900. *The British Union Catalogue of Periodicals* gives similar information. Joan P. S. Ferguson's *Scottish Newspapers held in Scottish Libraries* (Edinburgh 1956) [Scot. Central Lib.] gives locations of known surviving copies. The British Museum Library Catalogue, Newspaper Supplement (1905), gives copies held by that library at the date of publication. James Henderson Tierney's *Early Glasgow Newspapers, Periodicals and Directories* (Glasgow 1934) has the localised value its title suggests.

Aberdeen Chronicle 1806–32, cont. as *Aberdeen Herald* 1832–55—.
Aberdeen Constitutional, see *Aberdeen Observer*.
Aberdeen Free Press, see *North of Scotland Gazette*.
Aberdeen Herald, see *Aberdeen Chronicle*.
Aberdeen Journal, see *Aberdeen's Journal*.
Aberdeen's Journal, 1747–8, cont. as *Aberdeen Journal* 1748–1855—.
Aberdeen Observer 1829–37, cont. as *Aberdeen Constitutional* 1837–44.
Air Advertiser 1803–39, cont. as *Ayr Advertiser* 1839–55—.
Ayr Advertiser, see *Air Advertiser*.
Ayr Observer 1832–55—.
Banner 1840–51.
Berwick Advertiser, see *British Gazette and Berwick Advertiser*.
Border Advertiser 1848–55—.
British Chronicle or Union Gazette, see *Kelso Chronicle*.
British Gazette and Berwick Advertiser 1808–23, cont. as *Berwick Advertiser*, 1823–55-.
Chamber's Historical Newspaper, Edinburgh 1832–1836.
Chartist Circular, Glasgow 1839–42.
Clyde Commercial Advertiser, Glasgow 1806–[?]10.
Clydesdale Journal, Glasgow, apparently cont. as *Glasgow Sentinel* 1821–23. There was a later *Glasgow Sentinel* 1850–55—.
Constitutional, Glasgow 1835, cont. as *Glasgow Constitutional* 1836–55.
Constitutional and Perthshire Agricultural and General Advertiser, Perth 1835–55—.
Constitutional and Dundee Courier, see *Dundee Weekly Courier*.
Cupar Herald 1822, cont. as *Fife Herald, Kinross, Strathearn and Clackmannan Advertiser*, Cupar 1823–55—.
Dumbarton Herald 1851–55—.
Dumfriesshire and Galloway Herald and Advertiser 1835–43, cont. as *Dumfriesshire and Galloway Herald and Register* 1843–55—.
Dumfriesshire and Galloway Herald and Register, see *Dumfriesshire and Galloway Herald and Advertiser*.
Dumfries Times 1833–42.

Dumfries Weekly Journal 1777–1823, cont. as *Dumfries Weekly Journal and Nithsdale, Annandale and Galloway Advertiser* 1823–35.

Dumfries Weekly Journal and Nithdale, Annandale and Galloway Advertiser, see *Dumfries Weekly Journal.*

Dundee Chronicle 1830–40, cont. as *Dundee Herald* for few months after Jan. 1841.

Dundee Courier, see *Dundee Weekly Courier.*

Dundee Herald, see *Dundee Chronicle.*

Dundee, Perth and Cupar Advertiser, 1803–55—.

Dundee Warder 1841, amalg. with *Fifeshire Sentinel* 1845 and cont. as *Northern Warder* 1845–55—.

Dundee Weekly Courier 1816, cont. as *Dundee Courier* 1817–32 and as *Constitutional and Dundee Courier* 1832–34, then as *Dundee Courier* 1834–55—.

Dunfermline Chronicle 1853–55—.

Dunfermline Journal 1840–55—.

Dunfermline News 1849–55—.

Edinburgh Advertiser 1764–1855—.

Edinburgh and Leith Advertiser 1825–26, cont. as *Edinburgh, Leith, Glasgow and North British Commercial and Literary Advertiser* 1826–55—.

Edinburgh Correspondent 1810–16, 1818–22.

Edinburgh Evening News 1718–1855—.

Edinburgh Evening Post and Scottish Literary Gazette 1827–44, then amalg. with *Scottish Record* 1844–55—.

Edinburgh Gazette, see *Edinburgh Gazette or Scots Post Man.*

Edinburgh Gazette or Scots Post Man 1714–93, then *Edinburgh Gazette* 1793–1855—.

Edinburgh Guardian 1853–55.

Edinburgh Herald 1790–97, cont. as *Herald and Chronicle* 1797–1806.

Edinburgh, Leith, Glasgow and North British Commercial and Literary Advertiser, see *Edinburgh and Leith Advertiser.*

Edinburgh News and Literary Chronicle 1848–55—, incorp. *Edinburgh Weekly Chronicle* 1848.

Edinburgh Observer 1822–45, incorp. *Edinburgh and Leith Advertiser* Aug. 1826, *Edinburgh Star* c. 1827–32 and *New North Briton* 1832.

Edinburgh Star 1808–27, then amalg. with *Northern Reporter*, July 1826, and with *Edinburgh and Leith Advertiser*, Aug. 1826, then incorp. in *Edinburgh Observer*, c 1827–45.

Edinburgh Weekly Chronicle 1808–48, incorp. *Scottish Pilot* 1842, then incorp. in *Edinburgh News and Literary Chronical* 1848.

Elgin Courant 1834–55—.

Fife Herald, Kinross, Strathern and Clackmannan Advertiser, see *Cupar Herald.*

Fifeshire Journal and Clackmannan and Kinross Register, Kirkcaldy – Cupar, 1833–55—.

Fifeshire Sentinel, see *Dundee Warder.*

Forres, Elgin and Nairn Gazette, Forres, 1837–55—.

Galloway Advertiser and Wigtonshire Free Press 1855—.

Glasgow Advertiser 1783–9, then *Glasgow Advertiser and Evening Intelligencer* 1789–94, cont. as *Glasgow Advertiser* 1794–1802, cont. as *Herald and Advertiser*, Jan.–May 1803, cont. as *Glasgow Advertiser* 1803–5, cont. as *Glasgow Herald* 1805–55—.

Glasgow Advertiser 1855—, see *North British Railway and Shipping Journal.*

Glasgow Advertiser and Evening Intelligencer, see *Glasgow Advertiser* 1783–9.

Glasgow Advertiser and Railway and Shipping Journal, see *North British Railway and Shipping Journal.*

Glasgow Argus 1833–47.

Glasgow Chronicle 1767–79, then incorp. in *Glasgow Journal* c. 1779.

Glasgow Chronicle 1811–55—. [A publication unconnected with the *Glasgow Chronicle* of 1767–79].

Glasgow Constitutional, see *Constitutional.*

Glasgow Courant 1745–60, then inc. in *Glasgow Journal.*

Glasgow Courier 1791–1855—.

Glasgow Daily News 1855—.

Glasgow Evening Post and Paisley and Renfrewshire Reformer 1828–38, then *Glasgow Saturday Post and Paisley and Renfrewshire Reformer* 1838–55—.

Glasgow Examiner 1844–55—.
Glasgow Free Press 1823–35; 1851–5—.
Glasgow Gazette, see *Scotch Reformers' Gazette*.
Glasgow Herald, see *Glasgow Advertiser* 1783–9.
Glasgow Journal 1741–1845, incorp. *Glasgow Courant* 1760 incorp. *c.* 1779 *Glasgow Chronicle* of 1767.
Glasgow Looking Glass 1825 (June to Aug.) then as *Northern Looking Glass or Lithographic Album* to June 1826.
Glasgow Mercury 1778–96.
Glasgow Saturday Post and Paisley and Renfrewshire Reformer, see *Glasgow Evening Post and Paisley and Renfrewshire Reformer*.
Glasgow Sentinel, see *Clydesdale Journal.*
Glasgow Times and Scottish Daily Advertiser·1855—.
Greenock Advertiser 1802–55—.
Hawick Advertiser 1855—.
Herald and Advertiser, see *Glasgow Advertiser.*
Herald and Chronicle, Edinburgh, see *Edinburgh Herald.*
Independent, Edinburgh, 1824–6, then incorp. in *Northern Reporter.*
Inverness Advertiser 1849–55—.
Inverness Courier and General Advertiser for the Counties of Inverness, Ross, Moray, Nairn, Cromarty, Sutherland and Caithness 1817–55—.
Inverness Journal and Northern Advertiser 1807–48.
John O'Groat Journal, Wick, 1836–55—.
Kelso Chronicle 1783–84 (?) then as *British Chronicle or Union Gazette* 1784 (?)–1803.
Kelso Chronicle and Border Pioneer 1832–55—.
Kelso Mail and Border Gazette 1797–1855—.
Kelso Weekly Journal 1808–29.
Kilmarnock Journal 1834–55—.
Ladies Own Journal, Edinburgh 1844–55—. [as supplement to *North British Advertiser*, Jan.–Oct. 1844].
Loyal Reformers' Gazette, Glasgow 1831–2, cont. as *Reformers' Gazette* 1832–9(?).
Montrose, Arbroath and Brechin Review and Forfar and Kincardineshire Advertiser 1811–55—.
Montrose Chronicle, or Angus and Mearns Advertiser 1819–20.
Montrose Courier and General Advertiser for the Counties of Forfar and Kincardine 1815–6.
Montrose Standard and Angus and Mearns Register 1837–55—.
New North Briton, Edinburgh 1830–2, then incorp. in *Edinburgh Observer.*
North British Railway and Shipping Journal 1846–50, cont. as *Glasgow Advertiser and Railway and Shipping Journal* 1850–54, cont. as *Glasgow Advertiser* 1855—.
North Briton, Edinburgh, 1855—.
Northern Ensign and Weekly Gazette, Wick 1850–55—.
Northern Looking Glass or Lithographic Album, see *Glasgow Looking Glass.*
Northern News, Dundee, 1855, then, after first no., *Weekly News* 1855—.
Northern Reporter, see *Edinburgh Star.*
Northern Telegraph, 9 Dec. 1854–6 Jan. 1855, incorp. *War Telegraph* 9 Oct. 1854.
Northern Telegraph News, Aberdeen 1854–55—.
Northern Warder, see *Dundee Warder.*
North of Scotland Gazette 1847–53, cont. as *Aberdeen Free Press* 1853–5—.
Orcadian, Kirkwall, 1854–5—.
Orkney and Shetland Journal, London 1838–9.
Orkney and Zetland Chronicle, Edinburgh 1824–6.
Paisley Advertiser 1824–44, cont. as *Renfrewshire Advertiser* 1844–50, then incorp. in *Glasgow Constitutional.*
Paisley Herald and Renfrewshire Advertiser 1853–5—.
Paisley Journal and Renfrewshire Gazette 1853–5—.
Perth Courier 1809–22, cont. as *Perthshire Courier and General Advertiser* 1822–55—.
Perthshire Advertiser and Strathmore Journal 1829–55—.
Perthshire Courier and General Advertiser, see *Perth Courier.*
Radical Reformers' Gazette, Glasgow 1832–3.

Reformers' Gazette, see *Loyal Reformers' Gazette.*
Renfrewshire Advertiser, see *Paisley Advertiser.*
Ruddiman's Weekly Mercury, Edinburgh 1777–83.
Scotch Reformers' Gazette 1837–54, then as *Glasgow Gazette* 1854–5—.
Scots Chronicle' Edinburgh 1796–1801.
Scotsman or Edinburgh Political and Literary Journal, Edinburgh 1817–55—.
Scots Times, Glasgow 1825–41.
Scottish Guardian, Glasgow 1832–55—.
Scottish Herald and Weekly Advertiser, Edinburgh 1844–7.
Scottish Patriot, Glasgow 1839–43(?).
Scottish Pilot, Edinburgh 1837–42, then inc. in *Edinburgh Weekly Chronicle.*
Scottish Press, Edinburgh 1847–55—.
Scottish Record, see *Edinburgh Evening Post and Scottish Literary Gazette.*
Scottish Reformers' Gazette, Glasgow 1837, then as *Glasgow Gazette* 1854–55—.
Southern Reporter and Advertiser for the Counties of Selkirk and Roxburgh, Selkirk 1855—.
Stirling Journal and General Advertiser 1820–55—.
Stirling Observer 1836–55—.
Stonehaven Journal and Kincardineshire Advertiser 1843(?)–55—.
Teviotdale Record, Jedburgh 1855—.
True Scotsman, Edinburgh 1838–41.
War Telegraph, see *Northern Telegraph.*
Weekly News, see *Northern News.*
Western Star, Glasgow 1807–9.
Witness, Edinburgh 1840–55—.
Workman, Glasgow 1855—.

INDEX